Presented To:

_____

From:

_____

Date:

_____

DARE TO
Dream

DARE TO
Dream

If You Can See the Invisible Today,
God Will Make It Visible Tomorrow

MATTHEUS VAN DER STEEN

DESTINY IMAGE® PUBLISHERS, INC.

P.O. Box 310, Shippensburg, PA 17257-0310

"Speaking to the Purposes of God for This Generation and for the Generations to Come."

This book and all other Destiny Image, Revival Press, MercyPlace, Fresh Bread, Destiny Image Fiction, and Treasure House books are available at Christian bookstores and distributors worldwide.

For a U.S. bookstore nearest you, call 1-800-722-6774.

For more information on foreign distributors, call 717-532-3040.

Or reach us on the Internet: www.destinyimage.com.

Trade Paper ISBN 13: 978-0-7684-3879-6

Hardcover ISBN 13: 978-0-7684-3880-2

Large Print ISBN 13: 978-0-7684-3881-9

Ebook ISBN 13: 978-0-7684-8964-4

For Worldwide Distribution, Printed in the U.S.A.

1 2 3 4 5 6 / 14 13 12 11

Original Dutch Title: *Durf te Dromen–Wandel in je Bestemming.*

Copyright 2008: Mattheus van der Steen

Author: Mattheus van der Steen

Dutch Editor: Ingrid van Diest

Translator: Jill Nijdam Harris

English Editor: Jill Nijdam Harris

Publisher Holland: Rock Publications/Highway Media/Bread of Life

ISBN number: 978-90-79403-01-1

Cover photograph: Niels Stavorinus Photography

SPECIAL THANKS

I dedicate this book to my Lord Jesus Christ, with the hope that the people who read *Dare to Dream* will increasingly become more and more like Jesus, and go on to carry out His works on Earth and to build His Kingdom.

In addition, I dedicate this book to my wife and best friend, Rebekah, our sons, Zephaniah and Justice, and our precious new daughter, Destiny. You have brought so much balance and happiness into my life. Thank you, Rebekah, for selflessly giving me time during our holidays to work on this book—your love is overwhelming.

Also, many thanks to my father and mother. Your unconditional love and enthusiastic encouragement have helped me walk in my dreams and work toward reaching my God-given destiny. Thank you! Dad, thank you for all the hours you spent editing the original text of this book.

Special thanks also go to my spiritual parents, Angela and Larry Greenig and Heidi and Rolland Baker.

I would like to thank the TRIN team for their help, encouragement, and hard work, and thanks to Ingrid van Diest for editing the Dutch version of this book and Jill Nijdam Harris who edited the English version. You are all a great blessing to me.

And last, but not least, I would like to dedicate this book to my covenant friend, David Tari. I hope and pray that you and your generation will run with the dreams God has given you, and, like David, you will be called and anointed, a generation after God's own heart dedicated to fulfilling your God-given destiny to His glory!

ENDORSEMENTS

Dare to Dream, written by Mattheus van der Steen, is a fantastic firstfruit and shows how God wants to raise a whole army of worshipers who are committed to Him, and who are willing to give up everything to bring His glory to the ends of the earth. If I could duplicate Mattheus and Rebekah a thousand times, I believe that my vision to give one million orphans a home could be fulfilled. At this moment, God is releasing His sons and daughters worldwide to fulfill His Great Commission. The lives of Mattheus and Rebekah are examples of this. They have understood God's heart for the orphans and widows, and the love of Jesus in them is obvious for all to see. Their testimony and their lives are signs of what God wants to do in an entire nation. Read this book and be challenged to be the hands and feet of Jesus to the people who are brokenhearted as well as the lost and the dying.

Dr. Heidi Baker
Cofounder and director of Iris Ministries
Mozambique and Shara Lea Pradhan

We love Mattheus and Rebekah van der Steen. They are dreamers of the most extraordinary kind. They live to make God's dreams come true—His dreams for nations, for widows and orphans, and for Heaven on Earth. As you read the stories of dreams come true in this book, you will be encouraged to believe in miracles for your own life.

WESLEY AND STACEY CAMPBELL
Revival Now Ministries
Kelowna, Canada

This book releases the dreamer in you and will encourage you to walk in your God-given purpose. It is a book filled with hope and reminds us that we can do all things if we pray and believe that we will receive. Mattheus is a living example of this. When you read this book, let the fire and wind of God blow through the chambers of your heart and let it awaken again the dreamer in you so that you can go and walk in your destiny.

ANGELA T. GREENIG
Set Free Ministries
Seattle, Washington

I got to know Mattheus van der Steen and the TRIN team at a conference in the Netherlands and was deeply moved by their love for, and dedication to, the participants. They gathered the young and the old and made room for them to connect in various ways. However, most of all I enjoyed the freedom in the Spirit. When I learned of Mattheus' book, *Dare to Dream,* I was excited about it as we share mutual desires, visions, and the heart to encourage people to dream God's dreams for their lives. It is my prayer that many people will be impacted by this message and begin to walk in their destinies.

WALTER HEIDENREICH, President
Free Christian Youth Community
Ludenscheid, Germany

Dare to Dream is a wonderful story of personal transformation that leaves readers with a passion to see the same thing happen in their own lives. Only transformed people can become transformers. Mattheus van der Steen and his wife, Rebekah, have truly become just that, devoting themselves to seeing the transformation of cities and nations. The impact of this book will be great, bringing many into the Kingdom.

BILL JOHNSON, Senior Pastor
Bethel Church, Redding, California
Author, *When Heaven Invades Earth*

Dare to Dream is not just a title, but an accurate description of my dear friend, Mattheus van der Steen. He dreams big dreams, and he works hard and sacrifices much to achieve those dreams. Dreams will take you to places you have never before imagined. Dreams are the language of hope for leaders. Those who do not dare to dream have "died," although their funeral will not take place for many years! This book will challenge you to dream big dreams and inspire you to expect greater things in life. Get this book, not only for you, but for the people you lead, your dear friends and family. It is a book which must be read.

JAMES LEVESQUE
Engaging Heaven Revival Center
New London, Connecticut

Mattheus van der Steen has a genuine desire to reach the lost and bring the light and love of the Gospel of our Lord Jesus Christ to the world. His commitment and sacrifices are evidence of that desire. I strongly believe that after reading his book, *Dare to Dream,* you will start dreaming and believing you can achieve your God-given purpose. I pray the prophecy of the prophet Joel (2:28) will be fulfilled in your life. Think big, be ready to dream big dreams, and remember we serve a BIG GOD!

RAJKUMAR GANTA
National Director, TRIN India

Reactions from other Christian leaders, as well as readers of *Dare to Dream,* are found in the back of this book.

CONTENTS

FOREWORD

by Brother Andrew van der Bijl

Really, it's true! I finished this book in one sitting, with tears trickling down my cheeks and a smile on my lips.

So many of my memories came flooding back, and I especially remembered the saying, "He who doesn't dare to fall on his nose, will not dare to dream dreams or see visions, as they go hand in hand."

Acts 2:17 says:

> *In the last days God says, I will pour out My Spirit on all people. Your sons and daughters will prophesy, your young men will see visions, your old men will dream dreams.*

How Long is a Chinese. No, you read it correctly. It is not a question, but a statement. I think How Long is the name of a man from China I have yet to meet. You see, sometimes the meaning of a word is different from what you might have originally thought it would be. It's like dreaming.

If you think you were born too late to be an explorer, an inventor, a mountain climber, a conqueror, an adventurer, a world-changer, or even a revolutionary, then think again. We live in the most challenging time ever as there have never been so many people who have yet to hear the name of Jesus. However, it has never been easier to travel to them or to communicate with them by using the latest technology. We now have more resources, better knowledge, and, in fact, more of everything we need to do the job well.

We live in a world that desperately needs young people to reach out to others; and in doing so, experience the greatest adventure of all. Sound dangerous? Sure! But it is a lot more dangerous not to reach out. Without our intervention or word of warning, the many unsaved people of this world could go to hell. That is a very sad reality for everyone, including believers.

"How long?" cries the writer in Psalm 74:10. How long will the devil be the ruler of this world and have all the popular music in his possession along with the promising lives of millions of young people? How long will he mock Your name, God? Forever?

"No!" cry out the dreamers. "We will rise up, dream our dreams, and do spectacular things for Jesus!"

Like an army we will rise up, leaving our comfort zones behind us. We will win the world with our love—with *His* love. We will not be intimidated by our failures, nor by any insult or slander from the devil. He is the only one who wants to remind us daily of our failures, our sinful pasts, our lost generation, our empty churches, and our minimal influence on world affairs—but for how much longer? Until the dreamers rise up and remind the devil of his future, that he is the loser, that he has been defeated, and that Jesus is victorious.

Please, let this be the generation of young people who are on fire for Jesus, who will never shut anyone out—whether a terrorist, a criminal, a rebel, or a heathen. I say, "Do not put them on the evangelical blacklist of those we do not want to see in Heaven." God loves the sinner and that includes those we term our "enemies." Do we have to stay politically, religiously, or even culturally correct?

No! *Dare to dream!*

God wants this whole written-off generation reached through a new wave of dreamers. They will cross borders, climb mountains, demolish prejudices, make sacrifices, and exhibit the all-consuming love of Jesus. Even at my age, and I am almost 80 years old, I want to be part of it.

I think back to the early times in my Christian walk, which started almost 60 years ago. My joy, enthusiasm, and my desire to speak about Jesus knew no bounds. My loving father, a devout and serious Christian, once said to me, "Son, I was like you when I was young, but you'll get over it." Thank God I never got over it, and my prayer is that my passion for Jesus will only increase as time goes by. I certainly want to see that day when millions of young people, like an army of light, swarm across the world, disregarding forbidden borders, not held back by sanctimonious criticism, who love not their lives unto death, and are moved by the compassion of Jesus for the lost sheep (see Rev. 12:11; Matt. 9:36).

Let this be an encouragement to you. Whatever I did in the world and whatever Mattheus does, you can, and probably will do better than we ever did. You are surrounded by a new cloud of witnesses, which means there are so many more people praying for the dreamers among you.

Dear Mattheus, and all the readers of this wonderful book, go with God and never give up!

Your old mentor,
Brother Andrew van der Bijl
(also known as "God's Smuggler")
Founder, Open Doors

FOREWORD

by Rebekah van der Steen

My name is Rebekah and Mattheus is my husband and best friend. I was born and raised in Seattle, Washington, and moved to the Netherlands in 2003.

I was keen to give my testimony in this book because I really believe in daring to dream your dreams. It does not matter how desperate your situation is or how bad your past seems, there is always a way out. That way is through Jesus Christ, who is not only the Way, but also the Truth and the Life that leads to God, the Father.

As a little girl, I experienced severely traumatic events and often looked with longing eyes at the outside world and to the butterflies that were beautiful and innocent and were free to fly away. For years I dared not believe that there was a way for me to escape from my misery—but there was a Way!

After I accepted Jesus as my Savior, my life changed dramatically, and I dared to dream again. With my life safely in God's hands, I rapidly went from strength to strength and now, together with Mattheus and our sons, Zephaniah and Justice, and our beautiful daughter, Destiny,

I travel around the world in His service. We see thousands of people choosing to follow Jesus Christ and witness firsthand great miracles, signs, and people being set free. I encourage you to revive your dream. Dare to dream, because everything is possible with God, our Father!

I wish you great joy and revelation when you read *Dare to Dream*.

In the following testimony, I have quoted from an interview Mirjam van der Vegt did with me for the Dutch Evangelical Broadcasting program called *Vision*.

MY TESTIMONY

Even before Rebekah's birth, Anton le Vay, author of the satanic bible, saw in a vision that she would be the fifth bride of satan. He also saw the time and place where Rebekah would enter this world. Her family was cursed, and during her birth a satanic ritual was carried out. Rebekah was born into a world filled with spiritual darkness.

Who would ever dare to dream that this little girl would enter a Christian church, veiled and in white, 24 years later? A church where she walked toward her Christian husband, Mattheus van der Steen, to the glorious sounds of the song *Bride of Jerusalem*. Together with him she would later walk through the bright sunshine to an awaiting carriage drawn by two white horses. They were surrounded by hundreds of relatives and friends. A fairy tale? "It certainly felt like it," says the radiant Rebekah.

Together with her husband, Mattheus, she is sitting in front of me. She is determined to tell her story, even though satanists often try and intimidate her. At the wedding there were 20 bodyguards present to protect her. This interview is taking place under prayer covering.

"I am not afraid," says Rebekah. "I would rather die in God's presence, than sit in a satanist church."

CURSES

The story of Rebekah sounds like a scene from a horror movie.

"I grew up in an unstable family in America and our nanny was largely responsible for my upbringing. Only later did I understand that she was part of the plan to indoctrinate me. This woman took me to the satanist church. I grew up there, and, not knowing any better, I thought everything I learned was quite normal. I learned that I could make things move without touching them and could protect myself by making animal sacrifices. I also learned to pronounce curses on other people.

"When I was four years old, I was abused by one of the high priests in the church of satan. Being so young, I could not explain exactly what had occurred, but I was able to communicate to my parents enough for them to understand something unacceptable had happened. The man responsible was arrested and our nanny was dismissed, only to be replaced with a new nanny who also took me to the church of satan. I was a prisoner.

"On one hand, I would sometimes look outside during the services and was jealous of the little caterpillars that would one day turn into colorful butterflies. I felt that I was trapped in a cocoon and I would never escape. On the other hand, I also loved the supernatural powers that were in me, and I could even control fire. Fire was my primary element and the symbol of fire was tattooed on my arm."

THE CIRCLE OF BRIDES

"When I was nine years old, I was married to satan during a horrific ritual. I was given a dark dress to wear that was printed with pentagrams. Written in the inside of the sleeves were satanic symbols. All sorts of curses were sung during the ceremony and blood flowed as various sacrifices were being made. The other four brides then invited me into a circle. 'Welcome to the circle of brides,' they said to me. From that day on, I was allowed to sit at the round table where decisions were made. That table was where we made agreements on who was to be cursed next. One day, it was the turn of the American preacher Benny Hinn."

GREAT WHITE LIGHT

"Accompanied by a high priest and a female priest, I went to a meeting hosted by Benny Hinn. I had been taught that Christians are weak people with very little influence on the community they live in. During the time I had spent in their churches with other satanists I had learnt that they were self-absorbed, caring more about impressing themselves and others in the church rather than reflecting the love and compassion of Jesus to the outside world. To my surprise, when Benny Hinn entered the auditorium I could instantly see that, even though he was a Christian, he was not like them. I saw a big, white light around him and it was so pure that my eyes started to hurt. At one point, Benny Hinn stopped the service. He looked directly at us and said, 'You are witches, stop cursing immediately!' Then he looked at me and continued, 'You will soon be rescued and you will be called by God the Father in order to live and work for Him.' I began trembling and screaming. The other two satanists threw a dark cloth over my head so that I could no longer see the white light, and they dragged me away from the meeting.

"From then on I began to have doubts. In the church of satan, I only saw death and destruction. Babies were killed by priests as sacrifices, and the only way we survived these terrible scenes was by using illegal, mind-altering drugs. Along with another girl, I became more and more rebellious and we often escaped from the services and went our own way. One day she phoned me telling me that I had to help her escape immediately! I said I would help and went with her to a Methodist family she had come to know and where she would be given shelter. A short time later, people from the church of satan killed her. Her murder was a warning for others—including me—not to leave the church of satan."

FREE

"Not long afterward, I saw the film *The Blair Witch Project*. As I watched it, a veil was taken away from my eyes and I knew that if I ever attended the church of satan again, I would die. I fled to a Christian family that I knew, but soon the satanists discovered where I was. They tried to kidnap me, but I prevented them from succeeding by screaming very loudly in the middle of the street. The Christians with whom I stayed were also very scared and in order to frighten us and to show us that they knew where I was, the satanists surrounded the house with ritual objects during the night and pronounced curses on us. This proved to be effective, as the family asked me to leave their house. Assisted by their pastor, they burnt all my belongings and then sent me to another woman who was more familiar with exorcism.

"I was firmly convinced that the satanists would catch me. I took my last dose of heroin and went to the house where Angela Greenig lived. When I arrived at the house, I opened the door with my special powers without even touching it. However, the hand of Angela stopped the door halfway. 'I do not think so!' she said with authority. Behind her I saw a huge light. 'Do not worry,' laughed Angela, 'they are my personal angels.' It was the first time I had seen angels. I was then put in a closed room where nothing could be damaged if I decided to use my supernatural power to move things around. Angela looked right at me and said, 'You give your life to Jesus, or satan will take your soul to hell. You must choose now!'

"I started to scream loudly and uncontrollably and knew that it was impossible to do that by myself! Angela began to pray the sinner's prayer with me, and I could say the name of Jesus. I then fell into a deep, dreamless sleep; and when I awoke, it felt as if 90 percent of me was not there. My identity had been in satan, and he was now gone.

"Angela and a few others prayed that I would be filled with the Holy Spirit, and I started to laugh, sing, and speak in tongues. Then suddenly I heard the beautiful sound of a bird singing. I started to cry. Never, ever before had I heard a bird singing!"

STRENGTH

From then on, Rebekah has never stopped testifying about the miracle God has done in her life. She continues: "It's sometimes difficult to talk about my past. Some people think that I am crazy and wonder why I didn't inform the police about what I had seen. I didn't inform the police because one can't prove that the satanists commit murder. They are extremely careful in the way they operate. The babies who are sacrificed are often not even registered because they were born within the satanist community. Moreover, there are also satanists in the police force. Most people unfamiliar with this fact and who hear this story, find it almost unbelievable. Nevertheless, I want to testify to the truth of this to warn people against these dangers and rescue them from the darkness!"

The Netherlander, Mattheus van der Steen, met Rebekah under very unusual circumstances. He tells me, "I traveled all around the world for many years helping the disadvantaged. In Nashville, I was coincidently at a church gathering where Rebekah was sharing her testimony. When I saw Rebekah on stage, it seemed God spoke directly to me, 'This is your future wife.' I tried to talk to her after the meeting, but was unsuccessful."

Rebekah continues, "With my background of abuse, I had an aversion to men. It wasn't until later that I was able to speak with Mattheus in a park. There I saw his angels dancing with my angels! At that moment I knew that everything was going to be all right, but it was only after a few weeks that I had enough courage to send Mattheus an email, and in doing so, my relationship with him began. We are now married and live in the Netherlands."

Mattheus is aware of the dangers they face together. He says, "We have already experienced some very clear attacks, but we always see that God's power is a stronger force and, as a result, see a lot of breakthroughs."

Rebekah adds, "On Friday the thirteenth of August 1999, I was delivered and set free. I know that the satanists try to intimidate and frighten me at times, but I am not afraid. God protects me. I pray a lot and memorize and proclaim Scriptures." Mattheus agrees with her, "She is truly free. However, because she is proclaiming God so transparently, we sometimes have to deal with attacks that are a result of things that have happened in her past."

Rebekah has a number of special gifts, which she has devoted to use in her service to God. Says Rebekah, "I am compelled to work for the disadvantaged and have a prophetic gift.

"We as Christians must stand guard as this world is not our home. We are in the midst of a spiritual battle; and even in the Netherlands, satanists are sent into Christian churches to curse them. This has sometimes even affected the church's key leadership. We must put an end to our gossiping about each other and together begin to seek God's authority. He has all the power; so do not hinder Him as He seeks to do so much more through each of us. Let us show that we Christians are not weak, but strong in God!"

REBEKAH VAN DER STEEN
Cofounder
Touch, Reach and Impact the Nations (TRIN)

INTRODUCTION

My desire is that everyone who reads this book will be encouraged to become actively involved in seeing the Kingdom of God come on this Earth and to live in intimacy with the Lord. I chose the title *Dare to Dream* because I see around me so many Christians who have, for one reason or the other, become discouraged, and as a result, no longer dare to dream. It seems as if they don't know how to get from point A to point B in their Christian walk. They have given their lives to the Lord and, in the past, have had many visions and dreams. However, due to various adverse circumstances, they have abandoned any hope of ever accomplishing these dreams. Instead they choose to remain on the sidelines, while Jesus is still encouraging them to, "Go to the other side!"

His own disciples faced difficult circumstances, but despite storms and disappointments, despite religious currents and winds, they persevered until they reached the other side. Like them, we are also called to step out in faith, overcome our own obstacles, and go to the other side.

BRIDGE-BUILDERS

I hope to show you how to build a bridge between your conversion and your calling, and how you can effectively carry out the mission that you have been given by the Lord. The best bridge-builder is the Lord Jesus Himself, for it is by His death on the cross that he built a bridge between us, as sinful people, and God, our heavenly Father. The cross is the most beautiful bridge imaginable—a bridge that we must all cross if we surrender our lives to the Lord and want to follow Him successfully.

"Bridge-builder" is a name commonly associated with Dutch nationals. We are a nation of bridge-builders and we love challenges and pioneering. For centuries we have defied the encroaching waters that threaten a large part of our country by building bridges, dams, and tunnels. In 2005 we used our expertise to assist the U.S. authorities to secure New Orleans after Hurricane Katrina's winds ripped through it with devastating consequences.

(In 1613, the first Dutch settlers arrived in America establishing many villages and towns, including one called New Amsterdam, which is now known as New York. According to a 2006 census, more than 5 million Americans claim to have a total or partial Dutch heritage. This creates a bridge between America and the Netherlands, and even today we stand together to support Israel. My own personal bridge between the two countries is that I married an American from Seattle!)

However, in the Christian world, there is often little to remind us that we are bridge-builders. We are often preoccupied with building our own dams, our own kingdoms, our own systems, and our own church—and unfortunately, this scenario is echoed worldwide.

I believe that we are living in an era in which we can no longer play games. It is "Game Over" for religious systems and structures. It is time that, without compromise, we surrender all our selfish ambitions and personal agendas to our Lord Jesus. If we want to see revival in our communities and countries, we need to start doing things His way. We have to build bridges between each other, between churches, to our neighbors, to friends and family, and even to our enemies.

It is time for the Body of Christ to rise up and take the Good News about Jesus to the poor, wounded, and blind; in fact, to the whole world. The anointing was never meant to be only for ourselves; the anointing, or power of God, is so we can be witnesses in the world. This is why Jesus tells His disciples in Acts 1:8 to *go back* to Jerusalem where *"you will receive power when the Holy Spirit comes on you; and you will be My witnesses in Jerusalem, and in all Judea and Samaria, and to the ends of the earth."*

Luke 4:18 says:

> *The Spirit of the Lord is on Me, because He has anointed Me to proclaim good news to the poor. He has sent Me to proclaim freedom for the prisoners and recovery of sight for the blind, to set the oppressed free,*

Isaiah 61:1 says exactly the same thing and this same Spirit and this same anointing is available to every believer today. However, only those who want to see the Great Commission fulfilled will see real revival.

I wrote this book because I want to release something in you. I want you to once again believe that you can achieve your dreams and believe that God will provide. Go and walk in the authority that God has given you as a believer. Put simply, this means go and do what Jesus did by proclaiming His Kingdom, preaching the Gospel to the poor, taking care of orphans and widows, loving others, giving God all the glory, seeking first His Kingdom, laying hands on the sick and seeing them healed, comforting the brokenhearted, and seeing the captives set free—all in the name of Jesus.

It does not matter what your background is, what training you have, or what church you belong to—Jesus is the Way, He is the Truth, and He is the Life. He wants to bring revival in you and through you!

My prayer is that, as you read this book, you will realize that you can trust God with your whole heart; and when you do, He will do amazing things to help you make your dreams a reality.

> *Now to Him who is able to do immeasurably more than all we ask or imagine, according to His power that is at work within us, to Him be glory in the church and in Christ Jesus throughout all generations, for ever and ever! Amen* (Ephesians 3:20-21).

CHAPTER 1

A GREAT ADVENTURE

Life with God our Father, the Lord Jesus Christ, the Holy Spirit, and all the angels is a great adventure. From a very young age I clearly remember that we went to church every Sunday and, as my father was a pastor, we moved from one place to another quite regularly.

At the age of 14, I was at the Weena Skating Rink in Rotterdam, and I heard a voice saying, "Mattheus, why are you going to church?" It was a good question, and it shocked me.

I had been aware of God's existence from a very young age, and I remember warning people in the supermarket as a ten-year-old that they were going to go to hell if they did not accept Jesus as their Savior. I have to admit, this often caused great annoyance to my mother and sister. During one Christmastime, I wrote in big letters on my bedroom window that JESUS IS THE ONLY WAY, which further annoyed my sister!

However, talking about Jesus was one thing, but giving my life and my heart to Him was an entirely different matter. I did not have a personal relationship with Him. When I heard that voice at the skating rink, I felt as if a hot liquid was flowing over my body and I can vividly remember feeling large tears running down my cheeks. My friends with me at the rink that day were all members of an evangelical church. That night the youth pastor of the church prayed with me, and I surrendered my life to Jesus. Later that evening, although I felt shy about sharing my news, I was able to tell my father and mother that I had given my life to Jesus. They were so happy that we ended up having a party to celebrate! A few weeks later, my father baptized me in the Baptist church, and the whole youth group from the evangelical church came to witness this important event. We had a wonderful time.

In the following weeks, I continued to wrestle and reflect on the question I had heard at the skating rink. Why was I going to church? What is the function of the church? I came to the conclusion that I attended out of habit and that even though I was present during the sermon, I didn't really hear it, and ultimately didn't understand the message at all. In addition, I most certainly didn't understand the church culture! I also concluded that I went to church because my friends did; and I not only had no personal relationship with the Lord, but I did not communicate with Him either.

In 1993, I read an article by Brother Andrew van der Bijl (also known as God's Smuggler) in a magazine. The article described how retirement facilities are filled with people who are still waiting for a call from God telling them what He specifically wants each of them to do. He went on to say that we are all called by God and that we don't necessarily need to hear a clearly audible voice or a prophet who picks us out of a crowd and prophesies over us, before we obey God. It may happen, but is not absolutely necessary.

He then wrote that he just goes ahead and does what God tells him to do in the Bible. He often compares the voice of God to a traffic light, with green meaning "go" and red meaning, "don't go!" I began to see that indeed many people were complacently waiting for the green light in their lives when, in fact, 90 percent of the time, the light was already green! They just needed to go into everyday life following Jesus and being His hands and feet in whatever situation or community God placed them. Upon realizing this, I did just that and have come to learn that the light is more often green than red.

Later on, Brother Andrew became my mentor and, when my sister married his son Jop, we became part of the same family. Jop also became one of my best friends.

MARINE OFFICER

As a child I lived in the village of Pernis, which is on the edge of Rotterdam's large harbor. Some of my most treasured childhood memories are of the times I spent watching all the big seagoing vessels moving in and out of the harbor. I regularly saw one of the pilot boats going out to one of the many large ships waiting to come into the harbor. When the pilot boat came alongside, the ship's pilot would climb on board, via a ladder, and then guide the ship safely into the harbor.

I was fascinated and, in my dreams, I saw myself standing on the bridge of a huge ship in a smart white maritime officer's uniform.

I once prayed and asked the Lord if it was OK to go to the nearby maritime building. I didn't get a red light, so I got on my bicycle and cycled to the building. At the entrance there was a sign saying, "Prohibited Area," but I cycled past it and went to the harbor captain's office. As I arrived there, an older man came out of the building on his way to one of the ships. He introduced himself as Mr. Tazelaar, and he told me that he was a pilot and nearing retirement age. We started talking and, to my amazement, he invited me to accompany him. You can imagine how exciting this unexpected trip was for me! We went out on the pilot's boat to a big ship that had just arrived from China and, after a dangerous climb up the ladder wearing my wet shoes, I arrived on board.

On the bridge, the pilot gave me his cap to wear. That day was a dream come true for me and, after having had this wonderful experience, I wanted to experience more of this kind of life on board a ship. (Many years later, over a four-year period, I had the privilege of working with more than 300 different pilots in various parts of the world.)

When I researched what training I would need to achieve my dream of being a marine officer, my teacher discouraged me from pursuing the higher level of education required, saying it would not be "realistic" for me as I only had the ability to attain a medium-level education. She then advised me to pursue a lower, more technically-orientated course. Despite what I had been told, I chose not to abandon my dream of standing on the bridge of a ship in a white maritime officer's uniform. Disregarding all the advice I had been given, I enrolled myself at a marine officer's training school. Again I received the same warning that the first three months would be too difficult for me, and again I decided not to listen to people, but instead to follow my dream. I believed that I would get my diploma with the support of my parents and by putting my faith and trust in the Lord. I was determined to succeed.

The training was not easy, and sometimes it felt like I was going through some really "stormy weather," but five years later, I received my diploma from the Nautical College; and shortly afterward, my dreams became reality as I stood in a white uniform as a marine officer on the bridge of the ship MV *Anastasis*.

SINATARA

The *Anastasis* belonged to a Christian ministry called Mercy Ships which was, at the time, part of the Youth With A Mission (YWAM) organization. At the time, it was the largest floating hospital in the world. The aim of Mercy Ships is to spread the Gospel in third world countries while providing practical assistance to the communities in the vicinity where their ship is moored. This is a wonderful way to give hands and feet to the mission Jesus called us to do.

There were hundreds of volunteers on the *Anastasis,* ranging from the captain to surgeons, nurses, chefs, and waiters, and everyone paid a few hundred dollars per month to work on the ship. Every year the *Anastasis* went to a different port in Africa where, over a six-month period, thousands of medical and dental procedures were performed on those identified as being most in need. There were also dozens of people on the ship's construction teams, and they built wells and small clinics in the area.

While all this was happening, evangelism teams visited the villages and towns nearby to share the story of Jesus with the local community.

During my time on board the *Anastasis,* the ship was moored for a few months in a harbor in Madagascar, an island southeast of southern Africa. In addition to my work as a marine officer, I was also involved in evangelism and reached out to the local community on the days when I was not working on the ship. I was intensely affected by the poverty and the people I saw living on the streets there.

One day we were in the jungle, and I met a boy who was about 8 years old and who told us he had no parents. His name was Sinatara and he lived with a friend. The heartbreaking situation of this orphan touched my heart enormously. During the three months the ship was moored in the harbor, I visited Sinatara every Saturday to talk and play with him. When the time came to say farewell, he threw his little arms around my legs and screamed and cried in French, "Daddy, don't go away."

This touched me deeply and for the first time in my life I became acutely aware of the fate of orphans. I was deeply affected, and a new desire grew in me to help them.

PROPHECY

The *Anastasis* then sailed to South Africa where we stayed for a period of six months. Here, Peter Helms, a speaker from the Netherlands, joined the ship. I was told he had a prophetic ministry; but, because of my Baptist background, I was not that familiar with the gift of prophecy and did not know what a prophetic ministry was. However, I soon found out. During a meeting we both attended on board the *Anastasis*, Peter Helms pointed at me and my heart began to beat faster, both in fear and anticipation. He began prophesying over me according to what the Spirit of God was telling him. He said that I would play a key role in the endtimes by training an army of people and releasing them to do what they were called to do by God. He saw lots of fire and passion, waves of revival, and thousands of people in many nations who would come to know Jesus as their Savior. I was well and truly shaken. First, the orphan Sinatara, and now this word from God.

These two events brought me to a point where I felt that I had to make a choice. Should I continue my training to become a ship's captain, which would take another nine years, or should I stop sailing and commit myself to being trained to serve needy widows and orphans? I chose the latter, returned to the Netherlands, and put my white uniform and certificate in the closet at home. Today, years later, I miss the sea every day, but I'm still convinced that I made the right choice.

JESUS IS THE ROCK

In 1994, I became involved in Jesus Is the Rock Ministries and, at the time, there was a revival among the young people in a city in the center of the Netherlands. It was a wonderful time when non-Christian young people radically came to Jesus. Led by Jop van der Bijl and

Henk Foppen, we conducted services for non-churchgoing youth. There were mega-baptisms, worship celebrations, outreaches, and evenings of refreshing.

In the few short years I was with this ministry I gained a wealth of knowledge. Jop van der Bijl had just returned from Africa where he had facilitated major training campaigns for evangelists. Henk Foppen was, at that time, a member of the evangelism committee of a church. Both men had a heart for missions and evangelism, and they were very excited by the plans to generate new ideas to evangelize the youth.

In an effort to better understand the people they wanted to reach for Christ, Jop and Henk had gone onto the streets and talked with and listened to young people as they told them how and what they felt about their lives and their circumstances.

I believe that this is a very good and constructive approach. First, determining who your target group is; second, how they feel and think; and last, how you can reach them and those like them with the Gospel in the most effective way. It turned out that most of the surveyed young people found the message of Jesus and the Gospel too difficult to comprehend. They didn't like the traditional approach to "church" and how Christians related to one another.

Initially, Jop and Henk didn't dare bring young people like this into their church, but after much prayer, they plucked up the courage and did just that!

IRRITATING THE STATUS QUO

One Sunday morning, they invited 15 young men to church and sat them in the back row. Among them were young men who were addicted to soft drugs, were homeless, and had social issues. Jop and Henk were very excited by the large turnout of youngsters. During the service, the boys went in and out of the building, taking turns to smoke cigarettes outside, until one of the elders requested that they sit still. Other well-meaning members of the congregation were irritated as well and would even look back at them holding their finger to their mouth indicating that they should be quiet. At the end of the service, the 15 young people left the building very frustrated. They knew they were not acceptable as they were, and that was precisely the reason they had not wanted to attend church in the first place.

Jop and Henk were deeply frustrated too, and eventually the church developed a special committee to reach out to those outside the church who were lost and did not know Jesus as their Savior. After a year, they went onto the streets again and invited young people into the church. When they accepted and went to church, once again the reactions of the congregation drove them away. The young people and the way they behaved were simply not acceptable.

Unfortunately, this scenario is happening in many churches and communities worldwide because we value the man-made order and structure more than we welcome unbelievers. We do not give them time to be touched and changed by the Lord, and so we drive them away. I believe the Lord is pleased to see the lost come to church, but we left when the youth left, and I am sure He was shaking His head and filled with grief.

It is time for a radical change. We need to pray that God will give us compassion for the lost and we need to repent from the sin of valuing the order in a service more than the lost people God cares so much about.

In the same month, a few young people organized a house party, complete with the top musical hits of the '90s. All of a sudden churches were stirred into action and, at a meeting at the local town hall, launched a campaign against holding the party. Due to the immense pressure applied by these Christians, the party was canceled and many young people, angry at the older peoples' decision, asked why they had not been allowed to organize their own entertainment. After that, other recreational ideas for the youth were put forth and organized, but it wasn't long before the church objected to those as well.

Jop and Henk did not know what to do next. What could today's Church offer these young people who would not attend church? The church seemed so focused inwardly that there was no room for the children and young people from outside the church walls, who were looking to be loved and accepted, to find hope and friendship.

The city council eventually decided to allocate a place for young people to get together. It was right next to the town hall, and it was called the Plaza. Organizations were allowed to use the space during certain hours of the day, and Jop and Henk immediately jumped at the opportunity to use it for youth gatherings. They organized weekly Bible studies above the Plaza in a room where young people regularly met during the week to smoke cannabis and drink heavily.

In addition to the Bible studies, they also organized music concerts. Christian volunteers were part of the newly created Plaza Team. At first this new outreach to the youth encountered opposition from the churches as they felt that they needed to work together, so first a committee had to be formed. To honor the church leadership, Jop and Henk joined the committee on behalf of their church, but all the committee did was talk and deliberate and discuss ideas—it rarely managed to arrange any activities to reach out to the youth. In the end, Jop and Henk decided to follow their hearts and continue their outreach work to the youth without involving the church. They decided to pay all the expenses for future meetings out of their own pockets.

It was around this time, in 1995, that our family moved to this city. We soon came into contact with Jop and Henk, and there was an instant connection. One day, my sister Viviane (who was no longer attending church) and I were urged by our mother to go to one of the evening meetings at the Plaza. I remember the night of our first visit. We passed through a haze of cannabis smoke on our way up the stairs and as we entered the room, the smell of newly made coffee and freshly baked cake greeted us. The atmosphere was relaxed, and we immediately felt at home. There were five other young people that night as well as Jop and Henk. One was a boy from Amsterdam called Frits, who was partially blind. He was a very mischievous boy, but very funny. He had several bad experiences during his lifetime, and that evening he gave his life to Jesus. I felt like a fish in water. We continued to attend these meetings and eventually Viviane returned to following Jesus. She also fell in love with Jop, and they got married three years later.

Meanwhile, attendance of the Bible study group was growing so we had to look for a larger room to meet in. By then my sister and I were on the ministry team along with Jop and Henk, and I eventually became a full-time worker for Jesus Is the Rock Ministries. At that time, Jop and Henk, who were still paying for everything themselves, began organizing concerts with popular bands and singers like Darrel Mansfield, Rezz, and White Cross. As a result, the number of young people attending grew very quickly.

There were so many young people who were accepting Jesus as their Savior that it did not take long before we were ready to hold our first baptism service, which was held at a lake just outside the city where we lived. After we had conducted a few of these services, they became very popular for tourists, passersby, and the media to come and watch.

We thought it would be a good idea to organize special services for young church seekers and non-believing youth. The first service was a tremendous success, with more than 200 young people attending. We experienced a small revival. A "youth church" did not exist in the Netherlands at that time, and so we were one of the first in the country to introduce the idea.

WORKING TOGETHER

The surrounding churches witnessed our success and, for the most part, instead of cheering for Jesus, the councils of elders and church governing boards were deeply frustrated by the fact that we were experiencing such success and that, through this, young people were becoming active followers of Jesus—while they had only a few young people attending their churches. We had always stretched out our hands to them and blessed them, as it was our desire to work together with them. Some people took our outstretched hands and wanted to cooperate, but most of them were either too scared or too proud. They were afraid of losing the few young people they had. They were afraid we would steal their sheep.

To this I have only one thing to say. As long as churches have this attitude, they will have little impact in our communities and the fruits they produce will be those of division, jealousy, and ultimately the splitting of churches. In addition, a spirit of manipulation and control will emerge if we are not open to other believers. I believe that the time of building our own kingdoms is over and, personally, I do not believe in denominations any more.

If the whole Body of Christ wants to start moving and experience a revival, I believe that the whole Body of Christ, meaning every part of the Body, will have to cooperate with each other in a spirit of unity. Unfortunately, the Bride, the Body of Christ, is broken and infected by sin; but God can perform a miracle if we are prepared to work together and look beyond our own small worlds and at His bigger picture.

Jop and Henk's original plan to start a church in a pub was different—and it became a movement. In that movement, so many young people became believers that we started discipleship training, organized nights of refreshing, leading worship celebrations, and evangelism outreaches. We also established a place where young people could gather and relax, talk, have a snack, play snooker (billiards), or find a listening ear. It was an awesome time in which God showed His strength and where we, as pioneers in this field, learned so much.

We knew there were people outside the church walls who were lost and hurting, and we were passionate about reaching them with Jesus' love.

It is a sad fact that many people are so engrossed in church activities that they forget that they are commanded to "go into all the world" and make disciples. Many of these people prefer criticizing the behavior of the lost instead of asking God to give them His heart for them.

I have difficulty understanding this type of person, and so did Jesus. He even had a name for them—"*a brood of vipers*" (Matt. 23:33). These were Pharisees who lived their lives upholding all their religious customs and traditions, but didn't understand the real reason for doing so. They were without compassion for the deprived, the sick, and unbelievers. They were the type of people who turned a blind eye and a deaf ear, just like the Pharisees who, in the story of the Good Samaritan, hurriedly passed by a badly injured man who had almost been killed by robbers. They walked right around the injured man, even though they saw the pitiful state he was in, and attended their worship service. Ultimately it was the Samaritan, a heathen, who by stopping to help the injured man, showed the heart of Jesus.

KNOWING HIS HEART

Dear reader, we must repent of our selfishness and attachment to the petty things of this world. It's time to wake up and go and do something! "How?" you ask. Begin by taking the time to talk to God to see where your help is desperately needed. To this you might say, "There are needs everywhere and I cannot operate in emergency response mode." Or you might say that you aren't skilled enough. Nonsense! If you read Matthew 25:31-46, you will see that one doesn't have to have a special calling to help people in need, and that God even condemns a group of people for what they have *not* done.

I don't yet fully understand Matthew 25:31-46 because it is so radical and simple, but I believe that God has set a high value on us helping the outcasts, the poor, the orphans, and the widows in their distress—an action that results from spending time with God and learning to know His heart for these people. You do not need a special calling to tell people about the love of God.

Most Christians don't realize that people really do go to hell if they do not accept Jesus as their Savior. It is written in John 3:16:

> *For God so loved the world that He gave His one and only Son, that whoever believes in Him shall not perish but have eternal life.*

Almost every Christian is familiar with this Scripture. Whenever we hear it mentioned in a sermon, it makes us sigh deeply because we have to listen to the same message yet again, but then most still do not respond to it. For the most part, it just goes in one ear and out the other! Yes, God is *love,* but He is also powerful and holy. The Word of God says that, out of love God gave His Son Jesus to be sacrificed in order to pay for our sins, and that anyone who believes in Him and follows Him will have eternal life and therefore a home in Heaven. Anyone who refuses to believe in Him will be lost and spend eternity in hell.

My hope is that, if you have not accepted Jesus as your Savior, the Holy Spirit will convict you of God's Word. He is waiting for you to live a life where you are believing and teaching John 3:16 and sharing with others that God is love and that there is room in Heaven for everyone. There is no standard way to do this, but when you decide to follow Him wholeheartedly, He will give you various talents and gifts to equip you to do the job well.

I think there are far too many Christians who are complacent. They are so bored that they would rather sit at their computers playing games than go out and share the love of God with people and see His Kingdom come on Earth. Surrendering your life entirely to God, as I have personally found out, is both exciting as well as a great adventure!

OMAN AND KOSOVO

After a number of years in youth ministry, more and more doors were opened to me and I became involved with a ministry working in underground churches in Muslim countries. In 1999 in Muscat, Oman, the Lord woke me up one night and, in a vision, gave me an enormous amount of compassion for the nations and especially for third world countries. My heart was deeply moved by the burden the Lord had laid on me; and in the subsequent months, I would weep nightly as I felt His sorrow for the plight of these people. I began to realize that the Lord wanted me to focus on helping orphans and widows.

In that same year, after I had returned home to the Netherlands from Oman, war broke out in Kosovo, a country where Albanians were being brutally raped, murdered, or forcefully driven from their homes by Serbian militias. In Europe, several refugee camps were established for the displaced Kosovarans. In the city where I lived at that time, there was a very large refugee camp set up to accommodate them, and the Lord gave me the desire to go and work there as a cook. I was successful in obtaining the position and worked there for three months with a team of people feeding 3,000 refugees a day. My position afforded me the privilege of having personal contact and interactions with Kosovaran youth, so I was able to share the Gospel with them.

My heart became broken for these people, and I became filled with so much compassion for them that I decided to travel back with the young people to Kosovo as soon as the war was over.

Toward the end of my time working in the camp, I attended a Christian conference for three days to rest and be refreshed. The organizer of the conference, Bram Oosterwijk, was a member of Derek Prince's team and knew Derek personally.

I told Bram of the work that was being done among Kosovaran refugees in the Netherlands, and he told me that during that month, Derek Prince had received revelation from God about His heart for orphans and widows and that Derek was convinced that caring for them was a key for releasing revival. He had always wanted to do more than write books and teach about what was written in the Bible, and now he had the desire to reach out to the unsaved, especially orphans and widows.

Bram already had many contacts in Albania and Kosovo, so he was able to quickly establish a link whereby members of Derek Prince Ministries could start work there. They had to drive a car from the Netherlands to Kosovo as it was needed there in order to achieve their intended mission; I asked if I could accompany them. Three weeks later, Ingrid van Diest (a member at that time of Derek Prince Ministries and a missionary organization called De Brug), Chris Loos, and I left the Netherlands in the car and drove to Albania and Kosovo.

MASS GRAVES

I clearly remember that the first thing we saw when we entered Kosovo were mass graves. There were men in white overalls from the United Nations removing bodies from the graves and then zipping them into body bags before placing them in refrigerated containers. The stench of death was everywhere and the cry of women and children left to deal with the horror of what their lives had become was heartbreaking.

When we arrived in Gjakova, we found that 80 percent of the city had been destroyed and at least 2,000 of the city's men were dead or missing. Many of the women left behind had lost their husbands, sons, and homes. After consulting with the Lord, I made a commitment to stay, live, and work in Gjakova for a year with Bram's team.

Bram coordinated the work for the Balkans from the Netherlands for the first two years of the mission, and I was often alone with the Albanian team he had entrusted to me when he made me his executive assistant. I had complete freedom to lead the team as I saw fit, and I spent a lot of time at the feet of Jesus. It was the only option I had and the only way I could get the wisdom I needed to survive in that spiritually dark and traumatized place.

Using the car we had driven from the Netherlands, we went out every day and ministered to the orphans and widows whose fathers and husbands had died during the war. Sometimes while we were in what was left of their homes, we could see the blood of their dead men splattered across the ceilings and walls. When we visited them, we often risked our own lives as there were still thousands of land mines buried in and around the area where they lived.

With my small Albanian team, we not only visited the orphans and widows, we also baked 600 loaves of bread every day to give to the hungry. We supported them as much as we could with the few resources we had. On our daily visits, we could seldom do more than hug, embrace, cry, and pray with them.

After one year, we witnessed a great breakthrough! Seven of us were together in a room praying for the coming day when suddenly a white dove appeared in the open window. It was the first time I had seen a bird that was different from the thousands of black crows I had become accustomed to seeing. Seven people, including myself, started to shake and laugh, and gold dust appeared on our hands and clothes. This was the beginning of a long-lasting Christian revival among these Muslims. In three months, 200 Muslims received Jesus as their Savior; and instead of disease and depression, there was good health and great joy among them. Daily we saw God miraculously heal people who had been so hurt and traumatized by the war.

Every day our team spent time in God's presence to be cleansed of the horrific stories that we heard throughout the day. I often prayed, "Lord, do something in this misery." He was faithful; and instead of doing just one thing, to our great delight, He started to do many miraculous things for us!

THE ORIGIN OF TRIN (TOUCH, REACH AND IMPACT NATIONS)

During my time in Kosovo, the Lord gave me deeper insights through His Word concerning His heart for orphans and widows. What He said to me was life-changing. In Kosovo, my eyes were opened to the simplicity of the Gospel. Embracing people, giving unconditional love to people who own nothing, and distributing clothes, bread, and resources so that people had the basics to survive, opened the door for God to work. We saw teams from Western countries come and go, and all were deeply impacted and changed by the simplicity of this life and ministry of simply touching people in need with God's love. Even those with large ministries returned to their homes totally changed.

One night while I was reading a book called, *Plundering Hell to Populate Heaven,* which is about the vision given to the famous evangelist, Reinhard Bonnke, I saw in the spirit the words, Touch, Reach and Impact the Nations. I knew this was a word from God to me concerning my future ministry, so I asked Him for confirmation and went to sleep.

The next morning there was an urgent knock at my door and, as I opened the door feeling slightly dazed, I saw a Kosovaran man I had never seen before. He stood in front of me, looked straight at me, and repeated the words, "Reinhard Bonnke, bigger, nations," several times. Then he ran away. I continued to stand in the doorway and felt the strong presence of God on me as I realized, with joy and amazement, that my new ministry had just been born.

After I completed my term in Kosovo with Derek Prince Ministries, I returned to the Netherlands. Due to my traumatic experiences, I went through a difficult period trying to process the events I had witnessed, and eventually fell into a deep depression. After my recovery, I felt the Lord wanted me to spend three years working in normal society. I was wondering what kind of job He wanted me to do, but as it turns out, the Lord has a sense of humor! Ever since I was born, I have had a medical sleep disorder and where did the Lord lead me to work? He led me to a job in a store selling beds!

THE BEDDING STORE

When I returned home to the Netherlands, it was obvious that I needed to purchase a new bed, so my mother and I went shopping for one. We went to the town of Nijkerk and went into a bedding store. While I sat at the table waiting for the salesperson, the Lord spoke to me and said He wanted me to work there. I asked to speak with the owner and asked him if I could work in the store as a sales-person, but under the following conditions: 1) I would be allowed to speak freely and talk with people about Jesus, 2) I would be allowed to travel 30 percent of my time without taking a cut in my salary, and 3) that Christian worship music be played in the store—and that I had the owner's permission to pray for any sick people who entered the store.

The owner, a man named Dogan, didn't know how to respond to these conditions, especially since there wasn't even an opening for a salesperson. He did, however, take my phone number, and three weeks later I received a phone call saying he had a job for me.

After years of living and working as a missionary, having to settle into working in a bedding store was a major adjustment for me. However, I remembered what I had said at a youth conference just before I started working there, "Do you influence your environment or does your environment influence you?"

Deep inside I had a longing to bring about change in my society, especially among the large majority of people who have normal jobs, a family, and a home for which they have to pay monthly rent or a mortgage. Through the routine of daily living, it is easy to become discouraged if you do not see any godly change in your surroundings. I wanted to prove that if you are a child of God, His blessing, favor, and peace are on your life and will be a witness to others. In this way, even your work environment can become a place you influence for the Kingdom of God.

My first few days were intense and in the many weeks that followed, I received and memorized a lot of information about mattresses, bed frames, and box springs. I actually wasn't very interested in beds, but I knew in my spirit that this was the place where the Lord wanted me to be for the next three years. I decided to approach the work I had been given, not with a heavy heart, but as if I were doing it for the Lord Himself. After three weeks, I began to understand, in part, what selling was all about. Europe was, at that stage, in an economic recession and it was difficult to sell something to customers the first time they entered the shop as they were often "just looking," and nervous about deciding to buy something. I often spoke to these customers and, with a smile, asked how I could make them happy that day. This often worked and allowed me to continue my conversation with them.

I regularly received a word or prophetic insight, and sometimes I would sit at the table with a customer and over a cup of coffee, talk about life. Then, because the favor and blessing of God are on my life, customers would often tell me about their personal lives and share their struggles. I would then share the Gospel with them and often this led to me praying with them as they gave their lives to Jesus. My employer tolerated everything I did as long as I eventually sold a bed, and I nearly always did! On average, I spoke to 20 to 30 customers per day, and we would spend only 20 percent of the time talking about purchasing a bed and 80 percent talking about other subjects. The beds I did sell were often high-priced items, and in the second year I sold almost $1.3 million worth of product. I did not earn commission, but worked for the minimum wage allowed by law in the country, with some extras; so it didn't matter to me how many sales I made, but to my employer it did. It wasn't long before I was one of the best salesmen—and the only one who made converts to Christianity while selling a bed!

During my time there, the atmosphere in the shop changed. We had switched to playing worship music in the background, and there was a peaceful atmosphere in the store that touched every customer who came in. Many customers had just lost someone close to them or were recently divorced, and therefore needed a new bed and other articles for their bedrooms. There were sad stories, but most people would leave the store with a smile and had been touched by Jesus. Dogan was happy because of the sales—it was a win-win situation for everyone.

During my third year working at the bedding store, I entered the shop one Tuesday morning to find Dogan sitting in his chair with his hands gripping his jaw. His facial expression was blank, and I asked what had happened. He mumbled that he had a toothache causing him to have a severe headache. He was desperate to go and see his dentist to get the pain relieved. As he was about to leave for his dentist appointment, I asked if I could pray for him. He agreed. In faith, I put my hands on his jaw and prayed, "In Jesus' name, toothache disappear. Tooth, become healthy." Dogan looked up, smiled, and was very surprised that the pain was gone. I witnessed to him, explaining that it was the strength and love of Jesus that had removed his pain—not Jesus the prophet, but Jesus the Son of God. Dogan was moved and touched by the Lord.

After three years my time at the bedding store came to an end. I had learned a lot, seen a lot, and enjoyed my time there immensely. When you are available and prepared to walk in faith, nothing is impossible for God.

To be sure, it was not always easy, and I was occasionally laughed at. Several particularly unpleasant encounters involved a deliveryman who was also a churchgoing Christian, but he really disliked me. He found it unacceptable that I prayed for people to be healed and that people received Jesus as their Savior in a store. His opinion was that this sort of thing should not happen in a business, only in a church. He would say insulting things to me; but this only strengthened my resolve, and compelled me to pray even more. The warehouse, where I was often alone, became a place of worship and a place where the Lord gave me strength to continue. He even gave me words of knowledge about the customers who would come into the store.

I tell this story because I want to encourage you in your workplace or at school to speak frankly about the Lord. Yes, you may be laughed at, bullied, or ostracized, but that is only in the beginning. Those who scorn you will realize one day that there is something special in you. Through the love they see in your eyes, they will see Jesus. Your colleagues may be going through a difficult time right now that no one knows about but them. I encourage you to go to them (or maybe they have already come to you), pray with them, put your hands on them and bless them. Go to their homes and pray for their sick. Bless your colleagues and pray that they will become open to God's love for them.

The grace of God is on your life, and He wants you to be successful in whatever you do. When your employer and colleagues start noticing your success, they will soon realize that the favor and blessing of God are on you. Do everything as if you are doing it for Jesus, including the things you would rather not do.

I used to have to clean toilets, clean windows, and unload a 40-foot container of mattresses and bed frames almost every day. I can assure you, this was not light work; but the important thing to remember is to keep your eyes on Him. Thank Him every day for the opportunity to show His Kingdom to the people around you, to push back the darkness, and to lead people to Jesus. Your workplace is your best opportunity to step out in faith.

MEETING REBEKAH

As the time to leave the bedding store approached, I got in touch with Wilfred Gibson, a man of God whose vocation it is to coach people in identifying their calling and help them to map practical steps toward achieving it. It was extremely helpful to me to write down my dreams, prophecies, and my own desires on paper. In conjunction with the Lord, we developed a 'road map' for me to follow for the next five years. This was a good way to help me realize the next practical steps I should take toward giving hands and feet to the vision and dream of Touch, Reach and Impact the Nations (TRIN). Along with a few friends, we began work on the 'road map' for TRIN. It took three years before we finally realized the full vision the Lord had for us.

One of the things that I had so dearly wanted was to marry a woman who had the same passion for Jesus and calling to the nations as I did. Previously, while in Kosovo, I had met and befriended Bob

Fitts, a great worship leader from Hawaii. In September 2003, I invited myself to visit Bob and Kathy, his wife, in Kona, Hawaii.

It was there, on the beaches of Hawaii while eating a pizza that the Lord began to speak to me about meeting my wife soon. He wanted me to describe the wife of my dreams. I found this so considerate of God that I began writing down what the wife of my dreams would be like that same evening. I read it to Kathy Fitts, and the very next evening she arranged a blind date for me. It turned out to be with the daughter of the legendary singer, Keith Green. It was a pleasant meeting, but nothing of note came from it. I knew that God had to settle this through His heavenly "dating agency." I left Hawaii to go to Toronto, Canada, and on the way, I had a stopover in Nashville, Tennessee, where I and Bram Oosterwijk had been invited to speak about Kosovo at a Baptist church.

To fly to Nashville, I had to transfer to a different plane in Chicago. When I boarded the second plane, I accidentally sat in the wrong seat and only realized this when an older couple told me that I was sitting in one of their seats. The couple stood looking at me and, to my surprise, the woman began to cry. I was already a little weary from the long journey, so I didn't give this incident too much thought. I just noted how unusual it was. (Now, remember this incident for later!) When I finally arrived in Nashville, Bram was at the airport to pick me up, and he told me that he had bad news. The church where we had been invited to speak had canceled the conference, so it appeared that our long journeys had been in vain.

We both began asking God what His plans and purposes were, and we both had the feeling that there was a special reason why we were in Nashville. Indirectly, we had heard that there were three other Christian conferences taking place in the city at that very moment. We were particularly interested in one of the conferences because its topic was helping orphans and widows, a topic that wasn't very popular at that time but was very close to our hearts.

However, we had a problem. We didn't know the correct address, so we just started driving through Nashville, a very big city, in faith. We soon lost our way and arrived in a ghetto. There was broken glass and dirty needles everywhere and on every street corner sinister-looking individuals stood talking or watching people passing by.

The names of the streets had been removed so, praying for God's guidance, we drove around and arrived at an old building with a large, wooden gate. There was no poster on the billboard but we felt that we had to stop and knock. The door was opened slowly and behind the door we could see a group of people praying. The person who was leading the prayer meeting was the same woman who had became so emotional on the plane! She looked at me, screamed, started to cry, and all the while tried to explain to us that she had been praying for us to find them. She had already known on the plane that I had to be at this conference and that they had to "pray us in." A very bizarre experience indeed!

As it turned out, these people were hosting a small conference that focused on the care of orphans, widows, and the poor. Bram and I both knew that this would be a special experience for us. Soon after we arrived, a graceful older woman came to me with a large sword in her hand. She started prophesying about me reaching the nations and that I would meet my wife at the conference. The name of this prophetess was Angela Greenig. That same afternoon, the pastor of the church, Scott MacLeod, came to me and started praying for me. He said that God wanted me here, that I would be deeply touched (which actually happened), and that I would meet my wife here.

The next morning, Rebekah Krell arrived as a guest speaker at the conference. She was a strikingly beautiful young woman with a great passion for Jesus. She also had a very unique background and calling. I knew from the moment I saw her that she was going to be my wife! She was so beautiful, and all I could think was, "She will never notice me." Rebekah's spiritual mother, Angela Greenig, asked me whether or not I had met her spiritual daughter. With a thudding heart, I found Rebekah during lunch and, after I introduced myself to her, she simply shook my hand and then began talking with someone else. My heart was confident that she was the one. With only four days left in Nashville, I knew I had to create an opportunity to speak to her.

On the last evening of the conference, Rebekah was dancing near the front of the hall. I was seated on the other side of the hall, and I asked the Lord for a sign that she was indeed the one, and that this sign would be that within the next five or ten minutes, she would pass right in front of me as she danced. To my great astonishment, after only two minutes she ran through the audience and began dancing right in front of me!

I still had one day to go before I left Nashville, and still I hadn't spoken to Rebekah. I felt desperate, and I was afraid that I would soon be sitting on the plane without having made any meaningful contact with her.

Then Angela came up to me and asked if I still wanted to speak to Rebekah. I said I did and she told me to go outside, so I did—and there was Rebekah! I sat down on the grass next to her and actually dominated the conversation by nervously telling her somewhat exaggerated stories about myself! I received little response from her except for a few tears on her cheek as she continued to stare into the sky, and that was that. Nothing happened, and I flew to Toronto and then on to my final destination, the Netherlands. Three weeks later, on my birthday (of which she was unaware), I received an email from Rebekah. She asked me whether I remembered her, and she told me that since we had met, her life had changed.

I immediately called her, and she confessed that she had received a vision from the Lord during the conversation we had while sitting on the grass: she had seen our angels dancing together. She then knew that I would be her husband. In addition, she had seen how we would travel together to many nations, and in particular she saw an orphanage in Africa, that we would have a son, and that when he took his first steps he would be surrounded by black children. We married on May 21, 2005, and on March 8, 2006, we had our first son, Zephaniah. Eighteen months later, while visiting Iris Ministries in Pemba, Mozambique, Zephaniah took his first steps.

FULL TIME

A month before we married, we held a TRIN board meeting. At that time, my three years at the bedding store were over and several exciting doors were opening for TRIN. I felt it was now time to start working full time for TRIN. CP Helms and Theo Stouten, two friends of mine, challenged me to believe God for a fixed income every month so I could quit my job. I decided to trust God to give me $1,940 to live on every month, and together we began to pray for this amount.

For many years prior to this, I had been involved in the Soul Survivor ministry, and three weeks before our wedding on May 21, 2005, I had attended the Soul Survivor Festival, a large youth festival that attracts about 3,000 people. While Jason Upton led worship, Rebekah, Angela Greenig, and I went to meet a friend of ours who had brought his brother-in-law, a man who had backslidden, to the festival.

Rebekah and Angela prayed for him, spoke some prophetic words over him, and we walked on. Later we heard that this man had a powerful experience with God and had made the radical choice to give up his old life completely and follow Jesus. This man attended our wedding on May 21 and heard from God that he was to support us financially.

After a memorable wedding, we were in the hotel that evening, unwrapping our presents. In the basket of gifts, we saw a card on which was written, "I'm going to support your work by giving you $1,940 per month!" At first I thought this was a joke and so, at 1 A.M., I called CP to tell him the good news. He was as surprised and happy as Rebekah and I were at this wonderful offer. It proved not to be a joke and four weeks later we met this man and his partner.

Together, they were leading a young company and they wanted to support us. I gave up my job and starting running TRIN full time in September 2005. That first month, I went to India and invited our two sponsors to come along with me. We experienced such special things that we decided to work together. The company offered us office space in their building in Nijkerk, just behind the bedding store.

BREAKTHROUGHS

From that time on, the Lord has given us tremendous break-throughs! Many of the staff at the company who were supporting us gave their lives to the Lord and the number of TRIN staff grew to six in the first three months. In October 2005, we had the idea of holding Fire Nights and Christian conferences. We had few resources, but just went ahead and did it—night after night, conference after conference, the Lord's presence was with us. In addition, we began traveling over-seas more frequently to help orphans, widows, and the oppressed in various countries.

In a period of six months, we saw 15,000 people come to Jesus in Pakistan, Uganda, India, Cape Verde, Kosovo, and the Netherlands. Today, we still host a Fire Night on most Saturday evenings, and people come from all over the Netherlands, and even Belgium, to experience God's touch during the worship, preaching, and times of prayer. All this started very simply because we wanted to be obedient to the call of God and because our hearts were set to facilitate the presence of the Holy Spirit. We never advertise, but through word-of-mouth people hear about the Fire Nights and, with their curiosity piqued, they come from far and wide to attend.

People often receive healing, a new passion for Jesus, as well as encouragement, but what thrills us even more is that we see people start believing in their dreams again. Through our Internet broadcasts, many people in various countries around the world have been reached. Every month we have training conferences during which practical teaching is given by national and international speakers.

We have started a fast-growing church for people who are longing to see revival and transformation, and are prepared to reach out to places around the world to see it achieved. We also have a child sponsorship program called Project Held where we financially support hundreds of orphans throughout the world with offices in India, Uganda, and Pakistan—with more about to open in Europe. We have live streaming television via the Internet, and every month we lead two to three outreaches into other countries. Our amazing TRIN team works very hard to make all of these events possible. We see a movement arising that is touching nations with the Good News of Jesus and has a great impact on many people. I live in a dream together with Rebekah, our sons, and daughter. A dream that has become reality!

DARE TO DREAM AGAIN!

If all this is possible in my life, it's also possible in your life. As Oral Roberts would say, "When you see the invisible, you can do the impossible!"[1]

If you choose to believe in things that are not visible (which takes faith), God will help you do the impossible! Let the lion in you roar, for you are the head and not the tail. Remove the covering from your eyes and your heart; go; believe again; and shake off the restrictions you have put on what God can do in your life due to your "small-box" mentality.

"Yes," you might say, "but I've been hurt too badly. I am so disappointed, and I can't believe any more."

To this I say, "Stop licking your wounds! Leave your past behind and run to the Father who promises you a wonderful future. Dare to believe again. The time for self-pity and procrastination is over. It is now your time to rise up and shine!"

Perhaps you feel incompetent, or that you're stupid and good for nothing. Or maybe you're trapped into believing some other restricting force is at work in your life. Pay no attention to your own opinions about your ability or inability to achieve your dream if they do not correspond to the Word of God.

I love the example of a donkey. I often feel like the donkey that Jesus rode on Palm Sunday into Jerusalem. The only thing I want is the Lord Jesus Christ entering into areas where it is dark so that His light can shine there. Sometimes it seems like many Christians want to ride on the donkey, and they behave as if *they* are the king instead of Jesus. God is looking for an army of donkeys who simply want to carry His glory. Perhaps you feel paralyzed mentally or physically, and you feel that you are not good enough to accomplish the task. Maybe it goes further than that and you genuinely feel frustrated and discouraged. If that is so, then the Lord has this prophetic promise for you in Zephaniah 3:17-20:

> *"The Lord your God is with you, the Mighty Warrior who saves. He will take great delight in you; in His love He will no longer rebuke you, but will rejoice over you with singing. I will remove from you all who mourn over the loss of your appointed festivals, which is a burden and reproach for you. At that time I will deal with all who oppressed you. I will rescue the lame; I will gather the exiles. I will give them praise and honor in every*

land where they have suffered shame. At that time I will gather you; at that time I will bring you home. I will give you honor and praise among all the peoples of the earth when I restore your fortunes before your very eyes," says the Lord.

ENDNOTE

1.   Oral Roberts, *When You See the Invisible, You Can Do the Impossible* (Shippensburg, PA: Destiny Image Publishers, 2002).

CHAPTER 2

HOW CAN YOU FULFILL YOUR DREAM?

Do you have a dream in your heart that you feel is God-given? If you close your eyes right now, can you see yourself walking in that dream? God has a purpose and a destiny for all His children and He expects us to work hard to make the dreams He has given us become a reality.

My big dream is to see people set free from the bondage they are in to man-made systems and structures and see them released to become all that God intended them to be. It is an ideal that is described by David in Psalm 1 where it is written that we will be like trees planted by streams of water that yield their fruit in season and whose leaves do not wither. Whatever we do will prosper.

When your dreams seem too big or too difficult for you to achieve, remember that there is nothing, absolutely nothing, too difficult for God, or, as Oral Roberts said, "When you see the invisible, you can do the impossible."

"But," you might ask, "what is the secret to my vision or dream becoming a reality so that I can walk in my destiny and be successful?" I will give you several keys to help you do this successfully. They are principles that have helped me walk in my destiny, and I believe that they will do the same for you.

THINK POSITIVELY

"If you want to be successful in life, then you must follow your dreams" is a popular saying in the Netherlands.

Something to keep in mind is that your life will often be formed by your expectations. What you expect and think, in many cases, is what you will receive. What you sow, you will reap. If you fill yourself with positive thoughts and surround yourself with positive people, your life will also lean in that direction.

However, if you are constantly thinking in a negative way and surrounding yourself with negative people, you will probably have a life that is less than satisfying. If you expect a life filled with failures, disappointments, defeat, and mediocrity, your subconscious will not be searching for ways to succeed—and this will guarantee that you don't! Every time you try to break this vicious cycle, you are unlikely to succeed because the root of the problem, your negative mindset, has not been dealt with.

From my own experience I have learned that it is very important to raise your expectations if you want to have and achieve a bigger vision for yourself. You will never see change in your life if you do not change your thinking first. As this is such an important part of living a successful life, I am going to go deeper into this subject later on in the book.

If you have a specific vision, there will always be people and circumstances that try to discourage you. However, no matter how many people tell you that you will not succeed, if you maintain an attitude of faith, persevere through difficult times, and continuously claim God's grace and blessings on your life, then God will open doors for you and change your circumstances so that you do succeed.

INVEST IN YOUR FAITH HEROES

It should be clear that prayer, intimacy with the Father, and seeking God's wisdom are very important keys for accomplishing the plans God has for your life. However, there is something else that I want to share with you and it is something that is so easily overlooked by most people. One of the quickest ways to attain your vision is to help your spiritual fathers and mothers, your heroes in the faith, and those who have had a significant impact on your life, to achieve their own goals.

Perhaps your instinct is to erect various walls around yourself to protect both yourself and your dreams, but the truth is that the fastest way to reach your goals is by serving your mentors and those who inspire you.

I will give you an example. Suppose you have a dream of bringing millions of people to Jesus. You are an evangelist and you have already seen many people come to repentance through your tremendous passion for Jesus and lost souls. You have read books by Reinhard Bonnke or Billy Graham and you have the same dream as they have. My advice to you would be to invest in these pioneers, pray for them, buy their books, and bless them financially so they can achieve their goals. You are, in fact, part of their harvest and God will bless you and allow your area of influence to be enlarged as you enable them to do the same thing. As you sow, so shall you reap is such an important Kingdom principle that I will come back to further on in the book.

I am sure you have someone, an example or a role model, who has had an impact on your life and walk with God. It may be that someone has encouraged you when you were down. Or, perhaps when you hear a particular CD, watch a particular video, read books by a certain inspiring author, or even hear a certain speaker, your faith is built up. You are then able to claim back everything that satan has stolen from you and continue your Christian walk encouraged and revived.

It could be your pastor or youth leader who has helped you through your difficult times, or someone who has helped you to overcome the guilt from your past that has filled you with feelings of rejection and shame. This is someone who has taught you to look at yourself and your future from God's point of view, or someone who has instructed you, taught you many things, and helped you to walk by faith. It may also be a spiritual father or mother. These are faithful people who have trodden difficult paths with you and are deeply involved in your life.

The Bible says the following about this in Hebrews 13:7-8:

> *Remember your leaders, who spoke the word of God to you. Consider the outcome of their way of life and imitate their faith. Jesus Christ is the same yesterday and today and forever.*

There have been many people who have had an impact on my life and in whom I have invested. Among them are Brother Andrew van der Bijl, Angela Greenig, Reinhard Bonnke, Heidi Baker, Bram Oosterwijk, Ken Gott, Kris Vallotten, Professor Willem Ouweneel, Jan Sjoerd Pasterkamp, and many more. They are my mentors whether they are near to me or far away. They have accepted me as their equal, but for me they will always be my fathers and mothers in the faith. I ask them for advice, listen to their tapes, read their books, and try to go to their conferences. I learn from them and I honor them. These people have had such a major impact on my life that it would be foolish of me not to support them.

DO UNTO OTHERS...

In Luke 6:31 Jesus taught us to *"Do to others as you would have them do to you."* This means that if you treat others as you would like to be treated, you will reap the good deeds, kindness, compassion, etc., which you sow into their lives as these acts will be multiplied and returned to abundantly bless you.

In the same way, if someone has blessed you, it would make sense to return the blessing. If a friend paid the bill the last time you went to dinner together, make sure you pay the bill the next time you meet to share a meal. If a colleague has worked overtime to help you catch up with your workload, then return the favor the next time that person needs help to deal with their own workload.

Maybe you have a lot of questions about this aspect of Christianity, especially if you live in a country where financial matters are not an easy subject to talk about, but I challenge you to get involved and just do it! Sit down and carefully make a list of people who have been a blessing to you in recent years, people inside or outside the ministry. Bless them in return and watch what happens. You really will be surprised!

THE PRINCIPLE OF SOWING AND REAPING

Sowing and reaping is a principle God has given us and an important key to achieving your dreams. Sowing means giving financial gifts, time, love, and prayers with an attitude of love and joy. The word *sowing* in the Bible is an agricultural metaphor, where literally, the farmer sows seed in his fields, and in due course, will harvest its crop. Many countries still have farms in rural areas. The farmer does not sow his seed, which is his livelihood, reluctantly or with an unhappy face. The day he starts to sow is often a cause for celebration! And rightly so, as this very important act of sowing means that the farmer is not only investing in his future, but also visualizing the great return.

When he starts planting, the farmer sees only a plowed field; but in his mind he can already see how, in a few weeks' time, the first green blades of his crop will be visible and that, eventually, there will be a large harvest. He also knows his harvest will be so much more than the original amount of seed he sowed into the ground. Depending on the type of seed he sowed, it could multiply tenfold, or even a hundredfold. The farmer sees the invisible, and that is faith.

The natural often works in the spiritual, and we often see that the Lord meant the principle of sowing and reaping to be used spiritually as well. We can sow our seed in the form of financial gifts, time, love, etc., into spiritual ground, and give to the Kingdom of God, knowing that, in time, we will reap a harvest many times the size of the one we sowed.

Sowing should be done on a regular basis, and that means asking God every day what you can sow that day. This can take the form of sowing time, prayers, material things, or finances into God's Kingdom.

EXPECT A BIG HARVEST

Many people are very attached to their money and are very proud when, even though they are earning a good salary, they persuade themselves to give away $50.

Remember this: Whoever sows sparingly will also reap sparingly, and whoever sows generously will also reap generously. Each of you should give what you have decided in your heart to give, not reluctantly or under compulsion, for God loves a cheerful giver. And God is able to bless you abundantly, so that in all things at all times, having all that you need, you will abound in every good work. As it is written: "They have freely scattered their gifts to the poor; their righteousness endures forever." Now he who supplies seed to the sower and bread for food will also supply and increase your store of seed and will enlarge the harvest of your righteousness. You will be enriched in every way so that you can be generous on every occasion, and through us your generosity will result in thanksgiving to God (2 Corinthians 9:6-11).

Here it is very clear that those who sow abundantly will also reap abundantly. I challenge you to take the next three months and write down everything that you sow, including what you give away and to whom. On the left side of the page, make a column with the heading SEED, along with the date on which it was sown, and to the right of the page, make a column with the heading HARVEST. You will truly be amazed when you see what is in the right-hand column after three months!

Years ago, I was challenged to apply this principle of sowing and reaping to my own life. At first, I was rather hesitant and cynical and did not really expect a harvest. However, the Lord spoke to me and said that just as a farmer expects to sow and then reap his harvest, I should expect to do the same. And so I did, with outstanding results! I once gave away my last $65 and three months later I found an envelope in my mailbox with $325 in it. Some time ago we were having financial difficulties, and the instinctive response was to sow less financially during that month. But the Lord encouraged me to continue sowing by saying, "Seek first My Kingdom and My righteousness, and all these things will be given to you as well. Therefore do not worry about tomorrow, for tomorrow will worry about itself" (see Matt. 6:33-34a).

One night, during one of our services, I sowed $130, which was the only money I had. A week later, Heidi Baker was our guest for the weekend. She is a good friend and spiritual mother. (Heidi and her husband, Rolland, are committed to helping thousands of orphans in Mozambique and they have been experiencing a great revival during the last few years.) One evening while she was at home with us, the Lord Jesus said to her that she was to give us $10,000. The next morning, Heidi told us that she had a financial gift to give us on behalf of Jesus, and we were so surprised and grateful!

Few things are more important than learning how to sow into God's Kingdom, because it teaches us not to become attached to the things of the world. We are often trapped by being attached to material things and then find ourselves relying more on money than on God. What would you do if the Lord asked you to give away 30 percent of your income each month by sowing it into His Kingdom? What if He asked you to give away your new car? Would you do it?

A DEBT-FREE LIFE

In Deuteronomy 28:12, the following promise is clearly written concerning those who obey God.

> *The Lord will open the heavens, the storehouse of His*
> *bounty, to send rain on your land in season and to bless*
> *all the work of your hands. You will lend to many nations*
> *but will borrow from none.*

Reading this leads me to believe that God wants to bless us abundantly. He also does not want us to be indebted to others because when we are, we are in no position to give or sow anything because it is not our own. This means we miss a good harvest. Most houses and cars belong to the bank, not the individual. I believe that God wants to set us free from this. For example, during the time of the first disciples in the Book of Acts, people had land or houses, which they sold and all the proceeds were sown into the Kingdom of God. We see that everyone shared everything and everyone had enough, which allowed them all to live in abundance (see Acts 4).

In my life, people often look at me and what I have and think that there is some special favor of God on my life which they do not have. To these people I say that God has no favorites. The blessings I receive are results of obeying the principle of sowing and reaping. A natural result is that doors have been opened, and we have been able to live out our dreams with all the resources we need.

Go, sow, and become part of receiving the great harvest! Stop giving measly tips to God, and really sow, expecting a large harvest. The best thing you can sow is yourself, just as Jesus gave nothing less than His own life. In the Bible, Jesus is compared to a grain of wheat that has been sown into the ground to die. In John 12:23-25, Jesus speaks:

> ...The hour has come for the Son of Man to be glorified.
> ...I tell you, unless a kernel of wheat falls to the ground
> and dies, it remains only a single seed. But if it dies, it
> produces many seeds. Anyone who loves their life will
> lose it, while anyone who hates their life in this world will
> keep it for eternal life.

TRUE FRIENDSHIP

Another key to having your dreams come true is having true friendships. Make sure you have three or four genuine friends around you. These should be people you can trust completely, friends who believe in you but who are also honest and are not afraid to speak the truth to you. These are friends who want you to be successful; and while ensuring that everything goes well with you, are also able to see your blind spots and are willing to help bring out the best in you. They must be people who love you unconditionally.

We live in an era in which it has become increasingly difficult to find people who treasure, trust, and love; and, as a result, our society sometimes becomes a very lonely place. Whenever I am in Christian circles, the things I see surprise me. It is as if we do not know what real friendship is anymore. In many cases, people who claim to be friends are actually better categorized as acquaintances. What is even sadder is that when we look at people who are in the "ministry," their circles of friends tend to include only others in ministry.

Interestingly enough, in recent years, the number of people who want to be called my friend has steadily grown in direct relation to the success of our ministry, TRIN. However, during our most difficult times, the number of friends we had would suddenly decrease. Unfortunately, there are also those so-called friends who are jealous or full of self-ambition and are not able to stand it if things are really going well for a friend in ministry.

For example, there was a good friend of ours who was a well-known speaker. Everywhere he went, he experienced revival, and it seemed as if he had a lot of friends, or at least a lot of ministry friends. A few years ago, he and his ministry hit a rough spot and over time, he could count the number of real friends he had on just one hand. As it turned out, the rest were just "ministry friends" who had tapped into his success for the purposes of advancing their own positions. When his success came to an end, so did these friendships.

I know who my real friends are from the way they behave toward me. They are people I can completely trust, and with whom I can be myself. They often are not interested in my successes, but instead are interested in who I am and how I am doing. These are people who do not look at who I am from the outside but rather at who I am on the inside. It is with this foundation of real friendships that I dare to dream dreams and to live, because I know that they will be there when I fall, when I am tired, or when I need help. I know that they do not talk behind my back, gossip, or undermine me, but that they sincerely want to help me become successful. Everyone needs this kind of friendship. It is vitally important.

Perhaps you find it difficult to develop real friendships, but I would remind you that you reap what you sow. Start out by asking the Lord to give you real friends. Who is a person right now in whom you can completely trust and with whom you can build a strong friendship? Perhaps you can name only one person, and that's OK. Invest in this friendship by expressing your appreciation, opening your heart, and learning to trust again.

In my experience, people who themselves have been betrayed or have gone through difficult situations are the ones who know what true friendship is and what is required to sustain it. It is not always easy, so my hope is that you will persevere and soon be in the company of genuine friends who honor and respect you. Members of the Body of Christ still have much to learn about how to relate to each other as friends, as brothers, and as sisters. Important keystone values for a long-term friendship are loyalty, honor, and respect. Make the decision today to be a true friend to people in your community.

CHARACTER IS MORE IMPORTANT THAN ANOINTING

In your walk with God, it is important to remember that character and anointing are two entirely different things and they are not to be confused or compared with each other. God can appoint a person for a specific task or a specific mission and, in order to enable them to achieve the goal that He has given them, He anoints them with His supernatural power and grace. (To be anointed is to carry the manifest presence of God.)

It is important to note that even though anointing and character are two entirely different things, they need to be held in balance with each other. You can be highly anointed, experience all sorts of miracles and signs, and even see revival, but at the same time, you can be out of balance because your character has not grown with your level of anointing.

I know many people whom God has anointed, but who often have an unpleasant character and refuse to do anything to improve themselves. One can be anointed, but still live in sin. Just take a look around you. There are many anointed men and women who have fallen into sin and, as a result, the ministry that they devoted their lives to developing, simply disintegrated. Why? Because God, in His love and mercy wants to anoint us; and the anointing, according to the Bible, cannot be removed, but He is not willing to let us continue in ministry if we refuse to deal with our past and the things hampering the growth of our character.

Our character is much more important to Him. Therefore, if we are not willing to bring to light and address the flaws in our character—the hidden sins and things that we have been struggling with—God will. We are entering a time when God will no longer tolerate His people living with hidden sin while we have an anointing on our lives. All will soon be revealed.

First Peter 4:17 warns:

> ...It is time for judgment to begin with God's household; and if it begins with us, what will the outcome be for those who do not obey the gospel of God?

And Hebrews 10:26 says:

If we deliberately keep on sinning after we have received
the knowledge of the truth, no sacrifice for sins is left.

It is time that all men and women, young and old, looked inside themselves and dealt with old wounds, hidden sins, undealt with rejection, disappointment, bitterness, and being unwilling to forgive. We must release the past so that we can become sacred temples that God can work in and through. With God, everything is possible, and it is His will and desire to sanctify and release us. Anointing comes to those who are obedient to the call of God. We do not have to concern ourselves with whether or not we have received the anointing of God. Instead of focusing on the anointing, we each need to work on improving our character!

BE RELIABLE

The next important key to success is being faithful with the small things. We all want to do many big and important things, but that is not possible if we do not first learn to be faithful in the small things in life. Live your life with integrity, and always let your yes be yes and your no be no. Make it a practice to be reliable, and do not be deceitful. Honor your appointments, arrive on time, be helpful, pay your accounts before they are due, and be faithful and diligent in all the duties and responsibilities you already have, whether they are at home, at work, at school, or in the church. God will greatly bless your efforts; the favor on your life will increase; and it will open important doors for you.

Unfortunately, even in Christian communities, there is distrust, jealously, and the desire to position oneself high up in a hierarchical structure. I would encourage you to remember that if you are faithful in the small things, God will promote you and push you forward. You will be asked to do many different things because in many ministries there is a chronic shortage of reliable Christians who are faithful in the small things. There is so much miscommunication and even intentional attacks among Christians, that the result is often very destructive. Ironically, we Christians often present such bad examples to the world through our lack of love for each other, that people in the world do not want to go to church—and I don't blame them. We must repent of all our evil ways and personal agendas, and we must search our hearts and release everything that makes us bitter and unforgiving.

WHAT IF YOU DON'T HAVE A DREAM?

I hear this question often, "What if I don't have a dream?" God had a vision and a dream, and He created us! He created us in His likeness, so we, too, are creative beings. I believe that, like God, each of us has a vision or dream deep within us. In Jeremiah 29:11 we are promised that, as we seek God, He will give us a future filled with hope. I believe this is the hope that comes from working toward achieving the dreams and visions God has given us.

Maybe you have never asked God what His dream is for your life. Or maybe it is not yet the right time for the fulfillment of your dream because God is still preparing you for it. It may be that you have a vision or dream that is so great that you can't achieve it by yourself. If so, then it is important that you find an organization or church with the same dream or vision as you have and achieve it together. By doing this, you can contribute to a common dream and vision. We need each other.

Within TRIN, the majority of our staff members works to achieve their own dreams and are given the opportunity and freedom to realize these dreams, as long as they also fit within the vision and objectives of

TRIN. If their specific visions and dreams differ from TRIN's, we help them realize those dreams outside of TRIN and, in some instances, help them start their own ministries. We bless them with everything that is in us, and we partner with them. There is no competition in God's Kingdom and no tolerance for playing political games to become successful. This is the world's way of doing things, but the Kingdom of God is different. God's Kingdom is one of serving, encouraging, and helping each other.

PRACTICAL STEPS FOR REALIZING YOUR DREAM

There are a number of pointers that have helped me achieve my dreams, which I will share with you:

1. Write down your dream on paper and talk about it with other people. Through this process, you will be able to better articulate the specifics of your dream.

2. Make sure you have people around you who love you and believe in you. When you feel discouraged, they will encourage you.

3. Formulate a step-by-step plan and ask people you respect and have a strong relationship with to advise you in this process. Many plans do not survive due to a lack of vision and knowledge.

4. Determine what finances will be required to implement your plan and identify your key motivating factor for achieving your dream.

5. Dare to continuously release control of your dream and place it in God's hands.

6. Go and pursue it with perseverance and dedication.

7. Never give up!

CHAPTER 3

GOD'S WILL FOR YOUR LIFE

The Bible clearly states that if you believe that Jesus Christ is the Son of the Most High God; that Jesus died on the cross so that your sins will be forgiven; that God, His Father, resurrected Jesus from the dead on the third day; that the Holy Spirit is poured out on all flesh; then, by believing and accepting all these things, you are a son or daughter of God! Not only that, you are also God's heir and co-heir with Jesus Christ! That's certainly a reason to be grateful every day. And then there is the added bonus of the Holy Spirit living in you. The Holy Spirit communicates with your spirit that you are indeed a child of God. This is lesson number one in hearing God's voice and understanding His will for your life. You can hear His voice 24 hours a day, 7 days a week, because the Holy Spirit lives in you, right now, at this very moment.

I have met many people who struggle with trying to figure out God's will for their lives. Some have been struggling for years, and they are so tired that they have given up all hope of being able to discern and do God's will. They think they are unable to hear His voice and have become frustrated. This sends them on a downward spiral full of uncertainty and fear. I used to experience this myself, but I have now discovered that discerning God's will for me is easier than I thought.

Put simply, God's will for your life is that you, as the crowning glory of His creation, become all that He created you to be. The most important thing our Father asks you to do is to live, to be an ambassador for God's Kingdom on Earth, and that you become passionate about these things as you experience His love. God's will for your life is for you to be successful and happy; to love yourself and others; to care for the poor, orphans, and widows; and to really make a difference in this dark world.

Retirement and nursing homes are often full of people who have not achieved their dreams because they were afraid that it was not God's will. When we think like this we are being "religious"[1] and are succumbing to the voice of fear instead of listening to God's voice. We are too focused on our own limitations instead of God's ability to do the impossible in and through us.

GREEN LIGHT

Dear reader, as mentioned previously, I see a lot of Christians who are waiting at the traffic light, unsure whether the light is red or green. Too many people say they are waiting for the green light, and they keep waiting and waiting. I used to think just like that, but 14 years ago, I changed my thinking because of something Brother Andrew said. I then began thinking, "Let's say that God's will for my life is not as complicated as I think it is. Suppose that for the majority of decisions I have to make, the signal is simply green. And if so, what am I waiting for?"

Now, 14 years later, my conclusion is that there are more green lights than red. My daily prayer now is, "Lord, thank You for this great day. If something is not Your will for me to do, close the doors and make it obvious that You are showing me a red stop light, and that I should not follow that path any longer. I thank You, Lord, for all the other open doors."

Suppose you're walking down the street and you see an elderly man fall off his bike. What would you do? Would you get on your knees and beg God to tell you whether or not you ought to help this man? Are you going to text message your intercessors to ask what God's will is in this situation? Do you walk around the situation pretending you don't see it, because you think that you are not good enough to help this person? Or are you so proud that you would rather let someone else help the needy person? Of course not! You would simply help this person because that's God's will. That's not a difficult decision to make!

I, too, have often asked, "Lord, is this Your will?" And almost always the question is returned to me like a boomerang. God says, "Mattheus, what does *My* Word say about this situation?" Or, when the question is about things I would enjoy doing, He says, "What do you want to do, Mattheus?"

Our Father wants to give us His best! He wants to give us His blessings, His Word, His love, His gifts, and His talents—everything. He has even given us His Son. It is time that we begin to live as God's children. His will for our lives is that we fully come to life and bring others to life. Let's become less religious and increasingly pay attention to what the voice of the Spirit of God in us is saying, and do the things we are supposed to do.

SELF-TALK

The biggest obstacles in our lives can come from incorrect thinking. It is so important that we know who we are in the Lord and that we understand we are sons and daughters of the Most High God and no longer slaves. However, we so often have a negative attitude toward ourselves, about others, and even about God the Father, and these negative thoughts adversely influence us. This often happens subconsciously, and we simply don't recognize how destructive this is. These are lies that have filled our hearts and minds for so long that we think they are the truth! We have come to believe that God seldom hears our prayers. We have become convinced that the mediocre life we lead will probably not get any better. These are lies from our eternal enemy, satan, because God says something completely different! Hear the words of Jesus in John 10:10: *"...I have come that they may have life, and have it to the full."*

Make the decision to no longer listen to the lies and negative thoughts in your head. Self-talk means that you are constantly talking to yourself, about yourself, in your thoughts. This flow of thoughts, on the conscious and subconscious level, is in constant operation and is responsible for our moods and ultimately for our behavior. For each area in our lives that we continue to believe a lie, we give the father of lies, satan, the right to steal, kill, and destroy—not only in our own lives, but in the lives of those who have been placed under our authority. In order for deliverance to take place, these lies should be detected and dealt with.

To bind our negative, deceptive, wrong thinking has little meaning if we do not renew our minds and therefore our thinking. This is why the Bible says that we must renew our minds, and this can only be done by knowing the truth of God's Word. In Psalm 51:6 it is written, *"Yet You desired faithfulness even in the womb, You taught me wisdom in that secret place."*

It is much harder to destroy a half-truth than a whole lie. What you think and believe determines how you feel and what you do. We must expose the lies in our minds and replace them with the truth. Jesus is

the Way, the Truth, and the Life! Don't fool yourself into believing that
everything you think is OK, for then you will never work at eradicat-
ing the hidden, negative self-talk that is constantly discouraging and
intimidating you, or making you angry. There is a saying that "you
are your own worst enemy." Self-talk is often the result of a deep-set
pattern of thoughts and habits from as far back as your childhood and
is, therefore, already fixed in your thought pattern. Renewing your
thoughts begins by questioning old beliefs and the conclusions that
you have drawn from them.

First, we need the help of the Holy Spirit to recognize, discern,
and make it a practice to avoid negative thoughts and erroneous belief
systems that are in opposition to God's truth. Second, we need to ask
for perseverance every day to fight against negative thoughts until they
no longer have any influence in our lives.

Today, right this minute, it is time to revoke all wrong thoughts and
beliefs and declare war on them. Above all else, we must, with all diligence, guard our hearts for the heart is the wellspring of life. It is important to realize that our thinking and our perceptions form our reality
and thus our future; so what you choose to believe is vitally important
to your well-being. It not only determines how you operate and how you
handle situations in your life, it also determines how you view the world.

An essential key for making this change is the truth, which is free
and gives life. That is why it is so important to proclaim the truth of
the Word of God over your life and to fill your mind with the truth of
the Word. Fill your thoughts with Scriptures that can help you change
your thinking. I will give you some examples of Scriptures that have
helped me; but I encourage you to find scriptural truths in the Bible
for your own life.

*What, then, shall we say in response to these things? If
God is for us, who can be against us?* (Romans 8:31)

They triumphed over him by the blood of the Lamb and by the word of their testimony... (Revelation 12:11).

A thousand may fall at your side, ten thousand at your right hand, but it will not come near you. You will only observe with your eyes and see the punishment of the wicked. If you say, "The Lord is my refuge," and you make the Most High your dwelling... (Psalm 91:7-9).

It would also help for you to remember and repeat the following:

- I am the crown of God's creation, and I am His son/daughter.

- Negative comments from other people say more about who they are than about who I am.

- My self-esteem should no longer depend on what other people think about me; because if they give it to me, they can also take it away from me.

- I am not my body, I just live in it. It plays no decisive role in who I am or what I am worth.

- Failure is not fatal, as long as I learn from it.

- If I continue doing what I always do, I will continue to get the same results.

- This negative feeling I have about myself is a lie based on an unpleasant experience I had in the past.

- I will assume that other people like me, unless they specifically tell me they don't.

- I can no longer be afraid of people, because people only have power over me if I give it to them.

- If God is lonely without you in this life; you will probably be lonely forever in the next life without Him.

- Everything I do will prosper (see Ps. 1:3).

- Pain can make you bitter or better; it's ultimately your choice. Nothing that happens to you can permanently affect you, unless you choose to respond to it incorrectly. It is your reaction that ultimately defines whether you'll be bitter or better.

"WHEN YOU SEE THE INVISIBLE..."

"When you see the invisible, you can do the impossible." This statement by Oral Roberts has completely changed my life. I use this statement often, proclaiming and receiving it. I invite you to do the same. God's will for our lives is that we, His children, come alive and reflect His glory in the spiritual darkness that surrounds us.

For years I wrestled with trying to discern God's will for my life. Sometimes I would pray for days and it was as if my prayers didn't even go beyond the ceiling. I expressed doubts about everything. I questioned everything including: Was I supposed to go to that person? What is God's will regarding where I go on vacation? What is God's will in what I am doing today?

As a result, I became really stressed because I felt that I could not discern what God's will for my life was. I did not have the courage to talk about it with other people in my church, mainly because I thought they would consider me "unspiritual." Eventually I became so frustrated that I began to seek help.

I discovered later that almost every Christian struggles with discerning what God's will is for his or her life. Most of God's children who were struggling were frustrated and could no longer enjoy life. During this time, I started studying the Bible, and I concluded that God's will for our lives is that we live our lives to the full and enjoy the things that make us happy and bring us peace. He wants us to live close to Him and enjoy Him; to go out and enjoy the green grass, the blue sky, and each other. God wants to release the potential that He has placed in every one of us. He wants us to take dominion over all that has been given to us.

Too frequently we pray for God to show us what His will is for our lives when He has already shown us! A good example is Adam. After the Lord had created everything, He gave Adam the responsibility of naming all the animals because he had commanded Adam to:

> *"...rule over the fish of the sea and the birds in the sky, over the livestock and all the wild animals, and over all the creatures that move along the ground." So the man gave names to all the livestock, the birds in the sky and all the wild animals...* (Genesis 1:26; 2:20).

Imagine how things would be if Adam had responded, *"Hmm, Lord. I'm not sure if this is Your will. Let me first pray."* If that were the case, the animals probably would still be without names!

In the Bible, we can read what God's will is for our lives. He has already revealed it to us. God wants us to enjoy life, His friendship, and His creation. He also wants us to help the poor, the orphans and widows, and to establish His Kingdom on Earth. It is His desire that we tell people about His Son Jesus Christ; that we lay hands on sick people and see them healed in the name of Jesus; that we pray for our enemies; and that we love and bless each other. All this and more! Just read about it in your Bible.

We are so influenced by external elements, such as religion and culture, that many of us have stopped thinking for ourselves. In addition, through disappointing experiences, the spark of life in us has almost been extinguished, and we find ourselves stuck in a vicious cycle that seems almost impossible to get out of. We must realize that some of the most intense warfare takes place between our ears. We believe the lies that destroy our lives. We feel inferior and have put up walls in our efforts to protect ourselves; but as a result, have shut both God and people out. However, God wants to break through our self-made defenses. Everything is possible with God! Where is our faith? The Lord Himself challenges us by saying:

> ...if you have faith as small as a mustard seed, you can say to this mountain, "Move from here to there," and it will move. Nothing will be impossible for you (Matthew 17:20).

To this, many will say, "Yes, Lord, but what is Your will?" Well, I'm telling you that He is saying, "My will is that *you* come to life and become all that I created you to be. That is what will bring Me joy!"

Often the natural is a reflection of the spiritual. For example, when I look at my children, I am filled with great joy. It doesn't phase me that they are sometimes naughty, do unexpected things, or are just plain weird. In fact, that makes me really happy! Whether they are playing with their friends, each other, or are playing alone, I enjoy watching them. It would be heartbreaking and unhealthy if I gave one of them a gift and they responded, "Sorry, Dad, but I'm not sure that I'm able to accept this gift. I will need to first ask my neighbor to see if it is your will." That sounds like an absurd response, but unfortunately, the truth is that we too often respond to God, our Father, in this way.

PSALM 1

If you choose to live out your dream and obey the will of God, you will be successful. The word *successful* sounds worldly, but did you know that it is also a biblical principle? Another word for success is *prosperity*. God wants you to be prosperous. You might be asking, "How does one prosper? How can I live a successful life?" Well, we know that we have only one short life before we will see God face to face, so we want to make the most of it. God also wants the best for everyone. It does not matter where you live, what you look like, or what kind of training or education you may or may not have. God has written in His Word (the Bible) that everything you do will prosper (see Ps. 1:3).

We have all read about David in the Old Testament. He was a man after God's own heart, despite his sins and the terrible mistakes he made. We read that, in addition to doing other terrible deeds, he ordered a righteous man to be killed in order to cover his sin of adultery with the man's wife. But, once convicted by the Holy Spirit that what he had done was wrong, he was truly repentant. His heart sincerely sought after God, and David spent hours in intimacy with Him. In Psalm 1 we read:

> **Blessed is the one** who does not walk in step with the wicked or stand in the way that sinners take or sit in the company of mockers, but **whose delight is in the law of the Lord,** and who meditates on His law day and night. That person is like a tree planted by streams of water, which yields its fruit in season and whose leaf does not wither—**whatever they do prospers.** Not so the wicked!

They are like chaff that the wind blows away. Therefore
the wicked will not stand in the judgment, nor sinners in
the assembly of the righteous. For the Lord watches over
the way of the righteous, but the way of the wicked leads
to destruction (Psalm 1:1-6).

The Word of God is written for you—for you, for today, for right now. All the promises of the Word of God, inspired by the Holy Spirit, are meant for you. God's promise is that everything you do will be successful. Maybe you are laughing now, like Sarah did (see Gen. 18:12), or shrugging your shoulders and thinking, *Certainly this cannot be for me. This promise only applies to super-spiritual people.* But listen, God has no favorites in His Kingdom, and everyone has been given the same promises by God. Remember that you are the crown on His creation and you are clothed with His glory.

WHAT PATH DO YOU CHOOSE?

Psalm 1 is about how you choose to live and how you choose to behave. In other words, will you be obedient to what God says in His Word and through His Spirit? There are two paths made available to you: one without God and one with God. The first way is the choice of sinners, and as you act as your own god and make decisions based on your own limited understanding and wisdom, things will go wrong and your life will become stressful and unpleasant. Choosing this road will lead to nothing but despair!

The second way is to choose the way of the Lord by being obedient to His law. If you faithfully walk this path, in God's eyes you are a righteous one, justified by the blood of His Son Jesus, and He will lead you. As a result of His promises, you will be connected to Him, like a branch on the Tree of Life, and you will constantly be refreshed in a supernatural way which will ensure that you bear much fruit and never wither. You will be forever vibrant, attractive to both God and people. Everything you undertake will prosper.

Choosing this way of living is choosing to live out of heavenly joy and the riches of Heaven that are now at your disposal. You will be able to tap into the heavenly source, and it is the law, God's Word in the broadest sense, that is your source. When you read God's Word, you experience joy, and as you meditate and chew on it, this Word produces abundant life in you. As you become more familiar with the living Word, Jesus in you will increase as you decrease. God is alive in you, and He will be made visible in every area of your life. This is a life you will not be able to keep to yourself. It is a dynamic life, a life searching to bless and to be shared with others.

If you walk in the path of the righteous, God promises to lead you in your path with care. What a promise! He knows the path your life must take, and He is constantly going ahead of you; and as He does, He provides you with everything you need to live out His plan. He is a loving Father who takes care of His children. He is saying, "Just go now, live your life with Jesus. Go out and proclaim in word and deed My Good News to all the people in My world."

As it is written, *"Seek first His kingdom and His righteousness, and all these things will be given to you as well"* (Matt. 6:33).

What a great God we serve. He takes care of us in every aspect of our lives. How do we know we are on the right path, on the right track? In Psalm 23:3 the Lord provides a wonderful promise, *"He restores my soul; He leads me in the paths of righteousness for His name's sake"* (NKJV).

What does the phrase "paths of righteousness" mean? Perhaps when you hear these words, you picture a direct road from point A to point B. Did you know that this was the typical Greek way of thinking? The West is still heavily influenced by the ancient Greeks especially in the way we think. We have linear and logical thinking, which is of Greek origin. Unfortunately, when this is all we know and we apply it to our spiritual lives, this system leads to bondage and religion. All too easily, linear thinking coupled with our own human logic, can become overwhelmingly carnal and thereby an enemy of God! (See Romans 8:7-8.) God's Word is a book that presents a different way of thinking, the Jewish-Hebrew way. This way of thinking is circular and creative and leads to freedom and intimacy.

The word for "path" in Hebrew is *magal,* which means "circular."[2] Imagine you are climbing up a mountain. Is it better to go straight up or is it better to walk in a circle around the mountain, making gradual progress upward? While it may seem instinctive to go straight up, the best way to walk up is to take a circular path and to ascend gradually. In doing so, you probably won't be able to see the summit for the majority of your climb, but you will know it's there. As a result, with every step you take, your faith, patience, persistence, dedication, perseverance, courage, determination, wisdom, and diligence to reach your goal will grow. In your firm resolve, you will experience success and all the credit will go to God.

By choosing to conduct our Christian journey this way, we believe everything that God has said, and will never give up. The fear of the Lord will provide the wisdom for each of us, as sheep, to follow our Shepherd in our walk; and our righteousness, holiness, and true glory will be evident to all who see us.

> *He leads me in the paths of righteousness for His name's sake* (Psalm 23:3 NKJV).

Please note in this verse that it says He will lead us, and in some versions of the Bible it says He will guide us. Both words mean that

He will not hurry us but lead us carefully, so that we will achieve all He has planned for us to do in our lifetimes.

When we listen to the Holy Spirit and have the courage to obey Him against all the logic and wisdom of the world, we will learn to walk in faith with Him. It is through obeying this divine leadership that we learn to trust Him, so that we do not fall. Our own logic may try to prevent us from following Him, but we must have faith, trust, and the courage to go against all worldly logic. Walking with God in this way is completely opposite to the way the systems of the world operate, *"For those who are led by the Spirit of God are the children of God"* (Rom. 8:14).

Revelation 22:1-3a also speaks about being prosperous and bearing fruit:

> *Then the angel showed me the river of the water of life,*
> *as clear as crystal, flowing from the throne of God and of*
> *the Lamb down the middle of the great street of the city.*
> *On each side of the river stood the tree of life, bearing*
> *twelve crops of fruit, yielding its fruit every month. And*
> *the leaves of the tree are for the healing of the nations.*
> *No longer will there be any curse.*

Genesis 2:9 says that God placed the tree of life in the Garden of Eden. Then in Revelation 22:14 we read, *"Blessed are those who wash their robes, that they may have the right to the tree of life and may go through the gates into the city."*

Lastly, Revelation 2:7 says, *"Whoever has ears, let them hear what the Spirit says to the churches. To the one who is victorious, I will give the right to eat from the tree of life, which is in the paradise of God."*

It has been made clear to us that there is indeed a Tree of Life, a River of God, and a place we can lay claim to every minute of every day.

We don't have to wait until we are in Heaven, but right now, today, you may eat of the Tree of Life, which is Jesus Christ. We do this by choosing to be close to Him and soaking in His presence. This enables us to be the hands and feet of Jesus on Earth and to carry His glory into the spiritual darkness. The Source from which everything flows is Jesus and He enables us to help orphans and widows and to touch the untouchables.

When we begin to move in this dimension, we automatically experience the fruit, such as miracles, signs, and breakthroughs in situations. However, this is not to say that we will not experience hardship. We will also attract vultures—those who want to steal and destroy what God has given us. Therefore, it is important that we learn to protect all that the Lord has given us. That means His DNA, His dreams, and yours. Later in the book I will explain what I mean by this.

DON'T TRY TO MANIPULATE GOD

Among Christians, I have noticed that there is great shame associated with hearing God incorrectly—whether it is His voice or His will. We become so ashamed whenever we confuse God's voice with our own, or the voice of the world, that it paralyzes us to the point that we no longer try. I encourage you; do not feel discouraged or embarrassed, because as long as you are willing to be humble and transparent about it, and ultimately laugh at yourself when you get it wrong, there is no need to fear. Please do not shy away from actively hearing and obeying God. After all, we all make mistakes, and we will never be perfect while we walk on Earth.

On the flip side, there are instances when we try to manipulate God and abuse Him to advance our own agendas. Whether it's because we fill in the answers to our prayers because we want answers now and are tired of waiting, or we fulfill our own prophecies because again we feel we've waited too long.

A well-known example of this is seen in Abraham's behavior. He received a prophecy that he and his wife Sarah would have a child from which a great nation would arise. But after many fruitless years, Abraham and Sarah thought that it would be a good idea if they *helped* God fulfill His promise. Upon Sarah's request, Abraham slept with Hagar, one of her maids, and the child Ishmael was conceived and born. Ishmael and his descendants became the ever-present enemies of Isaac, the child Sarah eventually gave birth to, and to his descendants, the Israelites (see Genesis 16).

We see that it is dangerous to try to manipulate God and that it is a sin. If there are instances in our lives when we have tried to manipulate God, it is good to admit what we have tried to do so that we can be lovingly corrected by God and also to guard ourselves against becoming arrogant.

THE MOTORBOAT

Let me give you an example of this from my own life. For a long time I wanted a motorboat. I missed sailing, and whenever I saw a large lake or the sea, I was filled with the desire to go back to sea. Put me on a chair near the sea or on a big lake and you won't hear a peep out of me! I sit and think and stare for hours. For a long time I prayed for a boat, and in 2006 I thought I heard God say that I could buy a boat. I so badly wanted a boat that I admit I was not honest with myself or others. I had convinced myself that I had heard God's voice. In an impulsive mood, I bought, via the Internet, a secondhand motorboat. I had saved some money toward buying a boat and by borrowing from our savings account, I had just enough to pay the $1,565 the owners wanted for it.

However, my joy soon turned to sorrow as a series of miserable and unfortunate events took place. First of all, the boat was on a trailer and on the way back home the trailer axle broke off. After hours of dragging and hassling, we finally arrived in Harderwijk where we live, and launched the boat in the harbor. The following week, my trailer was stolen. The harbor master then called to tell me that my boat had sunk and was not retrievable. Surprisingly, I did not abandon hope, and I began to believe for a new boat and, together with a good friend of mine, we began to pray and ask God for another boat.

After researching the Internet, we saw a nice, eight-meter (26-foot) long motorboat and, as the owners were asking a reasonable price for it, we bought it together, sharing the costs. As we drove to pick up the boat, we were full of enthusiasm and felt that this time it was a gift from God. Upon arrival, the boat owner greeted us with a broad grin. He was a good salesman, and the motorboat was exactly what we wanted. The owner told us that this boat had been up for sale for a year, but nobody had wanted to buy it. Immediately we thought, "Thank You, Lord, what a great sign from You that this boat has been set aside and that You have kept it for us!" When the owner found out that we were Christians, he also claimed to be a Christian. He also told us that there was no guarantee on the boat. He said it so often that we thought we were experiencing spiritual warfare. An hour later, we left the happy seller and traveled from the port of Bunschoten to our berth in Harderwijk as two proud owners of a motorboat.

A few weeks later, we were out on the water in our boat with our family and friends and just as we were reentering the harbor, the engine stopped working. After repairing it as best we could, we entered the harbor. As the engine was still not functioning properly, we laid hands on it and prayed to the Lord to repair it. Nothing happened. It was Sunday and all the stores were closed. Early on Monday morning, we went directly to the harbor master and he provided a mechanic to fix our boat. After three days, we went to pick up the boat and we were told that we had made the worst purchase of the year! The mechanic said that the engine was beyond repair and that it had blown pure carbon monoxide into the boat. We were fortunate that there were no fatalities among us!

After all this happened, we ended up admitting to our friends and family that we had not heard God correctly and our supposed guidance from Him was nothing more than wishful thinking. Granted, there are times when we know beyond a shadow of doubt that something is from the Lord, and if it is the Lord who has spoken, what others think should not affect us. There are also other times when we try to manipulate God to fulfill our own agendas and desires. In doing this, we also manipulate and control people and situations.

We must exercise keen discernment as we pray for wisdom and revelation over situations and examine our motives. In my case, I really wanted to have that particular boat, and as a result, my clear and logical thinking was hindered because of my enthusiasm and desire. Of course, it would have been wise to seek the advice of a mechanic, or anyone else who knew about boats, but as the boat had been up for sale for so long, we were convinced that it was God's will for us to buy it, so we did not bother to ask anyone for a second opinion! In reality, the boat had not sold because it was in very poor condition.

I can imagine God sitting on His throne, shaking His head whenever He sees His children being manipulative or presumptuous. Let's just be real and honest with others and ourselves when we make mistakes or look foolish. In doing so, we make light of the mess we've made, learn an important lesson, and become nicer people to know.

ENDNOTES

1. Being "religious" can be defined as devoting ourselves entirely to the "practice of religion" by strictly adhering to the man-made rules and

regulations often found in more traditional churches. True Christianity is when we devote ourselves to developing a personal and loving relationship with God, our Father. Through this close fellowship, we are able to hear His voice, know what is on His heart concerning the things we see and do, and become all that He created us to be.

2. *Biblesoft's New Exhaustive Strong's Numbers and Concordance with Expanded Greek-Hebrew Dictionary.* CD-ROM. Biblesoft, Inc. (1993, 2003, and 2006) and International Bible Translators, Inc. s.v. "magal," (OT 4570).

CHAPTER 4

RENEWING YOUR MIND

Your thoughts have a greater impact on your circumstances than you might think. They ultimately determine the choices you make and your destiny. Your thoughts affect your attitude, how you respond to situations, what kind of people you associate with, and whether you live your life successfully or in defeat.

Subconsciously, we are bombarded with negative thoughts every single day. Knowing this, we have a great personal responsibility to monitor and control our thoughts; when we do, our lives change dramatically. There is a reason that the Bible insists on us renewing our thoughts every day and putting on the helmet of salvation to guard against harmful thoughts entering our minds (see Rom. 12:2 and Eph. 6:17).

God the Father says in Jeremiah 29:11 that His thoughts about you and me are positive and not negative. He also says that He has a plan for our future that is filled with hope. We read in the Bible that He is so proud of His creation that He calls us His sons and daughters, and that the angels are sent to serve us (see Heb. 1:14). In Revelation 5:10 it is written that God made us to be a kingdom of priests who will serve Him and rule on Earth.

God is a giving God. He always has an attitude of giving and blessing. It cost God everything to reconcile us to Him; it cost Him His Son Jesus. He knows the number of hairs on our heads, and He takes care of our every need. Perhaps we know these things with our minds, but we often do not really believe them in our hearts. When we finally choose to wholeheartedly believe in His love and how much He cares for us, we will then live positive lives filled with peace.

MORNING BLUES!

In the past, while waking up, I used to find myself thinking about all the bad things that had happened to me recently or difficult or unpleasant things I needed to do that day. As my mind wondered on, I would remember someone who had been nasty to me and then relive the sense of rejection, concern, or anger I felt about the words they had spoken. As I replayed all these scenes in my head, a feeling of depression and discouragement would settle in my mind.

I would then get out of bed, get a cup of coffee, and read a newspaper. As I read the stories of tragedy, violence, and failure in the world, a spirit of anxiety would creep into my mind to join the depression and discouragement I had already allowed into my subconscious that morning.

The first person I see in the morning is normally my wife and she was often the victim of my unhappy mood. It took me some time to realize that my bad temper and irritation had nothing to do with her, but was the result of me allowing negative, anxiety-producing thoughts into my mind from the moment I woke up. These thoughts drastically impacted my mood and emotions, which fueled my negative thought patterns. They, in turn, tainted the words I spoke as well as my actions for most of the day.

After this realization, I began my day differently. If I sensed a negative thought coming into my mind as I was waking up, I responded in the opposite spirit. I would make positive statements out loud. For example, some time ago I rented the Ahoy stadium in Rotterdam in faith, a project that would cost many thousands of dollars. Our goal was to hold a conference called Heaven on Earth, where we hoped to get thousands of people from different nations together to worship the Lord.

The day after I signed the contract to lease the stadium, I woke up and the first thoughts that came to mind were, *This is going to be a failure. What will happen if not enough people attend? We won't have enough finances to pay for everything. What will we do?* At that moment, I could have decided to respond in one of two ways: I could open myself to this flow of negative, anxious thoughts and let them completely take over my mind; or I could decide to stop them by saying aloud, "Thank You, Lord, that You are for me and not against me. Thank You that the stadium will be filled to overflowing. Thank You that we will have enough finances to pay not only for the entire conference but enough left over to support The Call Conference in Jerusalem and build an orphanage in Uganda." And this is exactly what happened!

By proclaiming positive things out loud, you immediately deactivate the power of negative thoughts that are trying to occupy your mind. Your positive words will build faith in your spirit and the heavens will be activated.

THE POWER OF NEGATIVE THINKING

I once put an elastic band around my wrist for an entire day. Every time I caught myself thinking a negative thought, I pulled hard on the elastic band and let it snap against my wrist. It was painful! At the end of the day, I had to take off the elastic band because my wrist had become black and blue from the bruises it caused. The number of negative thoughts that had gone through my head shocked me!

Without being really aware of it, negative thoughts can affect our day, our feelings, and our relationships. Therefore, we need a better understanding of how our mind works so that we can stop this attack on it.

We often think negatively about ourselves and this affects our attitude toward others in a negative way. Our poor self-image can also be a major obstacle to living our dreams. We make statements like, "I'm always late." "I'll never be able to pay my bills on time." "This promotion is too ambitious for me." "I'm not attractive." "I'm stupid and can't learn." "Prosperity is for everyone else, but not for me." Making these types of statements is effectively speaking curses over ourselves—and we need to stop doing it now!

These negative thoughts and words of unbelief have a negative impact on our lives because we conduct ourselves according to what we have said about ourselves. We are our own worst enemy. I believe that the negative flow of thoughts in our heads is the main reason why so many people in the world are struggling with depression and have to take antidepressant pills. It is also the reason why many relationships fail.

In some countries, the divorce rate is 56 percent, which means that more than half of all marriages there do not survive. And why? Because we are negative thinkers. We don't believe in each other or in ourselves. All sorts of negative thoughts creep up on us. Thoughts like, *Our marriage was a mistake. That other woman is more attractive. Does he really love me? This relationship will never work out. There is no hope for us*...and so on.

After years of habitually thinking these kinds of thoughts, we develop mindsets so steeped in negativity toward our spouses that we can neither be romantic nor loving toward them. The negative thoughts eventually become our reality, so we give up trying to make our marriages work and instead seek divorce. I am not saying that this is true in all cases, but the problem always begins in our thoughts. Even with things like adultery, pornography, and selfishness, it all starts with wrong thoughts. We must protect ourselves against what we see with our eyes and hear with our ears, and be very careful not to express our negative thoughts. When you reach the point that the mental state you have gotten yourself into seems like a deep, dark valley, know that God has a way out of it for you.

Perhaps it would be helpful to take this time to write a list of all the negative thoughts you have about yourself and your circumstances. By being aware of these negative thoughts, you can better fight against them by responding in the opposite spirit with positive thoughts and biblical proclamations.

A DAILY STRUGGLE

We must believe that the Word of God is true, and then we need to apply His Word to our own situation, to our relationships, to our work, or to our studies at school. God's Word says that you are the head and not the tail (see Deut. 28:13), that you will be so rich that you will give money to people and will not have to borrow from anyone (see Ps. 1:3). God is for you and not against you (see Rom. 8:31). No wall is too high, because with God you will overcome all obstacles. Speak God's Word concerning your life out loud. Say, "I fear no evil for You are with me. Your angels will protect me, no disaster will come near my home or surroundings" (see Ps. 23:4; 91:11-12; 91:10). Express these positive truths; apply only the Word of God and His promises to your personal situation, and after a while you will notice your attitude changing. The people around you will also observe this and your situation will change for the better, and new doors will open for you. This is all due to speaking God's truth about your life.

It is a daily struggle for us to change our old, destructive thinking habits and renew our minds with God's Word. We need to be alert each day to cast out any negative thoughts, to literally hold them in captivity, banish them, and then replace them with positive thoughts.

Recently, Rebekah and I were traveling from our home to my parents' home, a journey which normally takes only ten minutes when, because of construction work on the road, we were redirected along a narrow road that is regularly blocked by trucks picking up animals from nearby farms. As I looked at one of these trucks blocking the road while a long line of cars formed behind it, I grumbled and complained about the situation, "Why do we have to travel on this road and why does this truck have to block the way now? How inconsiderate of the truck driver! Look at the queue of cars in front of me!"

Then suddenly, *Bam!* I heard what I had said and I spoke out loud, "I'm sorry, Lord. Thank You very much for the beautiful road that the local authorities are having constructed. After it is open, we will be able to travel to my parents' home a lot faster. Thank You very much for this opportunity to pray for all the people who are in the cars ahead of me." I opened my car window and stretched out my hands to bless everyone in the line. Then I thanked the Lord for the driver and his hard work because without people doing the sort of work he does, we would not have fresh chicken or meat for dinner. I felt a lot better once I had changed my attitude, and the negative atmosphere in the car disappeared immediately.

If your thoughts seem to captivate and imprison you and you can't control them, I have good news for you! With God's help, you can! Your negative thoughts have formed a habit over the years. This mindset and thinking must be changed through filling your mind with positive thoughts. Make it a habit to express aloud the opposite as soon as you have a negative thought. Continue doing so until you see a change.

THOUGHTS OF SEXUAL IMPURITY

One of the great challenges in our time is sexual impurity. Marriages fail because one of the partners (men more so than women) is addicted to pornography. We can pray for you to be released from this addiction, but this will not help until you make the decision to renew your mind. Sometimes it is necessary to deliver someone from an evil spirit, but because he or she has granted access to this same evil spirit of impurity through impure, lust-filled thoughts—being set free begins with choosing to change the thought-life. We must first tackle the root of the problem because it is the mind that convinces someone to get involved in destructive behavior.

Suppose, for example, you are sitting alone at home, and your wife is at the gym or is out for the evening with friends. The following thoughts arise, *No one can see me; I can do it; everyone sins sometimes. I will only do it once; God will forgive me.* And as you step into the room where the computer is, an inner struggle arises in you, this time with the thoughts, *No, I won't do it; I'm just checking my emails.* Then you go to a search engine, or type in the Web address of a site that you really do not want to access, but you are so drawn to it that you are unable to log out and walk away. You then allow the images on your computer screen to pollute your mind for as long as you are able to stay logged on without being detected. You become a victim of lust, and the point of no return arrives when guilt and shame overwhelm you. Your thoughts go back and forth and, most of the time, they are negative.

When your wife comes home, you are irritable or pretend to be cheerful as you hide your sin. Your guilt makes you easily frustrated and angered and you take this out on your wife. Many marriages around me have been destroyed for this very reason. When we allow temptation to take hold of our thoughts and then allow them to be translated into actions, we usually end up regretting it.

We have to control our thoughts, and we can do so with God's help because we have received the gift of self-control from the Holy Spirit. We must learn to transform our negative, destructive mindsets into positive, productive, godly thoughts, and express them out loud. The first practical step you can take in terms of porn addiction is to not stay home alone without your wife. But the best and most radical solution is resisting the temptation to have a computer or television until God transforms the ingrained pattern of addiction. An ex-alcoholic has no alcohol in his home at the beginning of his transformation period. Likewise, you wouldn't have a gambling machine in your room if you were addicted to gambling.

Maybe you think this suggestion is too radical and that you cannot be without a computer because you need one to do your work. You can also start with the exercise of offering resistance. Suppose you are sitting at home and you feel a spirit of impurity rising up or an urge to access pornography on the Internet. Go to your computer, put a towel over it, and place a Bible on top of it. Proclaim out loud that God's Word is stronger than the temptation. Intercede for yourself and every-one else who is addicted to Internet pornography. Thank God aloud for pure thoughts because *"the pure of heart...will see God"* (Matt. 5:8), and proclaim that you do not want to participate in this wrongdoing.

Think of positive things, catch up on chores or take a walk, but don't give in to your thoughts of lust. Ask for forgiveness, listen to Spirit-filled worship music, call a friend, or read a book. Eventually you will have a feeling of great victory when your wife comes home and you have not succumbed to your impure thoughts. You are successful and you are on track to be set free of actions that can destroy your own life and lives around you. This is a daily process.

Also, realize that we have to live in the light and that everything we do in secret will eventually be shouted from the rooftops. In these endtimes, God is busy revealing secret sins that we have not confessed, and He is starting in His Body, His Church. In the last few years we have seen how God has begun to shake the Church and to sanctify the leaders. Sins are exposed and brought into the light. Never forget that God is a holy God, and if we want to see Him, we are to lead pure and holy lives.

ANXIOUS THOUGHTS

Anxiety is another reason why people are not able to achieve their dreams. Some people are anxious about everything and, as a result, they become mentally paralyzed, stress-filled, and are unable to make correct decisions. The physical consequences of stress, like high blood pressure, heart disease, and a weakened immune system, are destructive and sometimes fatal. The Word of God also cautions us about being anxious. In Luke 12:22-26 and 29-31, it is written:

> *Then Jesus said to His disciples: "Therefore I tell you, do not worry about your life, what you will eat; or about your body, what you will wear. Life is more than food, and the body more than clothes. Consider the ravens: They do not sow or reap, they have no storeroom or barn; yet God feeds them. And how much more valuable you are than birds! Who of you by worrying can add a single hour to your life? Since you cannot do this very little thing, why do you worry about the rest? And do not set your heart on what you will eat or drink; do not worry about it. For the pagan world runs after all such things, and your Father knows that you need them. But*

seek His kingdom, and these things will be given to you
as well.

Anxiety begins in our thoughts. Jesus commands us not to worry about our lives. Repeat these words out loud: "Lord, I am not worried about my life. I trust You to provide me with everything I need to meet my needs. I know that all the details of my life are known to You, even the number of hairs on my head, and that it is written that You will never leave me or forsake me."

God is always positive and He thinks positively, wanting only the best for you and your life; so turn your heart to seeking God and His Kingdom, and everything else will be given to you!

BE SALT!

In Luke 11:33-36, Matthew 5:15, and Mark 4:21, the Lord Jesus tells a parable. You can read this parable in all three Gospels because it is important! The parable is about our eyes and what we allow into our lives through our eyes. We are created to be the temple of the Holy Spirit. However, when we allow moral filth and impurity to enter, we no longer live in the light; instead we attract darkness. The Lord compares us to a lamp; a lamp is intentionally put in a dark room to illuminate it. It would be foolish to put it under a couch or in a dark closet as that prevents it from accomplishing its task. The Lord Jesus says in Matthew 5:13-16:

> *You are the salt of the earth. But if the salt loses its salti-*
> *ness, how can it be made salty again? It is no longer good*
> *for anything, except to be thrown out and trampled*
> *underfoot. You are the light of the world. A town built on*
> *a hill cannot be hidden. Neither do people light a lamp*

*and put it under a bowl. Instead they put it on its stand,
and it gives light to everyone in the house. In the same
way, let your light shine before others, that they may see
your good deeds and glorify your Father in heaven.*

Then we read in Luke 8:16: *"No one lights a lamp and hides it in a
clay jar or puts it under a bed. Instead, they put it on a stand, so that those
who come in can see the light."*

Here, our Lord Jesus is teaching us a number of important things!

1. You are the salt of the earth.

2. You are the light of the world.

3. When people see your good works, they will glorify
    God.

By the sacrifice of Jesus on the cross and the miracle of His resurrection and ascension into Heaven, we are given the command
and authority to be the salt and light on this earth and to do the
good works God has planned for us to do. There are far too many
saltless Christians and too many lamps hidden under our beds.
Hence, Jesus laments that the harvest is ripe, but the workers are
few (see Luke 10:2).

The Lord Jesus is quite radical about people who are saltless and
who live an obscure life in spiritual darkness and still consider themselves to be Christians. He says that such people will be thrown out
and trampled—not really something anyone would chose to do on
purpose. The good thing is that we can, once we are aware of our inef-
fectiveness, turn and repent of our saltless lives. We can reappear from
under the bed and go and shine in the darkness of this world and do

the things that Jesus did. Then, because of our good works, people will glorify God.

FALSE HUMILITY

Far too often we are falsely humble when we are actually afraid of being successful and becoming proud of ourselves. A few years ago we invited a missionary to dinner in our house. My mother, who is one of the best cooks I know, had outdone herself. She had worked hard for many hours in the kitchen preparing a special meal. The food was served and we began to eat. While eating, the missionary began to thank God for the delicious food that He had made. My mother, who is normally quite levelheaded and down to earth, hit the table with her fist and chimed in, "Yes, thank You, Lord, that You have blessed my hands and enabled me to toil for many hours in the kitchen to produce such delicious food!"

I could only laugh at the situation. So often Christians try to avoid the appearance of wanting honor and instead try to give it to God. Often I see someone after a church service give a compliment to the worship team or preacher; but the response is always, "It wasn't me, but God, so all the glory goes to Him." I'm sure this response saddens God because we are so afraid of offending Him that we refuse to accept compliments.

Imagine if you gave your son a jigsaw puzzle, and after working on it for days, he finally completes it. You compliment him on how beautiful the jigsaw puzzle is, but your son replies, "Oh no! You helped me so I give all the praise for its successful completion to you!" I would be so sad that even my eyebrows would frown! It is a wonderful thing to see that whatever I have given someone is appreciated and well-used. God has given us gifts and talents, and we should use them in the measure in which we live. So do not be afraid of compliments, for it is by seeing your good works that people will praise God!

WHO ARE YOUR FRIENDS?

Our thoughts are influenced by what we experience in the natural and spiritual worlds. I want to focus here on the question of who and what you are allowing into your world and how they influence your thoughts and surroundings. A question I often ask others and myself, "Do you influence your surroundings or do your surroundings influence you?" Who are your friends? Do the people you surround yourself with have a negative or a positive impact on you? It is normal to find that successful people spend the majority of their time with other successful people. Likewise, you will often find people who are depressed spending time with others who are also depressed. People who gossip and are constantly critical often have people around them who do the same things.

If you want to live your dream and lead a successful life, then you will have to make a number of radical decisions concerning the very important question of whom you chose to admit into your inner circle, the circle of family as well as friends. If you surround yourself with critical people whose communications are based on the rejection and pain they have not dealt with inside themselves, then you will be influenced and it is likely that you will communicate with others in the same way. You need to end these kinds of negative relationships. I am not talking about your spouse, if you are married, as you will have to learn to cooperate and to communicate with each other. I am referring specifically to the people you spend time with outside of your marriage and those whom you allow to be your close friends.

It is your choice as to who and what you allow to influence you. Suppose, for example, that you are at work and your colleagues are gossiping. Find another place to sit, and do not join in the gossip. Maybe your attitude will convict them, or they will try and salve their consciences by faultfinding and gossiping about you too. Don't fuss and do not waste your time on them. Instead, surround yourself with people who think positively about life. Find people who believe in their dreams and expect to achieve them. Study their lives, learn from them, and see how they deal with people, situations, and the things of God. Cut off friendships that negatively affect you. Life is too precious to waste on people who are always negative and critical about everybody and everything.

I am very selective in terms of who I permit to enter my inner circle. In my work I meet many people who are negative about themselves and others; I love these people, but from a distance. Of course I am friendly and cordial, but I will not allow their negativity and mindsets to affect my life.

I love faith heroes, men and women who have run the race and have dared to dream big. I learn from them and they are my heroes. I have a number of people with whom I can spend just a few minutes and it is enough to give me the strength to continue in my work and calling.

LIMITED IN A SMALL AQUARIUM

We often limit ourselves. For years I had a variety of aquariums. My first was a very small one. Soon I had filled it with dozens of exotic fish and the aquarium became too small to accommodate them all. Two years later I bought a larger one and to my surprise the fish grew in relation to the size of their aquarium. Still later I bought an even larger one and the fish grew again. The little fish had become big fish and continually outgrew their smaller aquariums.

This is just like us. If we remain small in our thinking through the restrictions we have placed upon ourselves, our world and the people with whom we associate will restrict our growth. We will remain unchanged until we choose to enter a river or ultimately, the ocean where we can grow. We are created to swim in oceans and not in aquariums. You decide for yourself how big you, your aquarium, and your world should be by the choice of people you allow into your life. I know people who feel it is safe and familiar in their small aquariums so, sadly, they do not grow at all.

I bless them, but I know that there is so much more for them. There is so much more to life than our daily and mundane existence. There is so much more to life than that famous Dutch expression, "Carry on as normal for that will be more than enough silliness." No, we are children of the King of kings. We must succeed in life; we must think and dream big, because in the Kingdom of God this is quite normal.

I remember well how, as a small child, one moment I wanted to be a cook, the next a pilot, then in another, a sea captain. I did not think about all the problems and disappointments that I would potentially face, and I most certainly did not think about the entrance exams I would have to take to qualify for these careers. I was a child and thought that everything was possible. I dreamed that I could fly, that I could walk across the water. Nothing was impossible in my mind. I was so innocent!

As we grow up, what we are told about ourselves, both through our surroundings as well as those in it, becomes very important. Many of us have stopped dreaming because of words that others have spoken to or about us, and we have become what other people have said we would become. We have come to believe the lies that were spoken over us while we were growing up—lies that we are stupid, ugly, doomed to failure, and that we will never amount to anything. We must be set free and loosed from these lies in our lives.

With whom do you surround yourself? Gather people and friends around you who think positively, people who do not react in worldly ways, but from God's love, and who apply His Word to their lives. Find people who have great faith, faith enough to dare to dream and speak of only positive things. Keep your distance from people who are always negative, and don't let them affect you. The Bible says in Romans 12:2 that you must be reformed and changed by the renewal of your mind. As it is written:

> *Do not conform to the pattern of this world, but be trans-*
> *formed by the renewing of your mind. Then you will be*
> *able to test and approve what God's will is—His good,*
> *pleasing and perfect will.*

That means it is up to you and me to make the choice to change our thinking to be in accordance with God's will. If we renew our thinking and think positively, if we put on a Kingdom mindset, then we will recognize the will of God and realize that the will of God is good, pleasing, and perfect! No one can renew their thinking overnight. Changing our thinking is a process. Therefore, we will have to start each day with proclaiming the Word of God over our lives. Before we open the newspaper, before we open our emails or go to work, we must start to think the way God thinks and see things the way He sees them.

His Kingdom thinking says in the same chapter of Romans 12:14-21:

> *Bless those who persecute you; bless and do not curse.*
> *Rejoice with those who rejoice; mourn with those who*
> *mourn. Live in harmony with one another. Do not be*
> *proud, but be willing to associate with people of low posi-*
> *tion. Do not be conceited. Do not repay anyone evil for*
> *evil. Be careful to do what is right in the eyes of everyone.*
> *If it is possible, as far as it depends on you, live at peace*
> *with everyone. Do not take revenge, my dear friends, but*
> *leave room for God's wrath, for it is written: "It is mine to*

avenge; I will repay," says the Lord. On the contrary: "If your enemy is hungry, feed him; if he is thirsty, give him something to drink. In doing this, you will heap burning coals on his head." Do not be overcome by evil, but overcome evil with good.

Take a moment to think who you have been influenced by. We all have our weaknesses. It may be that you are quickly angered, quickly feel dejected or impatient, or tend to talk negatively about others, and so on. For example, if you are quickly angered, don't spend time with people who have the same weakness, because then you will be throwing more fuel on your fire. If you become easily dejected, don't spend time with someone who is also downhearted. Seek someone who is cheerful and can encourage you. The Holy Spirit knows our weaknesses, and He wants to help and strengthen us.

GOOD COMMUNICATION

One of the most common causes of conflict is not communicating well. Often we speak from our flesh and, by using modern technology, are able to easily spread these thoughts to others. Today we can Skype, instant message, send SMS text messages, email, and phone, but many of these advancements do little to improve our ability to communicate. Much too often we respond from our pain when we express ourselves and we take no responsibility for the words that we send to others via these technologies.

In recent years, I have seen how much damage negative SMS text messages and emails can cause. This happens when we respond from our weakness instead of allowing the Holy Spirit to speak. If we are self-willed, we tend to repay evil for evil, and as a result we allow ourselves to be overcome by evil instead of overcoming evil with good.

One of my weaknesses in this area has been the way I deal with negative emails. I sometimes receive very nasty emails completely devoid of respect and love. They come from people who are envious either because we are successful, the ministry is growing, the favor of God is on our lives, or because we have a good marriage. Some people cannot stand that and will write unfavorable things to me.

RED FLAG

In the past whenever I read an email like that, I read it a few times and slowly the volcano of anger in me began to grow. The hot lava climbed up, and as I approached the point of eruption, I started typing, very hard and fast on my keyboard wanting to defend and justify myself. Deep down inside I knew that the Holy Spirit was saying, *"Be careful!* **No! No!** *Don't do it,"* but the need to justify myself always fought against this very sensible advice.

Then came the moment when I had to send the message. I read the email again and after a brief moment of rest, my fingers would grab the mouse to direct the arrow to send the message. In those few seconds, the Holy Spirit speaks, and I have the choice between obedience and disobedience. Should I allow my carnal self to speak or the Holy Spirit to speak? Which master and lord do I serve? In most cases I ultimately chose the Spirit of God, and I deleted the email while confessing my sin of letting myself become angry.

In the cases that I did end up sending the email, it has caused confusion, pain, and a lot of unnecessary damage that God has had to help me repair.

We have to take responsibility for our words and deeds. It would prevent so much misery for others and ourselves if we would respond to them according to what the Holy Spirit tells us. We would keep the peace, insofar as it depends on us, without compromise, without being overwhelmed by anger. Every time you don't send that email, every time you overcome a negative thought with a positive thought, you are made stronger. Your negative way of thinking will pass and eventually you will be successful.

Be positive in everything you say and think; do not look for problems; look for solutions. Surround yourself with victors and let those who are positive and who are God-chasers influence you—both you and your environment will change. You will be successful.

CHAPTER 5

DON'T ALLOW RELIGION TO DESTROY YOUR DREAM

Which church you belong to and how seriously they take their responsibility of helping you achieve your God-given purpose and dreams is a major factor in whether or not you will achieve God's will for your life.

This means you need to take an honest, unemotional look at the church you belong to now, and find out whether or not this is where God wants you to stay to achieve your dreams.

THE CHURCH YOU WERE "BORN INTO"

Few people are fortunate enough to come from godly families who attend churches that encourage young people to dream big dreams, finish their studies, and set out to achieve their dreams.

Many come from families who only attended church to celebrate Christmas or Easter, or to attend christenings, weddings, and funerals.

Others have, from a very early age, attended the churches they were "born into." These churches tend to be the ones both our parents, grandparents, and in fact several past family generations have attended. They are churches to which our families have particular, often emotional, attachments; these churches often give those the feeling that all is well between themselves and God.

This could well be the case, but often churches that have been attended by many generations have rules and regulations that go back that far as well. They may well have been introduced several hundreds of years ago by spiritual leadership who seldom saw their distant flocks and who may not even have had a Bible, or if they did, may not have been able to read or understand it. The leadership may then have tried to control the congregation by introducing harsh rules and regulations with the threat that those failing to obey them would go to hell.

These rules and regulations may have filtered down into the church today, and, although they are often man-made and have no bearing on what is written in the Bible, these laws have become "God's truth," to which people are still told to adhere or they will go to hell.

Today's Christians caught in this situation ponder what their chances of going to hell really are if they don't obey the man-made rules that seem so senseless to them. Their situation is made worse by pressure from family members, or from people in the church they have grown up in pressuring them to tow the line, crucify their flesh, stop rebelling against their elders, and do as generations of their family have done before them.

Deep inside they know that what they see around them are people who seem genuine and caring, but who have no intimate knowledge of who God is or even what Jesus dying on the cross really means to them. Most have spent their whole lives excelling at obeying the rules and regulations for which they themselves cannot give a sensible reason.

Their lives are one long religious performance and the better they are at obeying the rules, the higher their position within the church community normally becomes. The prouder they become at having reached this place of honor, the more self-righteous they become and the more God resists them. "...*God opposes the proud but gives grace to the humble*" (1 Peter 5:5).

With no revelation of who God really is, they seek to fill the godless, empty space within their souls by doubling their efforts to "please" God through adherence to their man-made rules. This vicious circle results in their becoming more and more like the Pharisees; as they seek to control others to make themselves feel better about their value system, their Christianity is a sham based on nothing more than the ability of their flesh to perform.

They do not realize what the grace and mercy of God entail or that Jesus did die on the cross to pay for the sins of all and no further debt needs to be paid except one of loving Jesus. At every opportunity they will imply that those under them are not quite good enough for God, and have plenty to feel guilty about. They then tell them to repent of their sins and to find a way to pay for them so that God may (but probably won't!) look favorably on them once again.

If you belong to a church like this because you feel obliged to, you will find these self-righteous, performance-motivated people will not take kindly to you wanting to leave their fold to achieve the dreams God has given you. If you tell them you want to work in a slum area on the other side of the world, they will tell you there are enough underprivileged people in your own area who need your attention. If you say you believe God is calling you to work among the street children in a large city with a bad reputation, they will tell you their own youth group needs workers so that's where you need to be.

In fact, because they know neither God nor Jesus personally, and therefore have no idea what is on their hearts, they will probably not even know what you are talking about or why you want to go to a "foreign" place. They are not led by the Holy Spirit but governed by unbiblical rules and regulations, and they will do everything they can to draw you away from achieving your dreams and into the same performance-orientated bondage they are in—so beware!

Unfortunately, besides these religion-bound people there are many other people who belong to churches on the basis of entirely wrong motives. They include those who adhere to New Age philosophies or are full-blown satanists or Freemasons who manage to work their way into the leadership to mislead God's people. We need to be aware of the destruction they can cause in the lives of those of us who wish to truly follow Jesus and become people after God's own heart.

A DIFFICULT DECISION

What do you do if you find yourself being manipulated by people like this? Should you strike out on your own to find a church that believes in doing what you have dreamed about doing and, in turn, risk being called rebellious or likened to satan by your previous church? Or should you forget about your dreams and stay in the church in order to please others?

This is a heartrending decision to make until you read what is written in Philippians 2:12-13: *"...continue to work out your salvation with fear and trembling, for it is God who works in you to will and to act in order to fulfill His good purpose"*; and Ephesians 2:10: *"For we are God's handiwork, created in Christ Jesus to do good works, which God prepared in advance for us to do."*

These verses make it quite clear that it is up to you to work out your own salvation and to do the good works that you believe God has called you to do. When you come face to face with God one day, it will be you and you alone who must answer God's questions about your life on Earth and how willing you were to do His will. Neither your family, church elders, nor pastor will be there to make an excuse for you, so make the right decision *now* so you can give God the right answer *then*.

BEWARE OF CHARISMATIC WITCHCRAFT!

You may think your troubles are over once you have buoyed up your courage and left the church that will prevent you from following your dreams; but this is not the case. You will often find people with backgrounds just like yours who have also joined the new church; however, if they have not been carefully pastored, they will have been born again, and even baptized in the Holy Spirit (and speak in tongues), yet their need to perform to gain approval continues. As they invent their very own *do's and don'ts* around spiritual gifts (and claim to operate in many of them), what the Holy Spirit is doing in this hour can become distorted. They may even prophesy and so impress others by their superior-sounding knowledge and revelation that people fall into the religious bondage of being controlled by what they say, rather than what God, says. This is charismatic witchcraft, so please be aware of it; let the Holy Spirit show you where it is, and actively avoid it.

THE ERROR OF COVERING

One of the offshoots of this kind of situation can be what people call "covering." This theory arose in the late 1960s in the United States and, in brief, it means that everyone is under someone else's authority, or under their covering. It means that you need to ask permission before doing anything you feel you must do from the person who is appointed as your "cover."

The theory arose with good intentions, namely for people to encourage each other to grow in relationship with the Lord, but soon it became a system whereby people started using manipulation to control those under their covering. Christian leaders who had introduced the teaching of covering admitted that it was not correct and asked for forgiveness. Unfortunately, this teaching is deeply entrenched and stubbornly refuses to go away; in fact, it can still be seen in Evangelical and Charismatic churches. We find it especially so among insecure or authoritarian leaders who use this teaching to reinforce their leadership positions and authority.

I believe that the teaching of covering opens up people to be controlled or manipulated by the person appointed as their cover. You do not need a cover from people because you already have all the cover you need in Jesus Christ. It is clearly written that he is the Head of the Body of His Church. Jesus even says in Matthew 23:8-10:

> But you are not to be called "Rabbi," for you have one Teacher, and you are all brothers. And do not call anyone on earth "father," for you have one Father, and He is in heaven. Nor are you to be called "instructors," for you have one Instructor, the Messiah.

I meet a lot of people who ask me, with a serious look on their faces, who my covering is. Most Christians are astounded when I say that Jesus, the Son of God, the Head of the Body of Christ, is my covering.

Unfortunately, many people have been injured or even destroyed by the teaching of the necessity of covering. People have become fearful or inactive because they have been told that they are exposing themselves to the works of the enemy when they have no covering. This is nonsense. It is written in the Bible, in Revelation 12:11-12, that by the word of your testimony and by the blood of Jesus, satan will flee from you. He has to depart from you because Jesus is your covering.

FINDING THE RIGHT CHURCH

Apart from feeling the need to escape from destructive leadership or from rules and regulations that make no sense, it is also possible to spiritually outgrow a church and so move from a quiet, traditional church to a more Charismatic church over a period of time. Someone may even be drawn to a church whose area of ministry is the same one they feel called to.

However, before choosing a new church to attend, or when checking to see whether your present church is the right place for you to be, it is important to find out what God thinks of your situation. In James 1:5 it says, *"If any of you lacks wisdom, you should ask God, who gives generously to all without finding fault, and it will be given to you."* So know that God will guide you into making the right choice if your intentions are pure.

In First Corinthians, a place in the Bible that has much to say on the subject of what a godly church should be like, it is written: *"Now you are the body of Christ, and each one of you is a part of it"* (1 Cor. 12:27). Here we see the necessity of belonging to a church which gives us every opportunity and encouragement to become a viable, working part of the Body of Christ.

How do we do this? Where do we start? In Ephesians 4:11-12 it tells us that in a godly church we will find that:

> ...Christ Himself gave the apostles, the prophets, the evangelists, the pastors and teachers, to equip His people for works of service, so that the body of Christ may be built up.

In Paul's first letter to the Corinthians we read:

Now to each one the manifestation of the Spirit is given for the common good. To one there is given through the Spirit a message of wisdom, to another a message of knowledge by means of the same Spirit, to another faith by the same Spirit, to another gifts of healing by that one Spirit, to another miraculous powers, to another prophecy, to another distinguishing between spirits, to another speaking in different kinds of tongues, and to still another the interpretation of tongues. All these are the work of one and the same Spirit, and He distributes them to each one, just as He determines (1 Corinthians 12:7-11).

From these Scriptures we see that in the right church God will not only give us apostles, prophets, evangelists, pastors, and teachers to prepare us to do His will, but that He will also give us various gifts, talents, and the anointing to enable us to carry out what He has called us to do. It is the role of our spiritual leadership to identify, encourage, and mentor us in our gifts until we are able to confidently use them to achieve our dreams and purpose. Without these God-given people, churches, and gifts, we will not get far.

Having said this, a church is more than a place we go to get equipped and mentored so that we can achieve our own personal dreams. It is also a place for which God has dreams, visions, and plans that He wants to see achieved, both in and through it.

For this reason it is wise to talk with the leadership, before joining the church, about their dreams and visions. In this way you can make sure they not only have the same values as you do, but that they are taking the church in a direction you agree with and can wholeheartedly commit yourself to helping achieve. This exercise is well worth the effort and will save you from both heartache and misunderstanding in the future.

OUR ROLE IN FULFILLING GOD'S PURPOSE

Once we have found a church that we know God will use to develop our gifts and talents for His glory, we need to know what He expects of us after we belong to the church.

In Hebrews 13:17 it says:

> *Have confidence in your leaders and submit to their author-ity, because they keep watch over you as those who must give an account. Do this so that their work will be a joy, not a burden, for that would be of no benefit to you.*

Please note that spiritual leaders are appointed by God and not by men and should have Jesus' heart for us and our spiritual welfare. They should not be the authoritarian sort of people who demand that we follow their every instruction without question.

According to Romans 8:14, *"those who are led by the Spirit of God are the children of God"* and that does not only mean our spiritual leaders, but us as well; and for this reason we should do nothing the Holy Spirit tells us not to do, even if we do have to go against our leadership. Acts 5:29 says, *"We must obey God rather than human beings!"*

Spiritual leaders have the awesome responsibility, not of lording it over others or of becoming arrogant, self-righteous, and unreachable, but rather, like Jesus, of being servant leaders. God expects them to take the task He has given them to lead His people as a holy, God-given responsibility. God will require an account of every decision they make with regard to those placed in submission to them.

As our spiritual leadership take their God-given responsibility seriously and pray for and lead us, we in turn should submit to them knowing that whatever they advise us to do has come through what God has told them as they seek His will for our lives.

As you do your best to submit to their authority, make sure that you know in your heart that they really do take your spiritual development seriously; and if you are not sure, please don't mutter or condemn them behind their backs. Make an appointment and discuss your concerns with them. They should be able to give you reasonable explanations of decisions they have made and back them up with verses from the Bible, if possible.

If you still have a difference of opinion, examine your own heart for signs of pride, rebellion, self-pity, or selfish ambition. If you continue to feel that the leadership does not have your best interests at heart, consult those to whom you are accountable and ask them to pray for you and then have them share what they feel God is saying and so advise you. Note: When you pray, don't do it with an attitude of looking for God to agree with you or feel sorry for you, but rather with an attitude of genuinely seeking His will. Remember, making one wrong decision from your flesh could take years, if not the rest of your life, to correct; so any effort to seek God's will is well worth the effort and humility required.

If, after discussion, prayer, and consultation, you and your leadership are still not in agreement, it may be time for you to seek God's will regarding whether you should move to another church or stay where you are. Pray and trust that God will work out everything that is going on for the good of those who love Him (see Rom. 8:28). If you quite genuinely have done everything possible to handle the situation in a godly way, God will guide you; and even if you do make a mistake, He will quickly correct you.

ACCOUNTABILITY

The Bible says in Ephesians 5:21, *"Submit to one another out of reverence for Christ."*

It is wise to be accountable to godly people who have already won the wars you are still fighting so that they can guide and pray you through them. They should be friends who have a higher level of spiritual maturity than you do.

Make sure you have a group of godly people around you who are role models for different areas of your life. These people should have more life experience, more wisdom, and a deeper prayer life than you. They should also be able to hear the voice of the Lord well. These wise counselors should be people who are willing to mentor you without wanting to manipulate or control you. Listen to their advice and then act on it. If there are things in your character that need to be changed for your own good and they tell you so in love, don't oppose it. That would be incredibly stupid. Listen to your counselors and change that which is not good. Work on correcting what others find disturbing in your life. Keep lines of communication open and move higher.

In my own life, I have seven men and women who are more mature than I am as a Christian because of their age and what they have experienced during their walk with the Lord. They are precious people who have invested in me without false agendas. I have given them permission to speak into my life. They encourage and correct me. These are people I trust, people who have weathered good and bad times with me.

In the New Testament we often see an older disciple, or even the apostle Paul, being mentored by an older, more mature Christian, but at the same time they themselves would mentor someone younger, as Paul did with Timothy and Silas.

We often refer to our older, more mature mentors as our spiritual mothers and fathers because that is the function they have in our lives. However, and just as important, as soon as we are spiritually old enough, we need to mentor someone less spiritually mature than ourselves. This is not only to guide and encourage them, but it is also enormously beneficial for our own spiritual growth as we study the Word and seek God's will for a person who is accountable to us.

NEVER THROW MUD

Never abandon your dream, regardless of what leaders or Christian brothers and sisters who are envious may say about you. Understand that people may criticize you because they are jealous. Deep inside, they actually want to do what you are doing, but they, for various reasons, have little fruit in their lives. Be careful how you deal with these people. Jesus tells us to bless them and not to curse them. Don't behave haughtily and arrogantly, and do not return mud for mud, because then you too will be on losing ground. Refrain from becoming bitter and negative and stop yourself from speaking negatively about them, because ultimately, the result will boomerang. You will receive, in full, the fruit of your negative thinking and words.

For example, I know someone who is in ministry but is always talking negatively about everything and everyone. She sees demonic strongholds everywhere and negatively judges others. She is constantly saying various people and organizations have a demonic leadership structure and this has offended and damaged others. Over the past few years, I have seen her health gradually decline and her eyes reflect only bitterness and loneliness.

Do not judge others, but instead bless them. Fast and pray for them, and remove from your lips all condemning statements and negative words. Distance yourself from a situation if you don't agree with it and stay in an attitude of love and prayer. Let time extinguish the fire of their critical words and persevere, never quitting. Stay close to God and seek out people who believe in you, people who have also achieved their dreams by the favor of God. Gather wise counselors, true spiritual fathers and mothers, and true friends around you. Do what makes your heart come alive! Dream *big!* And remember, with God, nothing is impossible!

A 2010 UPDATE: CHURCHES THAT EQUIP AND RELEASE THEIR PEOPLE

Some churches, under apostolic leadership, are refocusing their vision. They look to their own congregations, and through teaching, restoring, and equipping them, they build healthy churches that can release their well-discipled, Holy Spirit-led people into the world to reach the lost for Christ.

Their new converts then join the same or like-minded churches, and they are then healed, delivered, taught, restored, and discipled until they too can be released into the world to fulfill their callings and destinies.

These are people who are totally committed to following Jesus; they spend time with God every day and know His heart for the lost and dying. Like a "Joel Army" they will leave the churches that have equipped them and fearlessly preach the Gospel of Jesus Christ to the ends of the earth.

A church doing this with great passion and success is the Bethel Church in Redding, California. Their School of Supernatural Ministry caters to over a thousand students from all around the world, and their course is currently taught in other locations such as the Eaglesnest School of Supernatural Ministry in Kelowna, Canada, and the Forerunner School of Supernatural Ministry at IHOP (International House of Prayer) in Kansas City, Missouri.

For further information about where you can find your closest School of Supernatural Ministry, please visit the Bethel Church Website at www.ibethel.org.

If there is no school near you, then pray and ask God to show you where you can find a church that will not try and take you into bondage by making you focus on their man-made rules, but rather identifies your God-given gifts then equips and mentors you to the point where you are a powerful revivalist and are able to be released into the world to reach the lost. You will be empowered to do all that you have dreamed of doing, to reach the goal God has given you, and to see transformation and revival wherever you go.

CHAPTER 6

THE BLESSINGS OF ABRAHAM

Another key to realizing your dream is to recognize that you, as a born-again Christian, have inherited all the blessings God gave Abraham.

The blessing of Abraham is described in Genesis 12:1-3:

> *The Lord had said to Abram, "Go from your country, your people and your father's household to the land I will show you. I will make you into a great nation, and I will bless you; I will make your name great, and you will be a blessing. I will bless those who bless you, and whoever curses you I will curse; and all peoples on earth will be blessed through you."*

The blessing of Abraham is one of the most impressive blessings in the Bible, and through Jesus, the blessings Abraham received are passed on to us. Galatians 3:13-14 says:

Christ redeemed us from the curse of the law by becoming a curse for us, for it is written: "Cursed is everyone who is hung on a pole." He redeemed us in order that the blessing given to Abraham might come to the Gentiles through Christ Jesus, so that by faith we might receive the promise of the Spirit.

Everyone who has received Jesus Christ as their Savior and now follows Him, shares in the blessing that God gave to Abraham. The blessing on Abraham, and on you, can be read about all through the Old Testament as well as in the New Testament. We already read in Genesis 12:1-3 what the blessings of God are. It says that:

1. God promises Abraham land, a place to live.

2. God promises Abraham that He will make his descendants a great nation.

3. God promises to bless Abraham.

4. God promises Abraham a good name.

5. God promises Abraham that he will be a blessing to others.

6. God promises that those who bless Abraham will themselves be blessed, but those who curse him will themselves be cursed.

7. God promises that through Abraham the whole earth will be blessed.

It is clear that God's desire is to bless us. Many people have a false image of God and believe that God is against them; but here we see that God's heart is for us, that it is His desire to bless us with every good thing. Once you become aware that, because of Jesus, the blessing of Abraham is on your life, you can claim this blessing every day and make it part of your daily life. The promise that Abraham would be successful and prosperous now rests on your life 24 hours a day, 7 days a week.

GIVING TITHES

Proverbs 10:22 says, *"The blessing of the Lord brings wealth, without painful toil for it."* This applies to both spiritual and material things. We know that Abraham was one of the richest men of his time. This can be read in Genesis 13:2: *"Abram had become very wealthy in livestock and in silver and gold."*

A very important principle in receiving the blessing of the Lord is to give tithes. This means that you give away one tenth of your income by sowing it as seed into the Kingdom of God, which need not necessarily be a church. If you do this, the spiritual law of sowing and reaping will come into operation, a principle we discussed earlier. In Genesis 14, we read that Abraham gave his tithes (a full tenth of the plunder he recovered in battle) to the Lord. This means the giving of tithes is a spiritual principal and law that also applies to us. And as we gladly give our tenth, we can be assured that the same blessing rests on us!

> *Then Melchizedek king of Salem brought out bread and wine. He was priest of God Most High, and he blessed Abram, saying, "Blessed be Abram by God Most High, Creator of heaven and earth. And praise be to God Most High, who delivered your enemies into your hand."*

Then Abram gave him a tenth of everything (Genesis
14:18-20).

Let's see what the Book of Proverbs says about the relationship
between giving tithes and the blessing that rests upon this action.
Proverbs 3:9-10 reads:

> *Honor the Lord with your wealth, with the firstfruits of*
> *all your crops; then your barns will be filled to overflow-*
> *ing, and your vats will brim over with new wine.*

ABUNDANCE AND WEALTH

God wants nothing more than to bless His people. He wants us to
do well in all aspects of our lives and wants to see us secure and prosperous both spiritually and materially. He wants to give us His riches
in order to build and expand His Kingdom. Wealth ultimately belongs
to God; and God, as our Father, wants to give it to His children who
then choose to use these resources to honor Him. God's Word gives
us two important clues about wealth. In Deuteronomy 8:18, we read:

> *But remember the Lord your God, for it is He who*
> *gives you the ability to produce wealth, and so confirms*
> *His covenant, which He swore to your ancestors, as it*
> *is today.*

With this strength, we must build His Kingdom. In doing so, we
also need wisdom. As it is written in Proverbs 8:12-21:

> *I, wisdom, dwell together with prudence; I possess*
> *knowledge and discretion. To fear the Lord is to hate*

evil; I hate pride and arrogance, evil behavior and per-
verse speech. Counsel and sound judgment are mine; I
have insight, I have power. By me kings reign and rulers
issue decrees that are just; by me princes govern, and
nobles—all who rule on earth. I love those who love
me, and those who seek me find me. With me are riches
and honor, enduring wealth and prosperity. My fruit
is better than fine gold; what I yield surpasses choice
silver. I walk in the way of righteousness, along the
paths of justice, bestowing a rich inheritance on those
who love me and making their treasuries full.

And also in Proverbs 3:13-16, we read:

Blessed are those who find wisdom, those who gain
understanding, for she is more profitable than silver
and yields better returns than gold. She is more pre-
cious than rubies; nothing you desire can compare with
her. Long life is in her right hand; in her left hand are
riches and honor.

In the right hand of wisdom is long life, in other words, health and physical strength. In her left hand is wealth and honor, which amounts to prosperity. An interesting observation is that the Hebrew word for *prosperity* also means wealth or power. However, the same word also means soldier or army. If we accept and proclaim Abraham's blessing in our lives, strictly speaking, it is a military action that plunders the camp of the enemy and makes God's people rich.

OBEDIENCE

The blessing of God on our lives always depends on our being obedient to God. God wants to bless us, but He asks of us, as his sons and daughters, to listen to His voice and keep His commandments. The greatest commandment that God gave us is to love God above all others and to love our neighbors as ourselves (see Matt. 22:37-39). If we love the Word of God, His instructions and commandments, we will do what God says. The Hebrew word for listening to the Law, to God's directives for life, is *sh'ma,* which means "hear"!

Jesus said in John 15:14, *"You are My friends if you do what I command."*

And in John 14:21:

> *Whoever has My commands and keeps them is the one who loves Me. The one who loves Me will be loved by My Father, and I too will love them and show Myself to them.*

If we love God's Word, we will always rely on His mercy and compassion and live lives completely dependent on His Holy Spirit. We have realized that we need His help for every step we take. Keeping His commandments relies on our having pure hearts and correct behavior. They go hand in hand.

Jeremiah 31:33 says:

> *"This is the covenant I will make with the people of Israel after that time," declares the Lord. "I will put My law in their minds and write it on their hearts. I will be their God, and they will be My people."*

The truth of the New Covenant is that the law is not only written on stone tablets, but in our hearts, too.

SET FREE OF THE SPIRIT OF POVERTY

Lastly, let us look at Deuteronomy 28, a chapter that goes into the details of blessings and curses. What is described here is life-changing if you bring it into practice in your life. The blessing of God that enriched the lives of Adam, then Abraham, and then Moses, can also enrich our lives. I regularly proclaim Deuteronomy 28:1-15 over my own life and it has changed me and my environment completely. In the Netherlands, among Christians, there is still the spirit of poverty. There are Christians who will only own secondhand goods, and everything looks cheap and sober. This is often obvious among missionaries, as they bow to the spirit of poverty, walk around in secondhand clothes, drive old cars, sit on sagging sofas, and ride rusty bicycles.

I believe that God has better plans for His sons and daughters. He is the King of kings and everything is under His control. God wants us to be set free of this spirit of poverty. Read with me a paraphrase of Deuteronomy 28:1-14 (based on the New International Version). It is reframed in the first person, as if especially for us, because through Jesus we have become recipients of all these blessings!

> If I fully obey the Lord my God and carefully follow all His commands He gives me today, the Lord my God will set me high above all the nations on earth. All these blessings will come upon me and accompany me if I obey the Lord my God:
>
> I will be blessed in the city and blessed in the country.

The fruit of my womb will be blessed, and the crops of my land and the young of my livestock—the calves of my herds and the lambs of my flocks.

My basket and my kneading trough will be blessed.

I will be blessed when I come in and blessed when I go out.

The Lord will grant that the enemies who rise up against me will be defeated before me. They will come at me from one direction but flee from me in seven.

The Lord will send a blessing on my barns and on everything I put my hand to. The Lord my God will bless me in the land He is giving me.

The Lord will establish me as part of His holy people, as He promised me on oath, if I keep the commands of the Lord my God and walk in His ways. Then all the peoples on earth will see that I am called by the name of the Lord, and they will fear me. The Lord will grant me abundant prosperity—in the fruit of my womb, the young of my livestock and the crops of my ground—in the land He swore to my forefathers to give me.

The Lord will open the heavens, the storehouse of His bounty, to send rain on my land in season and to bless all the work of my hands. I will lend to many nations but will borrow from none. The Lord will make me the head, not the tail. If I pay attention to the commands of the Lord my God that He gives me this day and carefully follow them, I will always be at the top, never at the bottom. I will not turn aside from any of

the commands God gives me today, to the right or to
the left, following other gods and serving them.

Wow! What a revelation! We have direct access to the blessings of
God if we listen to Him and do what He says. All these blessings are
for you, right now! Take it, proclaim it, believe it, and live it!

If we listen and really do what God asks us to do, we will be placed
above all nations on earth. We will be the head and not the tail; we will
take authority over our lives and our circumstances. Everything we do
will be successful because of the grace of God in our lives.

It is God's ultimate desire that we continuously live in His blessing. As we spend time with Him every day and become more obedient
in doing what He tells us to do, so the favor of the God of the New
Covenant will increase on our lives and we will succeed in all we do.

In Deuteronomy 28:15 we read that if we do not keep the commandments of the Lord and do not listen to Him, many curses will be
released into our lives.

When Adam and Eve sinned in the Garden of Eden they brought
these curses both on themselves and on their descendants—every one
of us. We are all born under the curse of their sin, not under the blessing, and so bad things like mental and physical illnesses, depression,
animosity, accidents, disasters, and poverty are common among all
peoples.

However, to restore us to a place of blessing, God sent Jesus to the
cross to take upon Himself the curses we are born with. This is what
was prophesied about Jesus in Isaiah 53:5:

> But He was pierced for our transgressions, He was
> crushed for our iniquities; the punishment that brought
> us peace was upon Him, and by His wounds we are
> healed.

In other words, He absorbed completely into Himself the punishment we deserve both from our inherited sin as well as the sin we have committed. His goal in doing this was to reconcile us to God and restore to us the blessings of Abraham.

The apostle Paul had this to say about Jesus' sacrifice in Second Corinthians 8:9:

> *For you know the grace of our Lord Jesus Christ, that though He was rich, yet for your sake He became poor, so that you through His poverty might become rich.*

By saying Jesus was poor, Paul meant that Jesus had taken to the cross the overall consequence of the curse upon Himself, including the curse of poverty we are born with in all areas of our lives, including finances.

Psalm 23:1 says, *"The Lord is my shepherd, I lack nothing."* Jesus paid a high price to set us free so that God can prosper and bless us. Being rich in Jesus covers every aspect of our lives. He gives us the ability to acquire power and wealth. Are we open to receive these from Him? Do we expect God's blessing on and in our lives?

CHAPTER 7

THE POWER OF THE HOLY SPIRIT

In order to achieve your dream, you need the power of the Holy Spirit to be working in your life; because without this power, you will achieve very little. It is the power of the Holy Spirit working out the favor of God in your life that opens doors for you. He anoints you with the power of God you need to reach your goal.

Perhaps you have grown up in the power and the presence of the Holy Spirit, you know Him and recognize His voice—or perhaps all of this is completely new to you. You may have heard of the Holy Spirit, but may not have experienced Him yourself. Maybe you think of a dove that flutters around when you hear the Holy Spirit mentioned, or maybe you think that this is something altogether too vague for you. I can assure you that one of the greatest blessings you will ever have is to know the Holy Spirit and to be able to hear His still, small voice guiding you.

Many people have, in one way or another, experienced difficulty with the way the Holy Spirit works. These are often the very people who are afraid to release control over their lives to Him because it has always been the man-made rules of the church they attend that has controlled them. But know this, God wants to set us free from the religious spirit that seeks to control us because we really need the Holy Spirit to lead us with power and fire if we are to become all God wants us to be.

The Book of Acts describes how 120 people gathered in Jerusalem in an upper room waiting for the presence of God, when suddenly the Holy Spirit came as a wind—a thundering sound. One hundred and twenty flames appeared, and each person had a flame above their head and spoke in other tongues. This is the anointing and the baptism of the Holy Spirit.

If you are already baptized with the Holy Spirit, you do not need to ask for a further baptism of the Holy Spirit. Jesus Christ is the One who will give you whatever you need and will anoint you to do the things He has asked and expects you to do to achieve your God-given purpose.

MY QUEST FOR THE HOLY SPIRIT

My adventure with the Holy Spirit started at the age of 14 when I was skating and a strong inner voice asked me why I followed Jesus, and whether I really meant it. I had begun to read the Bible with great interest at that time. The Book of Acts and the four Gospels were my favorite books, and each time I read about the power of the Holy Spirit and how the disciples were baptized with the Holy Spirit and with fire, its impact on me was unprecedented. I read about people lying on the ground as they came into the presence of God, about glory, smoke, and earthquakes. I also read about the sound like a wind, and flames of fire manifesting and moving above the heads of the disciples, and them speaking in different heavenly languages. Then I read that the disciples went out and did all kinds of miracles by the power of the same Holy Spirit.

In the Bible I read about many things that I didn't see happening in the church in which I was involved. I started asking my father, who was a pastor, questions about the power of the Holy Spirit, supernatural healing, the casting out of demons, and speaking in other tongues. I also began to ask my youth leader the same questions, and to my surprise the only answer I received was that the Holy Spirit operated in ways which are written about in the Bible 2,000 years ago, and that He has not done so since then. That answer confused me. I prayed and asked God to bring me into contact with people who could tell me more about the power of the Holy Spirit.

ENGLAND

It was a few weeks later that I noticed a big blue bus parked in front of the only supermarket in the village where I lived. I was curious, so I went inside the bus and there I was welcomed by a friendly, wise man by the name of Kees de Vlieger. That week he was evangelizing in our village, and he seemed to know a great deal about the work of the Holy Spirit. He encouraged me to visit some of his friends in England. They were the founders of the evangelizing ministry that was done from the bus.

A few weeks later, I flew to England. A very friendly couple picked me up at the airport and we drove straight to a church meeting. I went inside the church and a warm sensation that felt like a blanket of liquid love covered me. The speaker, an older man in his sixties, stopped his sermon, looked me full in the face and said, "You are from the Netherlands, and you have come here for the baptism of the Holy Spirit. Son, the Lord is going to use you powerfully throughout the world, but first you will be trained and go through difficult periods.

God's anointing is on you, and He is now molding your character."
This was in 1992.

The man stretched out his hand toward me, and I suddenly felt
so much electricity going through me that I could no longer stand on
my legs, and I collapsed to the ground. My mouth started moving, and
I began to speak in another language, a language I had never heard
before, a heavenly language! I could not stop laughing and crying
at the same time. I had been baptized with the Holy Spirit and with
fire—and it felt wonderful!

A few days later I was back home and enthusiastically shared with
anyone who would listen to me what had happened. Not everyone understood what I was talking about but I knew that a fire had been ignited in
me and it has been unquenchable ever since! If you are not yet baptized
in the Holy Spirit, I encourage you wholeheartedly to seek it. Be filled
with the Holy Spirit, with His fire, and let go of all your objections and
misconceptions. It is an important key to a breakthrough in your life and
necessary if you want to achieve the dreams God has given you.

THE PROMISE OF THE FATHER

I am going to send you what My Father has promised;
but stay in the city until you have been clothed with
power from on high (Luke 24:49).

The promise of the Father is that the Holy Spirit, who was sent
to take the place of Jesus here on earth and was poured out onto the
believers and followers of Jesus Christ that night in the upper room
in Jerusalem, will also be poured out on us. The Spirit of God, the
Holy Spirit, is directly opposed to the spirit of the world, which is our
carnal mind. There is spiritual conflict between these two forces that
we face daily. God gives us the choice of not listening to our flesh (our

own will, the spirit of this world) and instead, to listen to His Spirit. Look at yourself and those around you and you will see what following this spirit of the world does. It causes confusion and circumstances that are far removed from those that we would be experiencing if we lived according to the Holy Spirit and the Kingdom of God.

God's promise is that anyone who is a follower of Jesus Christ can ask to be filled with His Holy Spirit. Jesus also promised us that the Holy Spirit will teach us and lead us in His ways in order to glorify Him. In John 16:13-15, we read:

> But when He, the Spirit of truth, comes, He will guide you into all truth. He will not speak on His own; He will speak only what He hears, and He will tell you what is yet to come. He will glorify Me because it is from Me that He will receive what He will make known to you. All that belongs to the Father is Mine. That is why I said the Spirit will receive from Me what He will make known to you.

The work of the Holy Spirit is to be our *teacher* and to give us instructions to lead us to the full truth. The more we are filled with the Holy Spirit, the more the fruit of the Spirit will manifest in us. The fruit of the Spirit is described in Galatians 5:22-26:

> But the fruit of the Spirit is love, joy, peace, forbearance, kindness, goodness, faithfulness, gentleness and self-control. Against such things there is no law. Those who belong to Christ Jesus have crucified the flesh with its passions and desires. Since we live by the Spirit, let us keep in step with the Spirit. Let us not become conceited, provoking and envying each other.

WE NEED THE POWER OF THE HOLY SPIRIT

The Holy Spirit is God! God consists of three persons: God the Father, God the Son (Jesus), and God the Holy Spirit. Most Christians know about God the Father and Jesus, the Son of God, but many have only a vague understanding of God the Holy Spirit. In the Book of John, chapters 14, 15, and 16, Jesus tells us about the Holy Spirit saying He will be His substitute after He has ascended into Heaven to be with His Father. He also tells us the Holy Spirit will be our Comforter and will lead us into all truth. I don't know about you, but that made me really eager to get to know the substitute for Jesus here on Earth a lot better!

The Bible also says that the Holy Spirit is the only One who knows God and all His plans and thoughts. Can you imagine! There is Someone who knows the character, the emotions, the plans, and the thoughts of God. He knows them all. He knows the future, what's going to happen and when, because He is the Spirit of God. Jesus also said that His substitute here on Earth wants to live in everyone who believes that He is the Son of God and is the Way, the Truth, and the Life, which leads to God the Father. This Person, who is part of the Holy Trinity, lives in your body, your spirit, and in your heart, and communicates the thoughts and will of God to you. He also communicates God's thoughts and emotions to you.

It is time we paid more attention to the Holy Spirit and showed Him the respect due Him. Through the Holy Spirit, you have access to the throne of God 24 hours a day, every day.

OUR COMFORTER AND HELPER

The Holy Spirit wants to reveal the promises of God and help us in our walk with God; however, He can only live in a clean temple, a clean body. *The pure in heart will see God,* according to the Bible (see Matt. 5:8). Therefore, the Holy Spirit will always convict us of any sin we commit and will speak to our consciences about what we have done wrong. If we show that we are truly sorry and repent and turn from our sins, God will always forgive us.

The Holy Spirit is a Person complete with emotions and character that we should refer to as *He,* not *it.* After you are born again, He comes to live in you. You may have heard of the Trinity, which is God the Father, God the Son, and God the Holy Spirit—they work together, in unity, as one being.

You and I are created in God's image, which you can read about in Genesis 1, and, like God, are also composed of three parts. We have a body, a soul, and a spirit. Although each has a specific function, they also work together in unity as one person.

> *If you love Me, keep My commands. And I will ask the Father, and He will give you another advocate* [Counselor] *to help you and be with you forever—the Spirit of truth. The world cannot accept Him, because it neither sees Him nor knows Him. But you know Him, for He lives with you and will be in you* (John 14:15-17).

MAKE SPACE FOR THE HOLY SPIRIT

We need the Holy Spirit in our lives to achieve both our own dreams and God's dreams for us.

First, the Holy Spirit convicts us of sin and of the most important truth in our lives—that we need God. In the affluent West, many people think they have everything, and there are many humanists there. They are impressed with their prosperity and, as a result, have become arrogant. They think they are God and can do everything without the help of anyone else. They do not believe that God is Almighty and that it is He who created us.

In contrast, in some third world countries, the acknowledgment of God is widespread because prosperity has not destroyed their need for Him. In itself, there is little wrong with prosperity, but it can become a problem if we allow it to become our idol and we start bowing to it as the people who had been following Moses bowed before the golden calf they made.

The result of the Holy Spirit convicting us of sin and our need for God lead me to have much hope for the Western world that has in recent years become more secularized. When revival comes, there will be a tremendous outpouring of the Holy Spirit. Many will realize that there is a God and that they need Him, and will want Him to become part of their lives. This is the reason why you have probably heard the word *revival* so often recently. Creation is pregnant with expectation. The difficult times the world has faced recently are simply birth pains, and we eagerly await the revelation of the sons and daughters of God.

In other words, when you and I start realizing who we are in God and start proclaiming the coming of His Kingdom, God can work through us and we will bring the spirit of revival to others.

Recently, Rebekah and I were on vacation in Egypt and as we sat on the beach enjoying the sun, the people who were lying near us said they had goose bumps and that they were strangely drawn to us because we had something that they desired. Some called it "positive energy," which is partially true, because that is how being filled with the Holy Spirit feels. Without us saying a word, they began telling us their problems and about the things that have not been good in their lives. Some even cried or laughed.

This happens frequently during our travels in Muslim nations as well as in the West and in developing countries. It is not about us, but people can sense the glory of God in our lives. God wants to use the Holy Spirit in us to make people aware of how much they need God in their own lives.

A WALKING REVIVAL

Do you radiate God's love? Have you authorized the Holy Spirit to work through you? The moment you become aware that the Holy Spirit is living in you, and that you are living in His love, you will be surprised by all that happens because you will have become a walking revival!

The Holy Spirit also enables us to realize the truth of the sacrifice Jesus made on the cross for us. When we receive this revelation and accept Jesus as our Savior, we are born again and our spirit is awakened to the things of God. We can find this written in John 3:5-8 and Second Corinthians 3:6. The Holy Spirit will also anoint and prepare us to carry out the tasks that God has given each of us to do.

However, anointing and character are two completely different things and while God gives you an anointing, you have to work at improving your character yourself. Most people are focused on the size of the anointing and its end result. However, God is more interested in developing your character, which must be in balance with the anointing on your life. This is why God will use the Holy Spirit to convict you of things that you do that are not in line with His Word.

Give the Holy Spirit permission and the opportunity to convict you of everything that is not right in your life—or that which cannot be tolerated by daylight. Let your character be formed by Him so you can continue the work Jesus started here on Earth before He ascended into Heaven to pray for us and prepare our mansions.

Jesus Himself started His ministry on Earth only after He had received the baptism in the Holy Spirit. (See Luke 3:21-23.)

EVEN JESUS WAS BAPTIZED

Jesus was conceived by the Holy Spirit. That in itself is a very special event and means that Jesus had the DNA of God in Him. Mary was pregnant through a supernatural conception by the Holy Spirit. Yet, later on, Jesus had to be filled and baptized with the Holy Spirit. So if Jesus had to be baptized and filled with the Holy Spirit, who are we then to argue that it is not for us? Many people refuse to do God's will in these areas, arguing about what is written about it in the Bible, and I am sure this is the reason why many people do not walk in their full destinies. They do not fully trust or believe in God's Word. There are things that we do not have to spend time debating or arguing over because these are simple facts and principles. Jesus Himself set the example of what we should do, so let's stop procrastinating and do it!

I am a believer in parents (or guardians) blessing and dedicating a baby to God because it is biblical, but I am against the idea that because of this blessing the child does not have to be baptized when he or she is older. I believe once a person is old enough to know his or her own mind, and makes the important decision to follow Jesus, that person should obey God's command to be baptized—and in the way He was baptized by John the Baptist, by full submersion in water.

If we truly want to follow Jesus, how can we refuse to be baptized when it is considered an act of obedience and a spiritual principle that Jesus has given to us personally? (It is also interesting to note that Jesus started His ministry almost as soon as He was baptized by being fully submersed in water.)

I regularly hear the question, "I was christened as a small child and I have already been confirmed, so is it necessary for me to be baptized as an adult?"

Christening and confirmation are things that have been instituted by the Church. They do not replace the need for each of us to make a personal decision to accept the forgiveness of our sin through the sacrifice Jesus made on the cross when we are old enough to fully understand what this means. This decision includes actively and responsibly becoming followers of Jesus and then following His example of being baptized by full submersion.

John the Baptist *"went into all the country around the Jordan, preaching a baptism of repentance for the forgiveness of sins"* (Luke 3:3); and so Jesus came to him to be baptized by full submersion, which is how we know what is expected of us. When we are lowered into the water during the baptism ceremony, it represents the burial of our sin with Jesus, after He was crucified. When we are raised up out of the water, it represents the resurrection of Jesus from the grave after He had conquered death and paid the price for our sins. We become new persons!

The Holy Spirit often convicts people of their need to be baptized during a baptism service, and they jump into the water themselves. In the past few years we have had hundreds of people who were watching us baptize people, spontaneously jump into the water to be baptized themselves. This happens because the Holy Spirit Himself is speaking to them, which is often better than if a person speaks to them, as people can often sound as though they are being judgmental.

WALK IN THE LIGHT

In the past few months we have had meetings where the worship was so deep that the glory of God hung above the people like a mist. Through the glory of God, people were changed and some were convicted of sin. Some people went home, returning sometime later with their previously hidden collection of pornography DVDs. They came forward to publicly confess their sin, and told us how they wanted to overcome their addictions to things not from God—they wanted to live in the light.

These kinds of radical confessions usually cause a wave of conversions, sometimes dozens of people at a time who publicly confess their sin. As there is no form of condemnation in our meetings—only love, forgiveness, and acceptance—people feel safe in confessing their sins. These are often spontaneous acts. This is the Holy Spirit!

After this happens, we often see great manifestations of God's glory. This is the way Jesus makes it clear to those whom He has trained to continue His work on Earth that the power of the Holy Spirit is needed to do this kind of work. Acts 1:8 says:

> But you will receive power when the Holy Spirit comes
> on you; and you will be My witnesses in Jerusalem, and
> in all Judea and Samaria, and to the ends of the earth.

The Holy Spirit was not just given to the generation that lived when Jesus poured out the Holy Spirit for the first time. It is a promise and a principle for all Christians in every generation. This power from God is available for anyone who longs for it and prays for it. The Holy Spirit came, not only to save us, but to enable us to serve God more effectively and to make us fruitful.

As Peter said:

> Repent and be baptized, every one of you, in the name
> of Jesus Christ for the forgiveness of your sins. And you
> will receive the gift of the Holy Spirit. The promise is
> for you and your children and for all who are far off—
> for all whom the Lord our God will call (Acts 2:38-39).

God did not create us to be robots or slaves, but instead, we have been called His sons and daughters, His own children! Living a life with, and according to what we hear from the Holy Spirit, is a life lived according to God's will. A life in which our sins are forgiven because of Jesus' sacrifice on the cross, and a life where we are empowered by the Holy Spirit within us and anointed to do what God has called us to do by Jesus Himself.

We enter a state of complete surrender—the opposite of control—openness, and obedience. Let us be transparent and honest and take off the masks behind which we hide ourselves, the fig leaves of Adam and Eve, and let us run to our heavenly Father. Let us be honest with Him, with ourselves, and with others, and stop making fools of ourselves. Be open and listen to the voice of God, the Holy Spirit.

Paul wrote in Ephesians 5:18: *"...be filled with the Spirit."* With the Holy Spirit which Jesus promised every one of us, you receive wisdom and revelation from God, and you receive the words to pray in accordance with God's will, especially when you pray in tongues. You receive the authority to overcome the way you lived in sin and death, with satan, and in the world. You receive the power to witness; you have authority over demons, disease, and suffering, and you can hear and understand the voice of God. You also have access to the mercy seat of God where you will receive everything you need.

As we read in Acts 4:29-32, it is because of the sacrifice Jesus made on the cross that we are now able to live in the power of the Holy Spirit. His presence in us helps us live as God wants us to live and do what God wants us to do. The Holy Spirit renews our lives from the inside as He renews our wills, our thinking, and our emotions. Through the Holy Spirit we receive and reflect the character and power of Jesus. Through the Holy Spirit, His Bride (the Church) comes alive, grows, and is a powerful light to the entire world.

THE HOLY SPIRIT SHOWS US THE FATHER'S WILL

The Lord Jesus only did what He saw His Father do (see John 5:19). Hence, He was never wrong and good things always happened to Him. Jesus was a walking revival. Jesus had to die on the cross, and rise from the dead to destroy the strongholds of satan forever. Through His resurrection and ascension into Heaven, room was created for the Holy Spirit. The Spirit of God was personally poured out on all His followers and they were born again, reborn, born from God. It is the Holy Spirit of God who knows everything—all His plans, His Word, and His thoughts. By consulting the Holy Spirit, we can know and see what the Father is doing.

Now I have one question for you, where does the Holy Spirit live? Seems like an easy question? He lives in you! What does the Holy Spirit do? What is His function? He convicts us of sin and injustice. He speaks truth against all of our lies. He says that you are no longer a slave to sin but a son or daughter of the Most High God and that you will inherit God's promises. He communicates with your spirit 24 hours a day, 7 days a week. Even now the Holy Spirit is communicating to you what He hears from the Father. Therefore, we can know at any time of the day what the Father would have us do, and we can respond immediately.

STREET CHILDREN IN KAMPALA

I will give one example. I was in the capital city of Uganda, Kampala, and we were in a taxi. There were swarms of people, and when we stopped at a red traffic light, my eye caught sight of two street children among the crowds. We drove on, and the Holy Spirit communicated with my spirit that I had to help those two boys. At that point, I could do one of two things. I could ignore the voice or obey it.

The easy thing to do was make all sorts of excuses and convince myself that it was simply a human reaction to seeing so much need, and that it would be unwise to suddenly stop in the traffic and turn around. It could also be dangerous and I didn't want to endanger myself, right? But after 30 seconds, I shouted to the taxi driver to stop. When he did, I ran back along the street, through all the people, and found the two boys. When I started to talk to them, they told me that they no longer had parents and that they spent their days on the streets begging in order to survive, but that it was their desire to go to school.

Together with Joseph Lubega, our contact person in Uganda, we took the boys to his family home where they showered, received clean clothes, and ate a hot meal. Now, a year and a half later, one of the boys is one of the best students at school and has given his life to the Lord. Things are going extremely well for him. The other boy, unfortunately, was addicted to drugs and after a few days he went back to the streets. Nevertheless, he has heard the Gospel and experienced the love of Jesus, and he now knows that there is a way out of his misery. Joseph and the children pray for him daily, and I believe he will come back to the children's village one day.

I believe that we were right to stop the car and share God's love with these boys. Did I fast, pray, and ask for permission from my leaders before stopping to talk to them on the street that day? No! I simply chose to be obedient to God. "Yes," you may ask, "but what would have happened if it wasn't the Holy Spirit that you heard?" Well, even if it was my own idea, it was still Jesus' heart. If you read Matthew 25, you will see that you don't need special guidance from God to take care of orphans and widows. In principle, it is a command for all Christians, from the moment that you are reborn. It is so simple and so easy. Jesus would say, "What you have done for these street children, you have done for Me. Thank you, My son. Thank you, My daughter!" This means you are free to respond to any situation you may be in, to help those God the Holy Spirit has told you to help; every day and wherever you are—at work, on the streets, in the super-market, or on the sports field.

Every day you meet people and every day the Holy Spirit speaks to you. Learn to understand His voice. I begin each day by asking for a greater ability to hear the spirits of wisdom and revelation, and that I will be sensitive to hear the promptings of the Holy Spirit. If I am in the supermarket and standing in a long line waiting to pay, I ask the Holy Spirit what He wants to say to someone near me. After He tells me, I obey immediately and leave no room for my own thoughts or fears that want to stop me. I immediately go to the person the Holy Spirit has pointed out to me and I tell him or her what I believe I have heard from Him. In the beginning, this is exciting to do but the results are often overwhelming. People suddenly begin to cry, look at me with disbelief, or shake my hand and ask for more. These are great opportu-nities provided by God to tell people about Jesus.

This is also one of the reasons why I like flying so much; it gives me hours to practice this on the people around me. Even if I am wrong sometimes, most of the people really appreciate the interest I show in them. My experience has taught me that most of the time they are very grateful. It is also a very special experience for me.

If you also do this, your daily routine will become an exciting chal-lenge and an entirely new world will be opened up for you! If you are really going to live from the Holy Spirit who is in you, then you can be sure that your life will be a great adventure, and you will influence many lives with God's love.

CHAPTER 8

GOD'S HEART FOR
ORPHANS AND WIDOWS

Another key to bringing revival and God's favor into your life is in understanding God's heart for orphans, widows, the poor, and the oppressed.

This subject is very important to me because it has become one of the keys to the prosperity I experience in all areas of my life. Caring for orphans and widows brings with it God's glory and favor. The Bible shows that it is an important subject for God and a spiritual principle. Christians who neglect to care for the orphan, the widow, the prisoner, the thirsty, and the hungry may well find it adversely affects their lives. I believe that there is a direct correlation between the blessings and spiritual breakthroughs we experience in our lives and the level of our concern for street children, orphans, and widows. Caring for the outcasts of society is a key to changing our lives, and we need to take practical steps to achieve it.

Many of us love large worship celebrations, soaking in God's presence, and anything else that involves singing, dancing, and passionately expressing love for God. However, expressions of love and passion, no matter how heartfelt, are not enough because from that joy and intimacy with God must spring action, the action involved in bringing God's love to the lost and suffering people whom He loves and cares about so much.

It is critical that we recognize that this is a priority for God's Kingdom. Spreading His love must be at the top of the agenda for every follower of Jesus. Often, as Christians, we can miss the simple reality that the substance of the Gospel is both practical and spiritual, a reality that can be seen clearly by reading Jesus' Sermon on the Mount:

> *Blessed are the poor in spirit, for theirs is the kingdom of heaven. Blessed are those who mourn, for they will be comforted. Blessed are the meek, for they will inherit the earth. Blessed are those who hunger and thirst for righteousness, for they will be filled. Blessed are the merciful, for they will be shown mercy. Blessed are the pure in heart, for they will see God. Blessed are the peacemakers, for they will be called children of God. Blessed are those who are persecuted because of righteousness, for theirs is the kingdom of heaven. Blessed are you when people insult you, persecute you and falsely say all kinds of evil against you because of Me* (Matthew 5:3-11).

For many Christians, the spiritual and practical aspects of their lives are often out of balance.

God opened my heart and eyes to see the needs of the disadvantaged and the addicts when I was 17 years old and walked past prostitutes on the street on my way to attend classes at the Maritime

College in Rotterdam. My heart would break as I saw these emaciated girls. At the age of 18 I borrowed a friend's mobile home, which was situated near my home, in order to shelter drug addicts and the homeless. I could write an entire book on that experience alone! There were things that didn't go well and things that did go well, but above all, in my heart, I felt the overwhelming love that Jesus has for these people.

IN A BAD NEIGHBORHOOD

I still remember waking up and finding that Frans, a drug addict we had helped and were caring for, had left during the night. Everyone was worried and began to search for him. Eventually we found him, out of breath, sweating, and with crazed eyes. He was having a very bad reaction to the illegal drugs he had taken and believed giant spiders were chasing him.

Often I had no answer to give to those who cried out, but I was able to simply be there for them. In their spiritual darkness I could bring the love and warmth of God to them. After school and at night I could often be found on the streets, especially in what people referred to as the "bad neighborhood." That was where the particularly troubled and needy families lived, and that is where I wanted to be found as well, comforting and ministering the love of God to those who lived in misery.

As I sat with teenagers who were in the difficult, but by no means unusual, situation of having to cope with a father who was a drug addict or a mother who was an alcoholic and living a promiscuous lifestyle, I could often only respond to their cries for help by showing them God's love. This is something all followers of Jesus can do; there is certainly no shortage of suffering people in this world who need to feel that warmth and love of God through our presence.

REFUGEE CAMPS FOR KOSOVARANS

One night in 1999, God revealed His heart for the widows and orphans to me. I literally felt God's compassion and the pain He feels for those who are suffering, but are often forgotten and neglected by the rest of the world. I felt as if I had painful cracks in my heart, and every night I begged God to take the pain away. After three weeks, God took this heavy burden from me, but the experience changed my life forever. His overwhelming love and His compassion for the widows and orphans remains with me to this day.

Shortly afterward, in June 1999, I had the feeling that the Lord wanted me to start working in a refugee camp for Kosovarans. The camp was near the city where I lived at the time and had been built by the Dutch government to house the refugees who were fleeing from the war in Kosovo. I presented myself to those running the camp and offered to assist them wherever I was needed, and was given a job. The first buses crowded with women and children arrived from the airport shortly afterward. They were thin from malnourishment and some still had blood on their clothing from the violence they had experienced. It was shocking and heartrending for me to see these people in this condition; but what will remain with me forever, seared into my memory, is the anxiety and fear of death that were evident in their eyes.

In the next three days, more than 3,000 women and children arrived at the camp. The big tent that had been erected served as a space to sleep, a kitchen, and a meeting place. It was an extremely chaotic scene. The televisions were tuned to CNN, which was displaying images of the war in Kosovo. Women would cry out in anguish and faint as they saw their villages burning. I will never forget those images.

In just three months we, as workers in the camp, were able to establish a tremendous bond with the refugees as we went about our daily tasks and served them in so many different ways. Every day we, as a team, provided the people with food, drinks, and all their other basic needs.

A CARVED CROSS

Most Kosovarans were Muslims and had never experienced the love of Jesus; nor did they know anything about God's heart for them as their heavenly Father. They told us about the horror of the elite groups from Serbia who were going from village to village, killing and plundering, leaving devastation in their wake. Often these soldiers were under the influence of hard drugs and alcohol.

A woman told me how her husband had been taken out one night and shot, along with her brothers and cousins. The killers carved crosses in the backs of their victims as a sign of victory. Many of the Serbian militias were Orthodox Christians and they considered the Muslim Albanians inferior. Through experiences like these, it made it difficult to explain the Gospel to them and for them to accept it. Just by us giving them love through deeds and not just words, by showing them compassion, understanding and respect, these people were touched by God in a whole new way.

In August 1999, NATO intervened in the war and bombarded the army of the then Serbian president, Slobodan Milosevic, effectively driving them out of Kosovo over the course of several days. Eventually, the nearly one million displaced Kosovarans could return to their country, including the 3,000 refugees in the camp.

During those three months in the refugee camp, I met nine teenagers who had been separated from their parents during their escape through the mountains of Albania and Macedonia. I was determined to go to Kosovo with them and, with the assistance of the Red Cross, help them find their parents, who were all, apparently, still alive. They attended a Christian conference with me during the last week of August and then returned to Kosovo.

As mentioned in Chapter 1, Bram Oosterwijk, the organizer of the conference, heard that I had a heart for Kosovo and that I wanted to work with the people from there. He was also the director of the mission organization called De Brug (The Bridge), which had been active in Kosovo even before the war, and had started dozens of churches and many Bible schools there.

After the war in Kosovo, the staff working for De Brug wanted to do something to alleviate the enormous distress and emotional wounds people across Kosovo were suffering. A few years earlier, Bram had founded a church in Tirana, the capital of Albania, where he had trained a man named Tori Muca to be the pastor. During the war this church (with the help of many donations from the Netherlands), had taken care of thousands of fleeing Muslims by providing for their basic needs in a sports hall. Many had been touched by God's love. It was, however, difficult for Muslim Kosovarans to understand how Christians could perpetrate the horrific genocide that had just happened to them, and how it could also be Christians who were now taking care of them.

As more and more refugees fled to Tirana, the Red Cross took over the sports hall to accommodate and help them. During this time, the friendship grew between Tori and the refugees he was serving. After the war they asked Tori to go with them when they returned to Kosovo so that he could help them bury their relatives and build up the homes that had been destroyed.

GJAKOVA

Once there, Tori started a ministry for De Brug in the south of Kosovo near the city of Gjakova. Roads had been bombed and land mines were still buried along the roadsides. NATO soldiers were working to remove or detonate the mines, which left craters in and near the road. To navigate the damaged roads, the first thing that was needed was a reliable 4 X 4 vehicle. One was donated by the Dutch and in August 1999, De Brug staff in the Netherlands agreed to arrange for the delivery of this four-wheel-drive vehicle to Kosovo. I saw God's hand in this situation and asked if I could join them. They agreed and two weeks later, I joined Ingrid van Diest of De Brug and another friend, and we drove the vehicle to Kosovo.

The devastation we found was indescribable. Entire villages had been decimated and the people looked on as we passed by. Numbed by the horrors that they had witnessed during the war, they showed little or no emotion. In Gjakova and the surrounding villages, hundreds of men were missing. Nobody knew what had happened to them and women and children were left to fend for themselves. (Over the next few months these missing men were found in mass graves and all signs indicated that they had been brutally murdered.)

Together with Tori, we began to help these widows as much as we could. In the following months we supplied clothes and bread to hundreds of widows, along with financial assistance to help them start rebuilding their lives. Fortunately, there were also larger organizations present that rebuilt many of their homes.

Despite all the physical help that was given, the people were still having great difficulty dealing with the emotional and spiritual trauma of the war. As we reached out with deeds and not just words, people started slowly becoming aware of God's love and became more open to us. As soon as we were able, we visited these people and, as we prayed for them, God healed many of them miraculously. This news spread like a wildfire and soon people came to us asking for prayer.

We began a church where we could further help and shelter the new converts. It was so special to see how God's glory manifested itself in an area that was so badly devastated; even today God continues to do great things among them. Many people are accepting Jesus as their Savior, and God continues to show His love to them through miracles, especially by healing them.

I worked for over a year in Gjakova; I saw how God feels about orphans and widows and how He greatly blesses those who help them.

GET ACTIVE!

In 1999, when we began our ministry to the orphans and widows in Kosovo, it wasn't a popular ministry to be involved in and although it seemed there were plenty of books and sermons on every other topic, there were few about looking after them. Through our work in Kosovo, and our connection with Derek Prince, he wrote a booklet about God's heart for the orphans and the widows. The booklet served as a wake-up call for the Church as it called attention to the way God feels about these people. What is written in the booklet is what we did in our daily lives while we were ministering in Kosovo. Little did we know that the message written during those times would have the impact that it has had.

Although it is important to know what God's Word says with regard to Christians caring for the orphans and the widows, it is not necessary for you to have it memorized before you do something to help them. Of course, studying the Bible and then doing what it tells you to do is always a good thing. The basis from which we operate is stronger when we know what the Word of God says on important issues and then act accordingly.

In the desperate case we faced, we didn't delay in acting on what we knew was right, we simply went ahead with what the Lord placed on our hearts. Derek Prince was able to document not only what we did, but how it corresponded with the Word of God.

Throughout my years of service, when I have finished preaching, many people have come forward, emotionally touched by God, crying that they want to help the widows and orphans. This is a direct result of a revelation that God gives them during the preaching. Sometimes I meet the same people a year later and they have not reached out to help anyone—they just continued waiting for the voice of God to tell them what to do.

If there is anything that makes me sad, it is people like this. I do not believe that unless we have had a personal revelation from God, we should sit and do nothing. There are many things people can do—just because they know it's the right thing to do. Some concrete steps of action to take in light of God's heart for the poor and destitute would be to financially adopt a child in an undeveloped country; visit people in prisons; visit patients in nursing homes; or pay a visit to a nearby retirement home, which is full of lonely people. Spend time with a single aunt, uncle, or grandparent, or send an encouraging card to someone who is having a difficult time. There are literally a thousand things that you can do to obey God's command to look after and care for those less fortunate than you.

SCRIPTURES ON THIS IMPORTANT TOPIC

There is no shortage of Bible teaching on how to deal with the marginalized and weak in our society. The Bible is very clear about how we, as Christians, should deal with the needy in the world, the war victims, widows and orphans, refugees, people who are rightly or wrongly imprisoned, and people experiencing famine or who have insufficient water, bread, or clothing to meet their needs. We often find that when we are reaching out to help others, that is, in fact, when God reaches out to help us.

The prophet Isaiah wrote:

Is not this the kind of fasting I have chosen: to loose the chains of injustice and untie the cords of the yoke, to set the oppressed free and break every yoke? Is it not to share your food with the hungry and to provide the poor wanderer with shelter—when you see the naked, to clothe them, and not to turn away from your own flesh and blood? Then your light will break forth like the dawn, and your healing will quickly appear; then your righteousness will go before you, and the glory of the Lord will be your rear guard. Then you will call, and the Lord will answer; you will cry out for help, and He will say: Here am I (Isaiah 58:6-9a).

In recent years I have seen many people who were healed when they committed their lives to help those who are less fortunate. Jesus' ministry was focused on the sick, the poor, and the outcasts. He often reached out to those who were on the margins of society. There are countless examples in the New Testament, as well as in the Old Testament, of God's character being one that cares for the orphan and the widow, the alien and the oppressed.

God the Father is a God of justice and we are the beneficiaries of His justice when we give our lives to Jesus. We wear His robes of righteousness and, as ambassadors for the Lord Jesus, we are all called to care for the weak and to fight against injustice in this world. This important calling is one that churches have regularly ignored with severe consequences. Similarly, the people of God in Old Testament times had periods when they neglected those whom the Lord specifically called them to care for. As a result, God closed His ears to their cries for help. He removed His hand from the people when they ceased to care for the strangers, widows, or orphans among them.

The concern God has for these people reveals His character and also establishes a principle in His Kingdom. The psalmist described it this way:

> *God sets the lonely in families, He leads out the prisoners with singing, but the rebellious live in a sun-scorched land* (Psalm 68:6).

> *The Lord works righteousness and justice for all the oppressed* (Psalm 103:6).

> *Surely the righteous will praise Your name, and the upright will live in Your presence* (Psalm 140:13).

God is a righteous God and His love compels Him to rise in action wherever injustice is. He is a just God and many have already experienced the blessings of that justice with Christ's death on the cross (see Phil. 3:9).

The concern on God's heart for this group was put into law and He has a number of commands for His people in which He instructs us to take care of orphans, widows, and foreigners. The foreigner was anyone we would refer to as refugees or asylum-seekers today. We read in Leviticus 19:9-10:

> *When you reap the harvest of your land, do not reap to the very edges of your field or gather the gleanings of your harvest. Do not go over your vineyard a second time or pick up the grapes that have fallen. Leave them for the poor and the foreigner. I am the Lord your God.*

In the Book of Deuteronomy we read:

At the end of every three years, bring all the tithes of that year's produce and store it in your towns, so that the Levites (who have no allotment or inheritance of their own) and the foreigners, the fatherless and the widows who live in your towns may come and eat and be satisfied, and so that the Lord your God may bless you in all the work of your hands (Deuteronomy 14:28-29).

THE WORDS OF JOB

We now see that caring for the foreigner, the orphan, and the widow, both physically and spiritually, is another key for a successful and blessed life. If you do this, God will bless you in everything you do! Let's look at Job:

Whoever heard me spoke well of me, and those who saw me commended me, because I rescued the poor who cried for help, and the fatherless who had none to assist them. The one who was dying blessed me; I made the widow's heart sing. I put on righteousness as my clothing; justice was my robe and my turban. I was eyes to the blind and feet to the lame. I was a father to the needy; I took up the case of the stranger. I broke the fangs of the wicked and snatched the victims from their teeth (Job 29:11-17).

If I have denied the desires of the poor or let the eyes of the widow grow weary, if I have kept my bread to myself, not sharing it with the fatherless—but from my youth I reared him as a father would, and from my birth I guided the widow—if I have seen anyone perishing for lack of clothing, or the needy without garments, and their hearts did not bless me for warming them with the fleece from my sheep, if I have raised my hand against the fatherless, knowing that I had influence in court, then let my arm fall from the shoulder, let it be broken off at the joint (Job 31:16-22).

What are these sins he did not commit? He describes very clearly that it is the sin of not taking care of the foreigner, the orphan, and the widow. Job is very serious about this saying that if he had not taken care of the foreigner, the orphan, and widow, his arms would no longer be part of his body and that it would be better if his arms were broken off.

Once again, the message is very clear: *do something!* Do not sit around waiting for something to happen. We should not be spending all our time watching television when there is work to be done! You don't have to go to a mission field far from home to do something for God. There are plenty of opportunities around you. Volunteer in a retirement home, hospital, prison, or in centers for asylum-seekers or those in need. Go and work in the care home where many people are lonely or be a "buddy" to an AIDS victim. You do not need to fast and pray for instructions about what you should do, as it has always been God's command to you to help these people.

SODOM AND GOMORRAH'S SIN

Ezekiel 16 is the story of Sodom and Gomorrah. Sodom was a city immersed in sinful living. Sometimes people refer to Amsterdam as being just like Sodom and Gomorrah. They refer to a city where everything is possible, a city that lives in overt sexual sin. I was always taught that God Himself turned against Sodom and Gomorrah because of the sin of homosexuality in those cities. I was always under the impression that it was because of this sin that the cities had fallen into such deep spiritual darkness.

But in Ezekiel 16, I read something very different! It says in verses 49-50:

> *Now this was the sin of your sister Sodom: She and her daughters were arrogant, overfed and unconcerned;* **they did not help the poor and needy.** *They were haughty and did detestable things before Me. Therefore I did away with them as you have seen.*

So, despite all their other sins, the sin that offended God the most was that they did not do anything to help the poor and needy!

There are generally three sins in the Bible that God gets very angry about, and often these are the sins that cause alienation between God and humankind. They are adultery, idolatry, and negligence. We have probably heard many sermons about adultery and idolatry. We know that they are not good; we know that God's judgment comes on us swiftly if we are involved in these things, and we know that these sins destroy not only ourselves, but others as well.

However, there seems to be very little said about the sin of negligence, or doing nothing when God is calling us to do something about a situation. We can read about the impact negligence can have in the New Testament, but let us now look at what's written in Proverbs, an Old Testament book, which is full of wisdom. Here we read some thought-provoking words from God.

Let's start with a promise from God in Proverbs 19:17: *"Whoever is kind to the poor lends to the Lord, and He will reward them for what they have done."*

In Proverbs 21:13, we read the following, *"Whoever shuts their ears to the cry of the poor will also cry out and not be answered."*

I have seen with my own eyes what happens when people commit themselves to serving the poor, the weak, and the outcast. They can suddenly hear and understand the voice of God so much more clearly. Sometimes it's easy for us to block out the cries of the needy if they are filtered through something our friends tell us about, the Internet, or media like television and newspapers. But the more we ignore what God is calling us to do, the less we will be able to form or maintain a relationship with Him. We can also convert this warning into a promise: whoever heeds the cry of the poor will be heard and helped by God when they cry out for help.

Before going to the New Testament, we read one last shocking warning and promise in Proverbs 28:27: *"Those who give to the poor will lack nothing, but those who close their eyes to them receive many curses."*

When I read that for the first time, I put aside my Bible and meditated on what I had read. Then I read it again and again and concluded—not least of all because I have seen its reality while praying for people—that it is possible to walk around with a curse on our lives because we do not take care of the poor or those in need. God promises in Proverbs 28:27 that if we do our utmost for this group of people, we will suffer no shortages in our own lives and will be abundantly blessed.

Although one of the keys to success in our lives is that we are committed to helping the orphans, the widows, and the poor, we do not necessarily have to do this as a full-time job. Most people who are committed to helping others have a job, a family, and bills that need to be paid on time, but have decided to devote some of their free time to helping those in need. For example, they set aside a few hours every week to work as volunteers in environments where people are cared for; or they financially sponsor orphans; or they contribute financially in areas of poverty.

However we help, we need to remember that God's Word is clear—doing nothing is not an option. Give to the poor, and you will be truly blessed!

I am convinced that one of the reasons why TRIN is so blessed and has produced so much fruit is because one of the pillars of our ministry is taking care of orphans, widows, and the poor. We allocate more than half of our finances toward helping these groups. We are seeing spiritual revival in many areas, including signs and wonders, and the key to this breakthrough and revival is, among other things, taking care of the orphans and widows and standing up for people who are affected by injustice in this world.

You can also see this in the lives of Rolland and Heidi Baker who live in Mozambique where they take care of thousands of orphans. We love being with Rolland and Heidi as they are a couple who have devoted their lives to helping orphans and widows. Together with their huge team of local and international volunteers, they are experiencing a huge revival. Many thousands of new churches have been planted as a result. They are abundantly blessed and prosper in whatever they do. Through their love of Jesus and the intimacy they have with the Father, they have understood His heart and come against the oppression of the poor, the sick, the widows, and the orphans in many undeveloped countries.

You may get excited when you read Rolland and Heidi's stories about their work in Mozambique, but the reality is that they are just like you and me. They have their own share of problems and plenty of ups and downs. Perhaps the only difference between Rolland and Heidi and many others like them is that they have put their faith into the concrete action of helping the poor.

It started with someone touching the untouchable and then the enormous love of God and the power of the Holy Spirit came. As a result, a great outpouring of the Holy Spirit took place. Entire villages, cities, and even countries were transformed!

Dear reader, you will find that if you do something, no matter how simple, for *"the least of these"* (Matt. 25:45), God's increased blessing on your life will surprise you! Step out of your self-centered world and give of yourself and your love, without expecting to receive anything in return—this is the kind of love that God gives us.

GRATITUDE

Often, we make the Gospel too complex, when in many ways, it is so simple. We all have a duty and a role to play in caring for the most vulnerable people in our society. Understanding this reality is an important key in obtaining a breakthrough and experiencing God's favor in our lives, but too often it is a subject seldom dealt with.

One of the blessings of caring for the poor is the opportunity to experience people as they really are. They often have nothing to hide and you get to deal with the real person, just as they are, without any hidden agendas. In Africa, for example, many people are not yet spoiled through prosperity or having too many material things. African children may dream of having toys and are so grateful when they receive one because they have so little. Sometimes those who are impoverished have a greater sense of appreciation than those of us who have too much to truly value each thing.

Recently, I stood at a market stall where all kinds of breads were sold; there were more than 30 different types. It was a holiday and people were lining up to buy bread. When I got there, several types of bread were sold out, but there were still more than 20 varieties available. There were four customers in front of me and they all seemed very frustrated that the type of bread they had come to buy was sold out, and some even stormed away angrily. I sympathized with the vendors. How immensely selfish we can be at times! When it was my turn, I said aloud, "Today 30,000 children will die due to lack of food and something to drink." Then I thanked God for all the loaves that were available that day for us to buy. It went very quiet, and the people stopped complaining immediately. I bought the loaves I had come for and walked home.

NO EXCUSES

Opening our eyes to the needs in this world makes us very aware of what we have instead of looking at what we don't have. Literally thousands of people are dying today, some of whom are quite young, and they are perishing simply because they have no bread and fresh water. Be grateful that you have these things plus a roof above your head and a place where you can sleep soundly.

Sometimes, people will point out that it's easy for me to understand the plight of the less fortunate because I often minister in impoverished areas. There is some truth in what they say because it is indeed quite different to have starving children in your arms and to see the need with your own eyes. This kind of face-to-face experience affects one deeply and is not easily forgotten. However, most of us watch the news on television or access it via our computers. We are also able to read enough newspapers to know what's going on in the world; but we often do not take up our God-given responsibility to help alleviate the suffering we see. In most cases, we shut off our minds from seeing the painful situations and continue focusing our attention only on our own needs and interests.

I have also heard people say that the need is so great that they don't know where to begin to help. There are just too many problems and too many children who are dying. Again, this is an excuse they are using for not taking their responsibility seriously.

I heard this beautiful story; maybe you've heard it too, which illustrates this point perfectly: There was once a writer who was busy writing his book in his hotel room. Through the window he looked out onto the beach. That morning, there were literally thousands of starfish washed ashore and the beach was littered with them. For a couple of hours a teenager had kept himself busy throwing the starfish back into the sea. The writer couldn't concentrate any longer on his writing, so he walked from his hotel to the boy on the beach and asked, "Why are you doing this? It doesn't make any sense because there are so many starfish on the beach!" The boy looked at the man and picked up a starfish. He held it in his hand and said: "Yes, but it does make sense for this one!" The boy then threw the starfish back into the sea. The man was so impressed with the young man's logic that he joined him for the rest of the morning helping him return starfish to the sea.

God wants you to stop for that one person who needs your help. Start with one. It will change you, and you will find a new perspective to your life. You will be better able to hear and understand God's voice, and signs and wonders will soon follow you.

JOHN THE BAPTIST ARMY

I believe that we live in a time when the Lord Jesus will return soon. A John the Baptist-type army is rising up and is proclaiming Jesus radically and with confidence, not worrying about what other people think of them. It is an army of God's people that has no age limit for new recruits. They are people who have broken free of their comfort zones and are aware that the Lord Jesus will come back very soon. The army is also known as the Joel generation. Young and old, they are preparing for the return of Jesus.

One of the hallmarks of this army is that they stand up against systems that produce injustice, and they proclaim the Gospel in a practical way, not only with words but with practical deeds, too. John the Baptist is a prime example of such a person. He was the cousin of the Lord Jesus and prepared people for His arrival. We read in Luke's Gospel that thousands of people flocked to him to receive teaching. John said the following:

> *"Produce fruit in keeping with repentance. And do not begin to say to yourselves, 'We have Abraham as our father.' For I tell you that out of these stones God can raise up children for Abraham. The ax is already at the root of the trees, and every tree that does not produce good fruit will be cut down and thrown into the fire." "What shall we do then?" the crowd asked. John answered, "Anyone who has two shirts should share with the one who has none, and anyone who has food should do the same"* (Luke 3:8-11).

What John is saying here by the power of the Holy Spirit is powerful! You can imagine what it would be like to have a pile of stones that God turns into children. God really can take the things that are impossible for us to do and make them possible. John also said something else quite radical—if we are born-again Christians, we should produce fruit in keeping with repentance. The ax is already at the root of the trees, and every tree that does not produce good fruit will be cut down and thrown into the fire. In verse 10 the people ask what they should do; in other words, what kind of fruit should they be producing in order to please the Lord? In verse 11 John says, *"Anyone who has two shirts should share with the one who has none, and anyone who has food should do the same."*

I have read this Scripture several times because it is so radical. I had expected John to say something quite different, more like, "I want you to pray more, live holier lives, study your Bible more, go to church more often." These are all good things, but God says here, through John, something very simple: "If you have two coats, give one away and do the same with your excess food."

In other words: take care of the weaker members of society because that is fruit in keeping with repentance!

A PICNIC FOR THE POOR

Perhaps we should examine our own fruit in keeping with repentance, and, if we have done nothing to make a positive difference, make a decision to do something to produce good fruit. This is what Job said about this subject: "My arm is created for helping the poor. If I don't help the poor, my arm doesn't belong to my body. As far as I am concerned, God can cut it off if I do not care for the foreigner, the orphan, and widow" (see Job 31:16-22). John went even one step further; he said that your entire body doesn't belong on this earth if you close your eyes to the misery of this world. I was shocked when I read this!

Let us look further in Luke 14 at what the Lord Jesus said about this:

> ...When you give a luncheon or dinner, do not invite your friends, your brothers or sisters, your relatives, or your rich neighbors; if you do, they may invite you back and so you will be repaid. But when you give a banquet, invite the poor, the crippled, the lame, the blind, and you will be blessed. Although they cannot repay you, you will be repaid at the resurrection of the righteous (Luke 14:12-14).

How many cripples, blind, beggars, homeless, asylum-seeking, lame, and poor people do you know of? This is what the Kingdom of God is about! If you organize a picnic, don't invite your relatives or rich friends, invite those who cannot repay you. God has a different view on things—and it is wonderfully non-religious! If you can do this, it will liberate you. This is Kingdom thinking; and if you think this way you will be blessed by the Lord, and your reward will be at the resurrection of the righteous.

How much do you have in your heavenly savings account? The righteous people are those who take action and do something about the injustice in this world. God wants you to belong to this group and wants you to do something to help others. He even gives you very practical tips: give your excess/surplus of clothing and food away; organize a meal and invite the weak, the disabled, lonely, the divorced, or the single mother with a low income who finds surviving financially so difficult. Invite a widow or widower from the retirement home, someone who is homeless, or a drug addict for a meal. If need be, transfer some money to someone who will help the poor and lonely—but in the name of Jesus, do something!

SHEEP AND GOATS

Now, let's look at what happens in Matthew 25. Fasten your seatbelts as you are in for another shocking discovery! The Lord Jesus is talking about the judgment He will give on the day when He returns to Earth—a day we should be looking forward to.

It will be the day that the works of satan will be stopped and God's creation as a whole will be restored. On that day there will be no more death, disease, pain, loneliness, quarreling, war, hunger, or distress. What a glorious day that will be for the righteous! It will be an awesome day for the people who have accepted Jesus as the

Son of God and as their Savior—people who are followers of Jesus and filled with the Holy Spirit. On this wonderful and exciting day, we will be taken to our final destination to be at home with God, our Father in Heaven. Right now, Jesus, along with hundreds of thousands of angels, is busy with the final preparation of our heavenly homes. The army of God is preparing itself to fetch us. The return of Jesus Christ to Earth will be spectacular, with signs in the heavens and on the earth.

However for another group of people, this will be the most dreadful day of their lives. This is the group who refused to believe that Jesus is the Son of God and who never accepted nor received Him as their Savior. The Lord Jesus also says something about another group of people. These are the people who didn't do anything to help take care of the orphans, the poor, the hungry, the naked, and the prisoner.

When Jesus returns to Earth as the King of kings, He will separate all the people into two groups. For the sake of convenience, He calls them sheep and goats in Matthew 25:31-46. (I believe He used these examples because He often calls Himself the Good Shepherd. A good shepherd will not put goats and sheep together in the same stable, because they might fight and injure each other.) Also, on this day, the Good Shepherd will come from Heaven, radiant, glorious, and surrounded by all the angels—millions of them! Then He will take His seat on the throne, and all of us will stand before Him.

As a shepherd, He will put the sheep on His right hand and the goats on His left. To the sheep He will say, "Enter into Heaven where you will all be blessed by My Father. Your reward is awaiting you in His Kingdom! Welcome because you have taken care of those who were thirsty, fed those who were hungry, housed the asylum-seekers and refugees, visited the prisoners, and taken care of the sick." The sheep will say, "When did we do this?" It may simply have been a lifestyle that they were not aware of or it may have been a result of a caring and compassionate nature; but what they did to help these people is of paramount importance to God.

To the goats the Lord will say the most dreadful words known to humankind: "Go away from Me, you are cursed, go into the everlasting fire prepared for the devil and his angels because you have not taken care of the hungry, the thirsty, the poor, foreigners, refugees, asylum-seekers, the sick, or those in prison."

Matthew 25:46 says that the goats will go to eternal punishment, but the righteous into everlasting life.

We have already read in Proverbs that we will be heavily cursed if we close our eyes and ears to the plight of the poor and needy. Again this shows that the Lord Himself says that there is a group of people who are cursed because they have closed their ears and eyes and didn't do anything to help them. To God, this inaction and neglect of what people are called to do is obviously a very serious sin.

The goats were apparently not aware of what is written in Matthew 25, because they asked, "When did we see you hungry, or thirsty, or a stranger?" How could this group be so negligent about something that the Lord so clearly tells us is so important to Him?

This should serve as a wake-up call. I can imagine that all this might sound threatening and condemning, but that's not my intention. The Lord's Word is to convince you, not to make you feel guilty. The Lord wants to speak to your conscience and open your eyes to understand His heart and His Word. Go to Him and ask Him to show you His compassion for the poor and needy, then go and do something to help them. Maybe it's something very small for you, but for God it is big and important. He says in Matthew 25:40: *"The King will reply, 'Truly I tell you, whatever you did for one of the least of these brothers and sisters of Mine, you did for Me.'"*

The entire ministry of Jesus was all about the simple ones, the misfits, the sinners, and the lost. We read important Scriptures about this in Isaiah 61. Both the ministry of Jesus, as well as yours, is described here:

> *The Spirit of the Sovereign Lord is on Me, because the Lord has anointed Me to proclaim good news to the poor. He has sent Me to bind up the brokenhearted, to proclaim freedom for the captives and release from darkness for the prisoners* (Isaiah 61:1).

This Scripture from Isaiah is repeated again in Luke 4:18-19. Jesus came back from the desert where He was invited to go by the devil. He returned in the power of the Holy Spirit to Galilee where His actual ministry began, and He preached his first sermon in the synagogue there. During His sermon, He described His ministry as it was prophesied in Isaiah 61. The ministry of Jesus is also described in Matthew 11:4-6:

> *...Go back and report to John what you hear and see: The blind receive sight, the lame walk, those who have leprosy are cleansed, the deaf hear, the dead are raised, and the good news is proclaimed to the poor. Blessed is anyone who does not stumble on account of Me.*

There is so much more to say about this important subject. It is something that all of us can do; you do not need training in order to provide for the poor and do something about the injustice in the world. I close this chapter with James 1:27, the Gospel in a nutshell:

> *Religion that God our Father accepts as pure and faultless is this: to look after orphans and widows in their distress and to keep oneself from being polluted by the world.*

CHAPTER 9

PRAYING FOR THE SICK

Another way to share God's love is to pray for sick people. One of the first times I prayed for a sick person was during a youth service. I was about 17 years old and had just read in Acts that the power of God which was on the disciples is the same power available to all believers today. I read that the followers of Jesus could heal the sick, cast out demons, and raise people from the dead when they prayed for them in the name of Jesus. From my Baptist background I knew about things like adult baptism by immersion, but the topic of "signs and wonders" was new to me. That is, until I preached in a youth service!

I had prepared a sermon that would take five minutes to give, and I was so nervous! I didn't feel the presence of God, the heavens seemed closed, and secretly I had already looked for the shortest way to the exit. At the end of my sermon, I did a short altar call and asked people who were sick to come forward for prayer. To my great surprise people came forward who were really sick. I closed my eyes tightly and suddenly I heard an inner voice saying, "Mattheus, don't just stand there looking so nervous, do something! I will put the words in your mouth, so open your mouth right now and speak." I opened my eyes, looked around and tried to speak, but my mouth was so dry that I couldn't!

PARASITE

Suddenly I saw Robbert, an acquaintance of mine, come forward. He had just returned from a missions trip in Peru. I asked him what was wrong with him and he whispered somewhat anxiously that he had a parasite.

I whispered nervously, "Lord, please help me, where exactly is the word *parasite* in the Bible?" I could hear my voice whisper, "Parasite, parasite, Lord, parasite? Help me." Because my microphone, which was pinned to my shirt, was still on, the whole congregation heard me! I closed my eyes tightly and didn't know what to do. I felt just like Peter when he had said with his own mouth to Jesus that he would walk on the water. I had the feeling that I had done the same thing by organizing a healing service.

In my mind I sat in the boat and I saw Jesus walking on the water. With great enthusiasm, I swung my legs over the side of the boat and I began to walk on the water. Suddenly I noticed that the waves were quite high and I started to doubt. *What if nothing happens and all these people have come to the front expecting to be healed, and they aren't? Could I even hear and understand the voice of the Lord?* Slowly, I began to sink into the water. I no longer looked to Jesus, but to the circumstances. I was listening to the lies coming into my head, and was filled with fear and uncertainty.

In the meantime, it had become very quiet in the hall. In a flash I recalled that I had seen a preacher on television who prayed for a sick person. It was the only time I had seen such a thing, and I remembered that this man waved wildly with his one hand while he put his other hand on the sick person and screamed something like, "I break and rebuke this disease." Because this was the only example I had ever seen, I did the same thing. I put one hand on Robbert, began waving my other hand in the air, and screamed into the microphone, "In the name of Jesus, I break this transvestite!"

I shocked even myself, and Robbert stood looking at me with his eyes wide open. At that moment I realized the huge mistake I had made. I had prayed for a transvestite to be banished instead of a parasite. Robbert roared with laughter and said cleverly, "How did you know?" That was a joke of course, but the people present began to laugh loudly and the tension was broken. That evening many were touched and healed by the Lord. Let me remind you, this was the first time I had prayed for sick people!

My prayer was certainly no great thing of beauty, but I think the Lord burst out laughing when He heard it. My mistake broke the tension in the room and in me, and everyone was very relaxed. The striving disappeared, and people came forward for prayer expecting that God would answer them.

Nowhere in the Bible do we read that we should pray for the sick in a special way. It is, however, written that we have to heal the sick, which is something quite different from praying for them. This was a great revelation to me, and I have no idea why it took me so long to realize there is a difference. I read through my Bible again just to make sure I wasn't being mislead, and nowhere did I find that Jesus prayed for the sick. He healed them, He addressed the disease or the demon, and the people were healed and set free. It is clearly written that all believers, like you and me, have received the same authority. Maybe we should stop only praying for the sick and should learn to stand in our God-given authority and heal them in Jesus' name.

PRAYING AGAINST CANCER

Some time after the healing service I have just described, I met William in another service that was held for young people. William was 17 years old and stood quietly in the back of the hall. Jop, my brother-in-law, and I went up to him and asked where he came from; he told us he lived in a small village not far from where we were. He also told us, with desperation in his eyes, that his mother, who was still a young woman, was dying at home. She had an advanced stage of cancer, and they were already making preparations for her funeral. Jop and I looked at each other and we were both thinking the same thing. We felt we should go to the house where William's mother lived and lay hands on her and heal her in the name of Jesus.

A little nervous and trembling, we arrived at the house that evening, a cup of olive oil in hand, and rang the door bell. William's father opened the door and with a weak smile asked us to come in. We saw such deep sadness in his eyes. William's mother was also there. I had never seen such a very thin and sick person so close up before; I could hardly bear it. I closed my eyes for a while, and I concentrated on Jesus. What I saw in the natural seemed so different from the supernatural reality. We explained to her what we were going to do. Although she went to church, she wasn't yet born again, but after we explained the significance of the sacrifice that Jesus had made on the cross for her, she received Jesus as her Savior and was baptized in the Holy Spirit. We then put our hands on her, anointed her with oil, and took authority over her illness in Jesus' name. The room was filled with peace, but we thought that nothing had happened in the natural because she seemed just as sick as before. She smiled a little and mumbled that she appreciated our visit very much.

On my way home I was relieved; I was glad that we had done it. But on the other hand, I was disappointed because I had really believed that she would be healed instantly. It was a struggle to deal with these feelings, but we had done what we had to do. We continued blessing the family in prayer and, three months later, met William again during our youth service. This time he was with his whole family, and he excitedly reintroduced us to his mother. She was completely healed and had become active in the church where she had grown up. We were so overcome we could not control our tears of joy. We were reminded yet again of how good God is, and we praised Him for William's mother's miraculous healing! For her, it was not yet the time to pass on.

SANDER

Some readers will have difficulty with the example I have just given. Perhaps you have experienced a similar situation. You have prayed, fasted, and done everything possible for your terminally ill loved one to be healed, and yet that person died. Perhaps through your disappointment you have questioned God and have even become bitter; but I urge you to speak to God and let Him comfort you.

Sometimes in life we can let something that has happened bother us for ages, and still be none the wiser. Sometimes we have to accept that many things that happen in life cannot be explained.

One example of this is Sander, a young, 20-year-old man. He was a beautiful person in all respects; he had blond hair, blue eyes, was strong, and had a great sense of humor. Unfortunately, he also had cancer and, according to the doctors, had only four months to live. His legs were already quite swollen, so he had trouble walking. We became close friends with him and visited him quite often. One day we asked him what his dream was. He said that his dream was to be healed and to go to America. We were planning to go on a ministry trip to Seattle and asked Sander if he would like to come with us.

In the beginning His family was strongly opposed to the idea because he was so seriously ill. However, his two best friends agreed and believed completely that Sander would be healed in Seattle. Both Rebekah and I had faith for Sander's healing, and all of us started fasting and praying. (In certain situations fasting and praying may be the decisive key and the difference between the success and failure of a petition we make to God.)

The doctor, who had already told Sander that he was going to die, made it clear that if he could still enjoy spending time in the United States, he should do it even though the trip to get there would be physically difficult for him to make. Eventually Sander decided that he would go along with his two best friends. They were all from a traditional church but believed wholeheartedly in revival and healing. We planned the trip in combination with a trip to a training seminar on spiritual warfare for our TRIN employees. The group that went to Seattle was comprised of our TRIN team, my parents (who joined us for the first time on such a journey), Sander, and his two friends.

When the time came for us to go to America, Sander's health had taken a turn for the worst, and he was no longer able to walk. We had to take a large wheelchair with us because his legs had swollen to five times their normal size. The favor of God was upon us and we were all given a free upgrade to the business class area of the plane. During the two flights we had to take to get to Seattle, many blessings occurred; passengers were moved by Sander's faith and God's loving presence in our group. In both aircraft, even the crew got emotional, and they said that they had the feeling that something special was happening, which only reinforced our belief that it was.

After a journey of 22 hours, we arrived at the airport in Seattle, but with a serious problem. Sander didn't fit into the wheelchair that we had brought with us as his body had become very swollen during the trip. Our team started praying and suddenly a man approached us with a very large wheelchair. He gave it to us, saying, "Keep it," and walked away. We believe that this was an angel because we couldn't find any natural reason for it. Nobody even knew that we needed a wheelchair, let alone such a big one.

Upon arriving at the church in Seattle, we had communion with bread and wine and felt God's strong presence. There was also a tremendous team spirit among us. We had arranged for a hospital bed to be put in the church for Sander so that he would be more comfortable, and Sander lay on it smiling, grateful that one of his dreams had been fulfilled.

Rebekah, my wife, comes from Seattle, and that evening we visited some of her friends and family, with near fatal results. Someone put a deadly poison in Rebekah's drink, and I noticed that she was not feeling well. I started to worry and wonder what was wrong with her; then she suddenly fainted.

I ran to her and felt her wrist—her pulse was very weak. Immediately I called for an ambulance, which fortunately came very quickly. She was rushed to the nearest hospital and put on several intravenous drips. I was told that they had found poison in her body and that was why she was in a coma. What a situation! Sander was desperately ill, staying at the church with the TRIN team and I was with my wife in the Intensive Care Unit of the hospital—and this was only the first evening of our trip.

Instead of panic or anger, which would have been a natural response, I looked to Jesus. I wanted to be angry and scream, but instead I decided, not with my mind, but with my heart, to trust in the Lord. I always have a little Bible in my pocket and started reading and praying Psalm 91 aloud.

That night I was able to contact my parents and Angela Greenig, our spiritual mother and pastor of the church in Seattle. They came to the hospital immediately. My mother was very concerned and upset and could not understand how we remained calm. While it is natural for a mother to be concerned, we were able to pray together and the peace of God came into our hearts.

Sander's condition deteriorated that night and he had to be admitted to from the hospital to remove the fluid that was building up in his body. After he was released from hospital, he had a very special week. One highlight was that one of his friends was baptized in a nearby pool. It was a special occasion, and Sander enjoyed it very much. After four days, Rebekah came out of her coma. She had suffered some damage to her ears and to some of her basic motor skills. In faith we thanked the Lord for her healing, which ultimately would take place during a TRIN healing service a year and a half later.

Sander died a week after we returned to the Netherlands. We were very sad and disconcerted because we could not understand why God had allowed this to happen. After a few months of wrestling and trying to find the answer, we decided to leave our questions about what had happened with the Lord, and to proceed with our work for the Kingdom of God.

Since then we have had to face similarly difficult situations within our own family. A 19-year-old cousin threw herself in front of a moving train because she heard demonic voices telling her the track was a stairway to Heaven. One grandfather committed suicide, and another died of heart failure.

QUESTION MARKS

We all have our own stories of loss and mourning. We can continue to focus on what did not happen despite our hope and belief that there would be a healing, or we can choose to focus on the miracles that God has done. To be honest, I could write a book about all the signs and wonders that Jesus has done in our midst over the last year.

In more than 11 countries, we have seen hundreds and hundreds of miracles, signs, people being healed, as well as people being set free from things that are not from God. The book I could write about the people who have not been healed would be very small in comparison.

I want to encourage you to leave your questions with God and not be hindered as you continue to proclaim the Kingdom of God on Earth. Later, when we are living forever with the Lord in Heaven, we will have enough time to ask questions and get answers. Perhaps that will not be necessary because, if we are incorporated into His glory, we will understand everything anyway.

So, my dear reader, son or daughter of the Most High God, do not let the disappointments of this life and the lies that come from them hold you back. Instead, make a decision to do what you feel you have to do. Do something in your community, make a difference, and get out of the boat and walk on the water. The worst that could happen to you is that you start to sink. But I assure you, if you go and walk in faith, Jesus will always be there to help you. He will always be with you; He is just waiting for you to get out of that boat!

CHAPTER 10

BE YOURSELF!

I think daring to be yourself is one of the most important keys to living your dreams and seeing the favor of God on your life. Many people are living as a copy of someone else instead of being their authentic selves. God has designed you as an original. You are unique; there is no one like you! You are probably quite aware of this, but I cannot say it enough, "Be yourself, and follow your heart!"

As chameleons change color according to their environment, so I often see people changing in order to meet the expectations of those around them. As a result, they lose sight of who they really are.

Those with a poor self-image and feelings of inferiority often feel they will be more acceptable if they become more like those around them expect them to be. They do not want to quarrel with people and try, instead, to alter their thinking and behavior to please others. I struggled for years trying to change myself to meet other people's expectations of me, and so become more acceptable to them.

I used to find great preachers fascinating, and I wanted to be like them. I behaved just like them hoping to get their approval. I tried reading the same books, wearing the same clothes, even having the same kind of hairstyle. I made the same kind of jokes and made the same statements as they did. I talked about the same topics and even tried to talk the way they talked.

As I tried harder and harder to become a copy of them, deep down inside I felt unhappy. I had become a clone of individuals who were important to me because I was so frightened that if I revealed my real self to them, they would reject me. I was afraid to say no, afraid to be used, afraid of embarrassing them.

I can tell you from this experience that the things you are frightened of, will probably happen! Why? Simply because if you cannot and will not appreciate and accept that God has designed you to be a unique person, He cannot work in or through you. This means that your chances of living in the victory He has for the real you, are almost nonexistent.

The stress of living in this unsatisfactory state can lead to burnout, as it did with me a few years ago.

UNCONDITIONAL LOVE

It was a great revelation to me that God would still love me unconditionally during my period of burnout, despite the deep mental darkness that I found myself in and despite the fact that I could do nothing.

I continued searching for the approval of other people by going through the motions of religious activities instead of trying to gain the approval of our God and Father.

Fortunately, one day, through a revelation of God's unconditional love for me, I discovered that I really am His son, and that He approves of the real, undisguised me! This revelation lifted a great burden from me and brought me so much relief and joy that I really was reborn from the inside out. I had learned a hard, but life-giving lesson, and was able to accept the real me and so establish a stronger foundation for my life.

I still work hard, but it is now very different. I know without a doubt that God loves me and whatever I do, whether it's right or wrong, has no effect on God's unconditional love for me. Everything I do now is a result of my passion for Jesus. It is a natural, almost involuntary, result. People around me so often say, "How do you do all this? How do you visit two countries per month while directing a growing ministry with a number of overseas offices, dozens of employees, a young family, and a church...and yet you are still so young?"

I look at them, beaming, and explain that the burden I carry is light because my motives are no longer based on impressing or being liked by others. I have embraced who I am in God and have set about achieving what His unique plans are for me and my life; and this has brought me the victory in which I now live.

Regardless of how I feel when I wake up every morning, I choose to be grateful and to see the day as God would have me see it. There will always be enormous challenges and opportunities and, if I face them in a godly manner and with the right attitude, there will be no day without miracles or God's favor and personal growth.

We read in the Book of Job that Job lost his wife, children, houses, camels, and sheep. In fact, his whole life as he knew it was taken away from him in a very short period of time. He had enough human reasons to become bitter and angry with God, but his attitude toward his sudden misfortune changed everything. Despite the pressure from those closest to him who ridiculed his faith in God and encouraged him to give up, Job with a grateful heart, said of God, *"Though He slay me, yet will I hope in Him..."* (Job 13:15). Wow, that's truly faith!

GOD IS HAPPY WITH YOU

Sometimes when I feel miserable, lonely, or am trying to deal with anguish, I verbalize what I know to be true by saying, "Father God, I know that You love me and, because You want the best for me, Your favor will reverse this situation." Oh, how I love the word *favor!*

Earlier I mentioned the word *favor;* I explained that it is the blessing of God and His grace on your life that will make your dreams come true—if you are authentic! This liberating truth means that, despite the fact that everyone is different, you can be yourself in the church or house group to which you belong. No matter what style of dress you prefer, whether you prefer sitting, lying, or standing while there, you are allowed to be yourself.

Repeat after me, "From now on I will be myself. It does not bother me what people think of me; I do not need the approval of people. I am myself. I am pleased with myself, and more importantly, God is extremely pleased with me!" If you really can say this from the bottom of your heart, you can begin celebrating as you enter into the adventure of discovering the gifts and talents God has given to the real, authentic you. These gifts and talents are given so you can achieve the specific calling God has placed on *your* life!

FAITH

Perhaps you are in a very difficult situation at the moment and feel as if the rug has been pulled out from under your feet. Let your attitude be, "God, I know that You can change my situation and that You are working all things together for my ultimate good. I believe that You will guide me through this difficult time and that I will emerge both victorious and stronger."

It is a biblical principle that as you believe, so it will be done. Decide today that you will take responsibility for your own life. Declare that whatever happens in your life, you will always say, "I believe in God. I believe He will never leave me or forsake me. Even though I don't always feel Him near me, I know and believe that He is always near me and has positive, constructive plans for my future. From today, Lord, I have positive expectations for my life."

Do you know that the faith of others standing in agreement with you helps? However, as important as it is for other people to join their faith to yours to see a positive outcome to prayers, it is also important for you to build and strengthen your own faith. This will come from hearing and believing the Word of God and letting it become part of you. It is when you have allowed this to happen that you will see God work in a mighty way. Do you remember what we have read about Abraham? God said to Abraham:

> I will make you into a great nation and I will bless you;
> I will make your name great, and you will be a blessing
> (Genesis 12:2).

At this moment God is saying the same to you!

You may think that promise was only for Abraham, but we read in the New Testament, in Galatians 3, that we, the Gentiles, share in all the blessings that God has given to Abraham. Who are the Gentiles? We are the Gentiles who accepted Jesus as our Savior and therefore share the blessings of Abraham.

It is important to realize what the blessing of God in Abraham's life means to us. As the spiritual descendants of Abraham, the blessing that he received has now been passed on to us. It enables us to do the impossible and to accomplish God's will for our lives. If you realize and proclaim and believe that He wants to bless you abundantly, you will step out in faith and be a blessing to the people around you. God will open doors for you that may lead to good things you can only imagine now.

> *being confident of this, that He who began a good work*
> *in you will carry it on to completion until the day of*
> *Christ Jesus* (Philippians 1:6).

If you currently see nothing happening with your natural eyes, you must learn to see with your spiritual eyes and you must believe that God is at work for you in the spiritual, invisible world. That world is real, just like hell and Heaven are real places.

I have often heard people say, "Seeing is believing." If you have heard this before, or maybe even said it yourself, God says the opposite: "Only if you believe will you see." In Hebrews 11:1 we read, *"Now faith is confidence in what we hope for and assurance about what we do not see."*

You need to learn to see through eyes of faith if you want to see something happen. If you can see it in the invisible world, it will become possible in the natural world. If you can see the impossible, then realize God can make it happen. Have a great vision and develop a dream for your life. Dream bigger dreams than you do now. Live your life in faith and be full of expectations. You will eventually become what you believe. Look at what you can do and stop focusing on what you cannot do. Begin focusing your attention on what God can do. What is impossible according to human understanding is possible with God. *"Jesus replied, 'What is impossible with man is possible with God'"* (Luke 18:27).

Be aware that you already have in you all you need to achieve your God-given purpose! God's grace and favor will make sure that people do their utmost to help you. His blessings, which are abundant, will ensure that you will always have what you need once you learn how to receive it. We all need to leave behind our poverty mentalities and whatever else is stopping us from dreaming big dreams.

GOD HAS GIVEN US EVERYTHING

So often we restrict what God can do in our lives, either by not embracing the dreams He has for us, or perhaps thinking we are incapable of achieving them. Living in sin, or being angry with God can have the same negative effect. This all stops us from receiving His best for our lives, and we shouldn't be surprised if we do not live in abundance.

God Himself created us as the crowning glory of His creation! People have hindered God from achieving His plans in their lives by listening to satan. God did miracle after miracle and sent many prophets. Eventually, He gave the most precious treasure He had and sent His only Son, Jesus Christ, to us. Jesus died a terrible death on the cross to pay the price for our sins. It is through His sacrifice on the cross that our sins are forgiven and the gap between us and God has been bridged. God sent the Holy Spirit to live in us after the resurrection of His Son Jesus, and He gave us His Word.

God has already given us everything. What more will it take to convince us that He loves us and that we are His children, His sons and daughters, freed from darkness, clothed with His glory, and the crown of His creation? Isn't it time we stopped behaving with false humility and settling for a less-than-victorious life? Isn't it time to accept all the gifts and talents God has put in us and use them to achieve the plans He has for our lives?

I have children whom I love dearly; I enjoy being with them for hours. They do not annoy or disappoint me, and never will. Like every loving father, I want only the best for them. When I am away from home traveling, I get tremendous pleasure from buying gifts to give them when I return home. They are too young to know the value of the gifts and often, after opening them, they will abandon them in favor of something they find more interesting. To me this does not matter because when I am thinking of them and what to buy them, my feelings of happiness know no bounds.

Imagine, however, if I come home and my children are wearing old, tattered, dirty clothing and looking thin. That would break my heart, just as it would break any parent's heart to see their children in this condition.

Unfortunately, this is exactly how so many Christians are walking around in the spiritual world. They feel humble when they walk around in old rags and drive old, secondhand cars. They believe this is the way to "suffer for Jesus' sake." No, this is false humility. God wants to bless us abundantly and even if you do not see it yet in the natural, proclaim it in the spiritual world by faith and believe you have already received it. Do not settle for second best when God only wants the best for you.

Come as if you are sitting at a table filled with good food, and eat with the Father. Come out from under the table where you have been eating crumbs, and know that there is so much more for you. Sit at the table where you belong, and eat good things.

THANK GOD

If you don't have the money to buy new clothes or a nice car, remember it's your attitude toward these circumstances that counts. Before my burnout, I had always been told that Christians should lead very sober lives; owning as little as possible was thought to be a sign of holiness. I was told that this was suffering for Jesus' sake.

After going through a period of depression and burnout, God started laying a new foundation for my life, one based on abundant blessing and not living at poverty level. Although I still wore the same shabby clothing and drove the same old car, I changed my attitude to one of thankfulness. I thanked God for the blessings He had already given me, but also the abundant blessings that were yet to come in my life. I then started to pray, "Thank You for my new clothes and for my new car."

Two weeks after this prayer my neighbor, who wasn't a Christian, came to see me. She told me her husband had just bought himself a new coat that morning, but they wanted to give the coat to me. With a grateful heart and many thanks, I took the coat from her, tried it on, and it fit me perfectly!

I prayed for a car for a long time. We had just been married and did not have the financial resources to buy one. One day my Muslim boss told me his wife had a car she did not use and asked if I would like to drive it for as long as I needed to. All I had to do was pay the insurance and the road tax on the vehicle. Of course I said, "Yes," as I thanked God for His blessings and grace on my life.

My attitude changed, and as I started believing God wanted only the best for my life, my environment started changing from one of poverty to one of blessing. I stopped feeling sorry for myself, and I started being grateful. I gave my tithes to the Kingdom of God and I began proclaiming God's blessing on my life.

You may think this applies only to people in the developed world and wonder about the people in poor countries. But the same blessing that was given to Abraham rests on all God's people, wherever they are.

Here are the special stories of Joseph Lubega, Abraham Kuchipudi, Rajkumar Ganta, and Joel and Jennifer Chuks. They are ordinary people who serve an extraordinary God, and each has played an important part in my life. As the favor and grace of God rests on my life and on the lives of these precious people, so it also rests on you.

Be inspired by these people who have simply done what they felt God was telling them to do. Nowadays they have an enormous impact in their environment and in their country.

On the other hand, you will not experience these things if you just continue to worry about what God's will is for your life. I was doing what I felt God was telling me to do, and met these people in special, God-ordained ways. The only key is obedience and willingness to go, the willingness to take risks. I hope these stories will inspire you to go too, and to experience God's favor on your life. The grace of God and the attitude of these people changed their lives completely, as well as the lives of many others in the countries where they work.

Let these true stories encourage you to go and to open yourself up to the strength and guidance of God. I did not receive a note from Heaven on which was written at what time or when I had to go to those countries. However, in 2005, I felt in my heart that I had to go to Uganda. I had no plan and did not know exactly what I would do. At the last minute, just before my departure from Uganda to return to the Netherlands, I met Joseph Lubega. In the same year, I felt that I had to go to India.

In these stories of Joseph Lubega, Abraham Kuchipudi, Rajkumar Ganta, and Joel and Jennifer Chuks you will read what happened as a result of the simple decision to simply go in faith.

JOSEPH LUBEGA'S STORY (UGANDA)

My name is Joseph Lubega. I am currently the director of the TRIN-New Lease of Life for Uganda, a Christian-based non-governmental organization (NGO). My vision is to provide care for orphans and street children in Uganda, and to help them become future leaders in our society.

Some time back, God drew my attention to the fact that many people in Africa who have huge potential, spend their whole lives in misery, battling to survive in an environment swamped by poverty and disease. This is all a result of a lack of opportunity. To illustrate this, I will give you a hypothetical example of a talented soccer player who happens to also be hungry and homeless. Obviously, if he spends all his time looking for food and shelter, his soccer talent will never be recognized or utilized. The same example could be used for musicians, authors, preachers, and many other professions. This is precisely the kind of reality we face in Africa.

For children, the death of their parents can become a sentence to a life filled with misery. There are cases where the family lives in a rented house. When their parents die, if no one is willing to give the children shelter, the only alternative for them is to live on the city streets. This means the children will not have access to education, health care, or a normal family life.

Children who move onto the streets to live will soon experience the harsh reality of their situation. Without proper guidance and someone to teach them the basics of life, including cultural and social norms and values, they are destined to become social misfits. They will not have the opportunity to apply for work and earn an honest living, as they have no idea how to behave in a socially acceptable manner. This means they are destined to lives in which stealing is normal and they will grow up as criminals. As we know, criminals do not live long lives.

After welcoming Jesus Christ into my heart in 1997, I felt called to do something to help the people of Africa overcome their poverty and misery. I believed that God could use me to achieve this goal because, if He had shown me the need, then surely He could provide me with the means to alleviate it. I started by taking in one child with the intention of providing him with a home, good food, a decent bed, and spiritual and intellectual education. At the time I started this ministry, I was jobless and homeless. The pastor of United Christian Centre church in Kampala, Uganda, took me in. He allowed me to sleep in a small room that was used to store the church's sound system. The kind people who attended the church gave me financial gifts with which I would buy food and pay for my new son's schooling. After a few months, God blessed me with a job as a teacher in a primary school. The pay was not good, but at least it restored my confidence so that I could be of use to myself and to the community in which I lived.

The need around me was great, so I took in another child, and another, until I was caring for eight children. I would bathe them, wash their clothes, cook for them, help them with their homework, and tuck them into bed every night.

Faced with my ever-growing family, the church administration asked me to move. We moved into an unfinished house that had a roof, but had neither windows nor doors. We lived in it for two years until God blessed me with a job as a news anchor at an FM radio station in Kampala. With the higher salary I was earning, I was able to rent a two-bedroom house, but it had no electricity or plumbing. By the year 2005, I was taking care of 21 children. My pay would have been adequate if I had been only looking after myself, but it was not nearly enough to provide the basic needs of 22 people. I figured it would take the income of a millionaire to achieve such a feat!

Within a short period of time, I had accumulated a mountain of debt from paying for schooling and for simple groceries; I feared that the debt might be insurmountable. In my darkest hour, I even considered the possibility of leaving the children to fend for themselves.

I started searching for help to look after my children locally, in churches and in government offices, but no one was willing to help. I searched for help internationally by looking at the Websites of foreign Christian organizations. I wrote more than 800 emails asking for help, but only one person replied, a woman who lives in Chicago, Illinois. She offered to help both financially and materially, but our need was so big that even with her help we remained in a desperate financial situation.

Toward the end of 2005, three men from the Netherlands came to Uganda. They were led by Mattheus van der Steen whom I later learned was the director of Touch, Reach and Impact the Nations (TRIN) ministry. I met these men on the very last day of their visit to Uganda. How could I know that in just one short meeting lasting only a few minutes God would change all of our lives forever?

This was the man whom God had sent to help us. As we communicated via email and telephone, Mattheus assisted us in obtaining the necessary funds to settle all our debts, to pay all the children's school fees, and even to rent a larger house that had both electricity and running water.

In April 2006, Mattheus, Lester Mulder, Hans Drijfhout, and Ingrid van Diest came to Uganda and stayed in the same house with us. At this point, there were 36 children in my care. The important lesson these people taught us is that pure Christian love knows no cultural or racial boundaries. They interacted freely with the children and put them at ease. They insisted on being called by their first names and not by titles like pastor or director. They allowed the children to touch them and they played with them. This experience has forever changed the children's outlook because they were shown that they were important enough for three tall, white men and a beautiful woman from the Netherlands to spend time giving them attention. They now had a model to look up to, an example of godliness that had been set by Mattheus and his friends.

The children were not the only ones to be blessed through all this. Through my divine appointment with Mattheus, even I have been blessed with international recognition and have been afforded the opportunity to travel. I have been to Europe twice, with his support;

and, as a result, I now have many friends in both Holland and Belgium. In short, meeting Mattheus has changed my life forever.

In conclusion, I have learned that God is Almighty. He can do all things big and small. What He needs is a point of contact between Him and the world. That point is the faith in the heart of a person or group of people, and the size of the faith does not matter. In Luke 17:5-6, the disciples asked Jesus to increase their faith and He told them that even if they had faith as small as a mustard seed they could order trees to be uprooted and planted elsewhere, and it would happen.

What the Lord wanted to teach them is that the potential is in the seed. In spite of its small size, it has the potential, with God's help, to become something big. In Romans 12:3 the Bible talks about a measure of faith. This faith does not come before it is needed. It comes in proportion to the job that needs to be done. It is like needing more oxygen when one is running. When you start running, your lungs will automatically need more oxygen and so they start taking in more. When I was unable to pay the school fees for my children, God did not provide millions, but rather just enough to keep me out of debt. When the time came to support students attending university, God provided just what I needed to do that, too.

Faith is like an electric fuse. It controls the flow of electricity into the house. If it is working well, all the lights in the house will work. If it is faulty, the whole house will be in darkness. The lower the resistance, the more energy will flow through. If the resistance of the fuse is higher, then the amount of electricity that flows through will be lower. I could put it this way: God is looking for effective conduits of His power from Heaven to Earth.

Having had this truth revealed to me, I realized that the Lord wanted to use me as the fuse through which to channel His power to light up the area around me, my community, my country, my continent, my Earth, and my universe.

God shows us the darkness around us so that we might believe Him to use us to dissipate it. If we refuse to believe in His ability to use us, the darkness will remain and may even overpower us. However, if we behave like well-functioning fuses, God is ready to let all His power stream through us like the electricity flows through a high-tension electric cable. The power is ready to light the house, but it needs a good fuse through which to work

I thank God for my brother Mattheus, because he saw the darkness and believed the Lord would use him to chase it away. The Lord used him to help me chase away the darkness in my community. The Lord is using me to light up my world, and the light of His victory is spreading. We now have 97 boys and 13 girls in our care. They are all healthy, well-fed, and attending good schools. The youngest are in kindergarten and we have three who began attending university this year.

I thank God for people who just get up and go when the Lord says so. One of the first people to do this was Abraham, and he became the father of nations. It is my prayer that even more people will believe in the power of His might and no longer doubt Him. I pray that people would not sit and ask questions of God when He has already told them what to do. In short, I wish more people would behave like humble donkeys that never question their master's will.

A 2010 Update

God has increased the number of children in Joseph's care from 110 to 280 in the past three years. You can read more about his project on www.bulamuvillage.org.

ABRAHAM KUCHIPUDI'S STORY (INDIA)

My name is Abraham Kuchipudi, and I am the founder and director of Save the Unsaved Ministries in Tenali, India. I would like to share the story of how God brought Mattheus and me together and the abundant fruit that has resulted from that meeting.

It was the beginning of 2005 and I was prayerfully seeking the right person to support our ministry because I wanted to do the ministry according to the will of God. At the time, the ministry was in debt and struggling financially to provide for the 25 orphan children and 200 pastors in our care. Although we worked hard to feed them both physically and spiritually, it was still very difficult. It was in that context that I began searching on the Internet.

I had gone to an Internet cafe to use the computer and the person before me had accessed Mattheus' Website and had left without closing the window on the computer.

I stared in amazement at the Website! I could hardly believe my eyes! I prayed as I perused the site carefully and in its entirety. My heart was filled with such a joyful sensation as I learned about such a young and dynamic personality who, not yet 30 years old, was doing so much for the Kingdom of God. His vision was to touch the untouched, to reach the unreached, to impact the nations, to help the poor and the sick who had no one else to tend to them. I was being impacted by his vision then and there as I learned that we held very similar views on what the message of God to the world was, and the best way to carry that message forward. I sent him an email describing the difficulties we were encountering in our ministry, and I invited him to visit us. Even as I sent this email, I was already beginning to praise God with confidence that a miracle would occur. I was both surprised and excited to receive a reply saying that he would come to India to visit us.

In September 2005, we welcomed him joyfully as he arrived with six dedicated servants of God. He was very moved by the difficult conditions in India. Despite heavy rainfall, he went from one slum area to the next preaching the Gospel. He also participated in a large conference for pastors where servants of God in our area were abundantly blessed by him and his ministry. During the many Gospel outreaches he did with us, the Word of God was presented in clear, bold ways, and we saw many people accept Jesus as their Savior. Thousands were touched and many signs and miracles took place. Many nonbelievers, among them many Hindus, experienced God's love and also accepted Jesus as their Savior. Many who were sick were healed; blind eyes were opened; and, the lame walked. The glory of the Lord became visible and many people became enthusiastic.

During their stay, the TRIN team visited slum areas and assisted in distributing food. They catered to more than just physical needs, they made themselves available to the people they met by hugging them and sharing God's message of love. Mattheus visited the orphanage; tears streamed down his cheeks when he saw the awful conditions there. He promised to commit to reaching out to every orphan there with God's love. From then until now, the orphanage has flourished, with the number of children increasing from 20 to 50. Now every orphan receives food, shelter, schooling, medication when needed, and good clothing.

God gave us the privilege of seeing him again in October 2006 when he came to visit accompanied by seven dedicated servants of God. A big conference for the youth was conducted where quite a number of young people were drawn toward the wounded feet of Jesus. These young people learned who they were in Christ and dedicated themselves to carry out the Great Commission. There was heavy rainfall during his second visit. Quite a number of villages suffered because of these floods, but Mattheus and his team reached out to them and shared the message of God's grace. We saw how the Holy Spirit worked in powerful ways, and saw many people with hands raised to accept Jesus Christ as their personal Savior.

On his third visit to India, Mattheus was accompanied by an army of 40 people from many different nations. This was a historical event for our city of Tenali. An unprecedented and massive crusade took place over four days and three nights. Thousands of people were blessed. We enjoyed heavenly music played by the Dew Worship Band from the Netherlands and they were an immediate hit in the city. No one had ever heard such music before. Indeed, our city itself was influenced by this event and it got the attention of many government officials and dignitaries as an event of this nature and scope had never before occurred during their careers.

Just as they had in previous visits, Mattheus and his TRIN team visited multiple slums, distributed food, and shared the message of God's eternal mercy and unconditional love with all they encountered. They also visited the orphanage, distributing toys and clothing, which blessed our children very much.

We were thrilled to be invited by Mattheus to participate in the 2007 Holland Freedom Fire Conference. The conference was a huge success as thousands of people from many different countries attended, and God was glorified. I can really say that because of Mattheus' multiple visits to India, our ministry has been blessed and is flourishing—we are able to do much more now than we could previously. We had a network of 200 pastors before and now there are well over 300. Mattheus effectively became the overseer of the Save the Unsaved Ministries and has made an indelible impression on the hearts of the orphaned children. We will never forget his love and affection for the orphans, widows, and the untouched.

It is our prayer that he will be used in many different countries and that many signs, wonders, and miracles will take place. I thank God that Mattheus is blessed to have Rebekah, whose loving heart makes them perfect partners in their ministry as they bless many people. Her obedience, loyalty, faithfulness, and sincerity are an example to every woman. We also thank God for the blessing of their sweet children. It is our prayer that they will grow in likeness to their parents and glorify the Lord with a double portion of their father's spirit.

I can personally attest that the fellowship of Mattheus influenced me greatly in my time of grief and trauma that stemmed from our poverty. Now, as this ministry flourishes and grows each day with the help of TRIN, my joy overflows and I am grateful for his spiritual and material encouragement. Mattheus is a man of God with an encouraging and generous heart, always blessing every individual. He is blessed with the Spirit of Jesus, who always brings into practice the eternal words of our mighty Lord.

For more information, see our Website: www.savetheunsaved.org or info@trin.nl.

CAPE VERDE ISLANDS:
IT'S NOT ABOUT NUMBERS

When you are faithful in small things, God will entrust you with larger things. For example, evangelists who attract huge crowds to their events don't start out that way. It's not as if they had an audience numbering thousands or millions right from the outset. Generally, such ministries start off small because the Lord is interested in first developing our characters; during this time He often allows us to go through disappointments to test and build our faith.

Just recently, I was standing before thousands of people in India and preaching the Gospel with fire and passion. There were miracles, people were healed and delivered, and many were filled with the power of the Holy Spirit. While people came forward to give their lives to Jesus, I experienced such joy that my eyes were filled with tears because the Lord was reminding me that some years earlier, my situation had been quite different. I had visited the Cape Verde Islands where He taught me an important lesson.

We had been invited, along with the TRIN team, to the islands by Joel and Jennifer Chuks, a missionary couple who ministered on one of the islands. We were planning to hold a convention and, as an evangelist, I had prepared to share the Gospel in simple terms using examples from my own life and the Word of God. This was the first time that our family had ever been to the Cape Verde Islands and our son, Zephaniah, was only five weeks old at the time.

After the long journey to get there, we met Joel and Jennifer Chuks for the first time. Joel had originally come from Nigeria, and Jennifer was an American. Right away I felt a connection with this couple and began to eagerly anticipate what the next five days would bring. We were hopeful that many souls would be saved, even in spite of the fact that we learned that there were very few good churches in the area and that people were generally not very open to the message of the Gospel.

By the time evening fell, I felt well-prepared and looked forward to the convention. We arrived at the venue to find a large old trailer with posters stuck on the side of it, two fluorescent tubes as lighting, and an old audio system. When the scheduled time to begin arrived, no one had showed up. Joel laughed and told us that the people were not very open to the Gospel, but that we had to start anyway. There was nobody except our small team from the Netherlands, Joel and Jennifer, and the owner of the trailer. I got up and stood on the trailer in the cold light of the fluorescent bulbs and, with bugs swarming around me, and my team as my only audience, I began preaching. Inside I felt as if I wanted to run away! I was ashamed of the poor turnout at the convention because several of TRIN's financial supporters were present and I was afraid of what they might be thinking.

Then God spoke to me: "Mattheus, it's not about you, and neither is it about TRIN. It is all about My Kingdom, so speak like you have never spoken before, and it will bring about a change in the spiritual realm here." God's strength came over me, and I began to preach with more passion and compassion than I had ever done before. At the end I gave the invitation to those who wanted to give their lives to the Lord to come forward, and no one came, but we all felt that something had been broken in the spiritual world.

The second evening was exactly the same, but at a different venue. On the third night, five young people attended the Gospel campaign. To be honest, they were on the streets to waste time as they had nothing else to do, but God's power came on them and they gave their lives to the Lord. On the fourth day I felt a tremendous urge to visit a prison. With Joel, Jennifer, and the team, we went to a prison. We went through security into the building and what terrible conditions we found there! Hundreds of prisoners were locked up in a small room. But as we proclaimed God's love to them and gave them our testimonies, people gave their lives to Christ.

There was one person in prison who attracted my attention. He was an older man and had already spent 11 years in prison as he had been convicted of drug smuggling despite his numerous claims that he was innocent. The Lord spoke to me and told me to pray for him. I laid my hands on him and immediately the Lord gave me a word for him. "Within the next three months you will be released from this place. You will lead a church from in this prison and through you many will come to know Jesus, and you will be their shepherd." The man began to cry and told me that before he was accused of drug smuggling, he was a Christian and that he knew that he was called to be shepherd of a church. However, he had decided he did not want anything to do with what he knew to be God's calling on his life, and had stopped following Jesus. He became involved in all kinds of wrong things, which ultimately sent him to prison.

After I prayed with him, he recommitted his life to Jesus with conviction. Two months later we heard from Joel that this man had been released and had started a church for the converts in prison. Joel and

Jennifer's church also prospered as the people in the surrounding area become more open to the Gospel.

What a lesson the Lord taught me there! In spite of being a lonely preacher on top of a trailer after a long journey from the Netherlands, and with almost no one in the audience, God did something miraculous. It impacted me deeply; I have been taught not to look at numbers but simply to be obedient. We must all start somewhere, so do not set the bar too high for yourself. Just be faithful in the small things, and the Lord Himself will open bigger doors for you!

JOEL AND JENNIFER CHUKS' STORY

Then the Lord replied: "Write down the revelation and make it plain on tablets so that a herald may run with it. For the revelation awaits an appointed time; it speaks of the end and will not prove false. Though it linger, wait for it; it will certainly come and will not delay" (Habakkuk 2:2-3).

It is one thing to have a vision or a dream, but it's something quite different to achieve it. So many people are too afraid to make the first move when it comes to realizing their dreams. They have beautiful dreams and goals that they want to accomplish in their lives, but they are too afraid to effectively implement what is required to achieve their dreams. Their lives are the very picture of inaction and complacency even as God is telling them to *Go!* Perhaps they tarry because they do not feel they have the proper conditions or the right situation to go, but sometimes the Lord says go even if we seemingly do not have the means. We need to know that God will always help us at the very moment we step out in faith.

I, Joel, accepted the Lord in 1997. I was so on fire for the things of God as a young man that I wanted to do everything for Him. In 1998 God called me into the ministry. Before I could go, I needed a period of preparation. I was not afraid to go through the preparation time, but I was actually afraid to make a move toward achieving my dreams. There were many things that made me hesitant, such as my family background and my perceived personal weaknesses. I was like Gideon who was called by God and he answered God saying that he was the least of his entire family and his family was the very least in all of Israel (see Judg. 6:15).

Although Gideon may have been proclaiming the earthly reality, he was not proclaiming the spiritual reality by faith. We must understand that it is not about our ability, but our availability to allow God to work through us that counts. The disciples were all "nobodies," and some had no formal education; but they were filled with a knowledge of God, and He filled them with His power. This enabled them to do the things for which God had called them.

I knew that God had called me to reach out to this broken world, and the many prophetic words that I had received, confirmed this. However, I still refused to set up the work, because I waited until God provided the financial resources. I did not understand that God gives the resources as soon as a person decides to do His work.

Eventually I got to a point where I had decided that I was going to do God's work. In 2003 God told me to go to Cape Verde. It took time to accept this, and we did not actually go there until 2006.

From the moment that my wife, Jennifer, and I started making definite plans for the trip, God began to provide the finances that we needed. When we arrived in Cape Verde, we learned a very different way of life, and we had to adapt to a different culture and environment. From the moment we arrived, our life was very difficult. Satan fought us in every area of our lives. He tried to destroy everything, even our marriage. I thank God that Jennifer and I decided to work hard on our relationship, and today we have a wonderful and blessed marriage. That is why we must stand firm as satan tries to lead us into temptation. We must always keep standing in faith and never give up. Winners never give up; and those who give up will never win.

We started to work with an existing organization in Cape Verde while we were waiting for God's direction for our lives. We then came into contact with Mattheus van der Steen. I do not recall exactly how we met, but I do remember very clearly how I felt when I met him for the first time. I knew that meeting him was a divine appointment and that it was from God. I believe that every time God sends you on a mission, He will also send the people to come alongside you to encourage and help you with the job for which He has called you. When we came into contact with Mattheus, Rebekah, and their friends, we knew that we were in a relationship that would affect the rest of our lives. Thus, we made plans for them to come visit us in Cape Verde.

We had received a word from God that we were to start a church and a logical starting point seemed to be an evangelism campaign. We set this up and invited Mattheus and his team to be with us, but almost no one attended the meetings. I was disappointed because the team had spent so much money to get to Cape Verde and it seemed to have been a wasted trip if no one attended the meetings. I did not realize that God had something special in mind for their visit to us. The TRIN people said, "Maybe we have come here to encourage you and your wife," which was certainly the case. I admired the courage of these men and women when they said, "Let's just evangelize in the old style; let's go preaching on the streets."

On Thursday, June 1, 2006, we went to the prison to share the Gospel. While the team was praying for the prisoners, the Lord told me that at that very moment a new ministry had been born and that it was His desire that we establish a prison ministry. Although we had never really thought about this before, we were obedient to the call and that is how the King's Prison Ministry in Sao Vicente, Cape Verde, began. Through this ministry, the lives of many young men in prison have been changed forever.

On the same day, Mattheus prayed for a man in prison. Later this man told us how he saw a light from Heaven during the prayer and it was shining on him. After three months, this man was miraculously released from prison and began to help us with the work among the prisoners. Then last month, a young man, who had been involved in occultism and witchcraft, repented and gave his life to Jesus Christ. As soon as he was released, he also wanted to join the ministry to reach out to prisoners. TRIN has helped us buy 40 Bibles for the prisoners, and the prisoners are very happy to have God's Word. Many of the prisoners have been converted, and we see more fruit in prison than in the church.

We have experienced many difficulties, but God has always provided a solution. God has given us a few personal miracles. For example, on October 19, 2006, we were in dire straits. We had not had a real meal for three days and we had exactly $8.36 in our bank account, which was actually too small an amount to be able to withdraw it from the bank. We asked ourselves what we could eat without oil, onions, meat, or hope. We had only half a cup of rice. So we did as we always do, we prayed.

We then got the idea to phone the bank. Before we had a chance to say anything, the bank employee told Jennifer that because of an error on the part of the bank, she would credit our account with $9 but that it would take two to three days to post to our account. We prayed that somehow God would allow the money to be credited to our account earlier than that. After our prayer, we called again and miraculously there was now $17.36 dollars in our account! We began to shout with joy and that evening we were able to eat a good meal.

On October 27, 2006, we experienced another miracle that was very similar to the first. We had only $6 in the bank and had no food in the house. We called the bank again and were told that we suddenly had $18.90 in our account. We praised God because that evening we could eat hamburgers and chips, instead of the rice and tomato sauce we had survived on for such a long time!

You have to understand that it is not important what dream God has given you because God has already deposited in you everything that you will need, both the abilities and power, to achieve what He has called you to do. He is the One who gives you dreams and He is the One who can make these dreams become reality. The only thing you have to do is know what God is calling you to do, and then, in obedience, go and do it. If you do, God will support you, no matter how difficult it might be. Take a stand, believing in your dreams, and God will help you through your difficulties. Even as I write this, God is opening many doors for His followers to go and preach the Gospel and God's power is manifesting itself in many ways.

We are even getting invitations to go and preach in other countries, to witness and to proclaim the Gospel of our Lord Jesus Christ. In each case that God says "Go," and as we are obedient to Him, He provides for our every need.

So stand up and *Go*!

THE STORY OF RAJKUMAR GANTA (BIRAVAN, INDIA)

I am very happy to meet you through this wonderful book. I am Evangelist Rajkumar Ganta, the founder and president of Harvest Plan. Our goal is "Reaching the Unreached—Telling the Untold." Our purpose and passion is to see people *won to Jesus Christ*.

"Everyone belongs to Me" (Ezek. 18:4) says the Lord, and Jesus said, *"Go into all the world and preach the gospel to all creation"* (Mark 16:15). God has given us the burden to reach the lost; He says in Mark 13:10, *"And the gospel must first be preached to all nations"* (all the people). Jesus tells us in Matthew 11:4-5: *"...The blind receive sight, the lame walk, those who have leprosy are cleansed, the deaf hear, the dead are raised, and the good news is proclaimed to the poor."*

Yes, the Good News is preached and the Good News is reaching the poor. When I met brother Mattheus van der Steen and the TRIN team for the first time, I felt very happy and much joy in my spirit, because God knew our hearts and our Lord has put TRIN and Harvest Plan together for a great purpose.

> *...whoever wants to become great among you must be your servant, and whoever wants to be first must be slave of all* (Mark 10:43-44).

I saw that the TRIN family is always seeking to reach the lost and help the poor. They are like humble servants. The TRIN team is not bosses or leaders appointed by man, but they are God-made servants. I personally saw them in action, and all the members of the TRIN team love the poor, preach the Gospel, and heal the sick.

I am thankful that we are partners with TRIN; and since God put us together, our ministry here in India has grown considerably. We have started three orphanages in the village and recently opened a new orphanage in Island with the help of the TRIN team. We have already held crusades with TRIN, and many people accepted our Lord as their personal Savior. We went to a village for a two-day Gospel crusade, and an old man said to me, "TRIN is the first team to come to this village with the Gospel of our Lord Jesus Christ." He remembered his forefathers telling him that 100 years ago some missionaries came to this village and preached the Gospel from door to door. Since then, no one had visited his village with the Good News of the Gospel of Jesus Christ until the TRIN and Harvest teams arrived to do it. I cried when he told me this.

Miracles

A Hindu brother allowed his rice field to be used by us to hold a crusade, although many other villagers had not been keen to rent their fields to us. During the crusade, many people accepted Jesus as their Savior and many were healed. However, perhaps one of the greatest miracles was that the man who had rented us his rice field for the crusade reported that he had planted his rice plants, and weeks before its due harvest date, his crop was ready to reap—and he reaped more rice from that field than ever before! I took the TRIN team to this place in October 2007, and they all saw that while the other rice fields were not ready to be harvested and the yield looked to be small, the crop on the land used for the crusade was abundant and ready to be harvested. We praised the Lord!

With the TRIN team, we preached the Gospel of our Lord Jesus Christ in many unreached villages. Many people heard the Good News for the first time and they accepted our Lord Jesus as their Savior; many were delivered and healed.

After the crusade with TRIN in our district, we started many village churches and house gatherings. We also started a follow-up service, and I am very happy to inform you that many of the new believers asked us if they could be baptized. Our beloved "Dad," Mattheus' father, Sjaak van der Steen, conducted 11 baptisms in our district. Although we have done many ourselves, even more people are waiting to be baptized, and we are giving them special classes to prepare them.

This has fulfilled and is still fulfilling Matthew 11:4-5. After the TRIN team preached and ministered in the villages, many people came to us and gave testimonies. Some said they had been healed, the blind received sight, the lame started walking, and the deaf started to hear. Many came feeling empty inside, and they received peace. Some of them were delivered from evil spirits, some of them came hopeless and afterward said they now have hope. Many said they felt alone, but after the preaching they said they no longer felt alone and now feel they have God to take care of them.

Along with TRIN, we are reaching all kinds of people, no matter if they are poor or rich, and regardless of skin color, because a soul has no color! TRIN exists to fulfill the Great Commission and the Great Commandment to "go and make disciples of all nations."

I hope this book encourages you to dream great dreams, both now and in the future. Always dream good dreams—dreams about the end-time harvest and about your purpose and plans. Dream about God, because you are God's dream. In Ephesians 1:4 it says, *"For He chose us in Him before the creation of the world to be holy and blameless in His sight...."* Honestly, God, our Father, chose us before the creation of the world. You are special to God and He has great dreams and plans for your life.

In First Peter 2:9 it says:

> *But you are a chosen people, a royal priesthood, a holy nation, God's special possession, that you may declare the praises of Him who called you out of darkness into His wonderful light.*

Let me also give you a thought from Acts 20:24:

> *However, I consider my life worth nothing to me; my only aim is to finish the race and complete the task the Lord Jesus has given me—the task of testifying to the good news of God's grace.*

You have the absolute victory in Jesus Christ. Victory is a gift we receive from God. Think about it, talk about it, feel it, dream it, and you will live it. Do not confuse God's dream with those of the devil because they are two different things. God is for you and with you, but the devil is always against you, which means that if God is for you, the devil can have nothing against you. Therefore, dream God's way, then you will have His authority to achieve what you have dreamed. Again, I pray you will achieve your dreams. Please visit our Website to learn more of our work for God: www.trinindia.org or www.harvest-plan.org.

A 2010 Update

A year after this report was written, the TRIN team once again returned to Biravam, India, to host a crusade with Harvest Plan, called Blessings Festival and International Music Celebrations. The following is the report from that crusade:

During the four days of the crusade, a total of between 140,000 and 150,000 people attended. Many were already born-again Christians but still, 120,000 decision cards were handed out and, to date, nearly 91,000 have been returned to us by new converts who have accepted Jesus Christ as their Savior. The services were broadcast on the local television station and those who watched, but were unable to attend the crusade, are still phoning us requesting decision cards as they choose to accept Jesus as their Savior while watching these programs.

The 90,000-plus new converts are starting to fill up existing churches in the area and these churches are planting more churches in other areas to accommodate the thousands looking for a church to attend. Some of Harvest Plan's pastors are going from village to village with local pastors, youth leaders, and elders to find the new converts there. When they find new Christians, they introduce them to the local church leader and then have a Bible study and pray with them.

In areas where there are no churches, home groups are started. If this is not possible, a simple family group is started. This is particularly useful to new converts who are part of a caste system that prohibits people from mixing with members of another caste and so cannot attend their churches.

Hundreds of youth in "religious" churches are being touched by the Holy Spirit and moving to Christian churches where the Holy Spirit is allowed to move freely. Students in a nearby youth hostel have been given teaching materials and are being taught how to run their own church services because so many of them have accepted Jesus as their Savior. Other hostels are looking to follow their example.

Believe with me for *one million* souls for Christ before 2013. My call is evangelist, to reach the lost in and around India. Always the fire is burning in my bones to reach the lost. Our aim is Reaching the Unreached—Telling the Untold. The purpose of our ministry is to reach 1,000 unreached villages and towns of India with our pastors, evangelists, and our team each year. My vision and goal is 100 big crusades in India. Our battle is for the Kingdom of Christ—it is our duty; it is our war.

CHAPTER 11

THE "NOT POSSIBLE"
HAS HAPPENED!

I am sure many readers of this book long to do great and mighty things for and with the Lord. Perhaps it's preaching the Gospel to 50,000 people and seeing the Spirit of God move mightily with signs, wonders, and healings as He does when Reinhard Bonnke preaches in Africa. Perhaps it's preaching the Gospel in some faraway, hostile land; or maybe it's just seeing every seat in your church filled with people eager to hear about God.

As you may have noticed elsewhere in this book, I often quote Oral Roberts who said: "When you see the invisible, you can do the impossible." I have often realized that, as much as I believe this to be true, and as often as I have seen the impossible happen in my life, there are still things I do not consider doing because I think they are impossible to accomplish! My mind has been programmed this way by many years of reading and listening to bad reports about an area into which

God wants me to move. As a result, I dismiss the desire He puts into my heart and I label it: "Not possible!"

It has taken a closer walk with God and being open to what His Spirit tells me to identify and overcome these areas. Then I am able to move into a place from which I know that, if I trust God, He will make possible what seems impossible to me.

One of the things I never considered doing was to preach the Gospel in Myanmar (formerly known as *Burma*). "Everyone" knows it is a closed country in which Christians are not treated well. It is difficult to gain entry to Myanmar and "impossible" to preach the Gospel there. After a discussion with some fellow Christians who thought this way about the country, I suddenly realized that I had agreed with their negative statements—in spite of what God says about *nothing* being impossible for Him!

Thankfully, I was quick to realize that my negative thinking had restricted what God could do in and through me, and I repented promptly. How God must despair at our unwillingness to consider certain assignments from Him, especially when our resistance is based on negative things we have heard or read—things which may not even be true!

After this awakening in my Spirit, I spent some time thinking and praying about Myanmar. Slowly but surely God put a dream in my heart to travel to that country and reach out to both the saved and unsaved there. I wanted to do what I could to help strengthen the church and see the Spirit of God bring the people a fresh wind of hope and healing. When I attended a conference at International Full Gospel Fellowship, Gereja Injil Seutah International in Indonesia, I met a pastor from Myanmar. He had God's heart for the people there. It was then that I saw how God was making possible what so many (including me) had felt was impossible!

This precious, humble man is Pastor Philip Thang. He told me about the children's home he had started and which now gives shelter, love, and care to many children. He also has a Bible seminary that has graduated many who are now pastors, church planters, youth workers, and missionaries throughout Myanmar.

He told me what it was like to live in Myanmar and shared some of the challenges he faced as a Christian. After hearing these things, I felt that my time to go to Myanmar and achieve my God-given dream was fast approaching. And I was delighted!

After praying with Pastor Philip I made the decision to take a small group of people into Myanmar in January 2010. The purpose of the trip was to see the reality of the situation on the ground. Before our arrival, Pastor Philip asked the government for permission to hold a meeting in which we would encourage local pastors. Fortunately, permission was granted.

Despite being told that we would be observed by secret police wherever we went, we felt very safe as we proceeded from Yangon (the city of our arrival and the largest city in Myanmar) and moved around the country. We saw the most heartbreaking poverty and heard of people dying from easily preventable and curable diseases; nevertheless, I fell in love with the people and their rich and ancient culture. The streets are always filled with young monks going about their business and there are many beautiful golden temples scattered throughout the city. Those following Buddhist teachings worship at these temples.

Our meeting, which was held in a building belonging to a Christian institute for the blind, was attended by 600 Christian pastors, church leaders, and house- and cell-group leaders. The Holy Spirit moved in a powerful way; I quickly realized that God was about to do something quite extraordinary amongst these people. It was clear that Myanmar was on the edge of a great outpouring of the Holy Spirit.

I challenged the spiritual leaders at the meeting by asking them about their beliefs, dreams, and desires. After a moment's thought, they began to cry out to God for revival and transformation. As they did, I encouraged them to dream bigger, because our God is a God of the impossible. It was then that they told me of their dream: they wanted to rent a hall for a multi-day public gathering of hundreds of Christians from all denominations. They wanted to worship the Lord and agree together in prayer that God would send the "rain" of the Holy Spirit to transform their spiritual desert into a place of life-giving revival.

I was so encouraged! Positive statements give birth to hope for the impossible to happen. We immediately jumped into an old taxi with Pastor Philip and visited various halls that might be suited for such a gathering. This was no easy task, as the military police kept stopping us and asking us what we were doing. Eventually, we arrived at the very beautiful, government-owned Myanmar Convention Centre, which holds 3,500 people. If available, it would prove to be one of the most impressive venues I had ever preached in!

While we took photographs of the facility, I remembered the Bible passage about the authority of two or more believers to ask whatever they wish in the name of Jesus and see it done (see Matt. 18:19-20). We prayed, asking God to go before us, make our crooked ways straight, and get for us the permission needed to hold a four-day music festival in this wonderful venue. Three months later, He did just that! With our prayers answered, we were one step closer to seeing our dreams become a reality.

Once I and the small team accompanying me returned to the Netherlands, Pastor Philip formed a committee to organize what would be known as the *Gospel Music Festival*. Backed by the prayers of Christian congregations across Yangon, the committee managed to achieve truly remarkable things. Not only did they work through the formidable stack of paperwork needed to get permission for such a large gathering, but they also organized an inter-denominational choir of 150 young people, including several outstanding solo singers and dancers who would perform at the festival!

Back in the Netherlands, I gathered the TRIN team to tell them about the doors God had opened for this historic event. We set about praying and asking God to form the exact team He would send for Myanmar's Gospel Music Festival. We prayed for candidates who had dreams similar to the one He had given me—people who knew and felt God's heart for Myanmar.

Eventually, 20 people applied to be on the team. It was amazing to listen to their individual dreams of going to Myanmar. One man had been moved by the Lord to pray for an outpouring of the Holy Spirit, and had been praying that way for the previous five years! One of the women described a dream she'd had in 2009 in which she saw the faces of Asian children. It was only when she saw the photographs of children from our initial Myanmar visit that she realized God was calling her to go there.

We knew prayer would be vitally important in achieving all God wanted us to accomplish. Wytze Valkema, leader of the Daniel Prayer Network in the Netherlands, mobilized intercessors to pray for the team and for their mission in Myanmar. The team members also recruited family, friends, and members of their home churches to pray for their trip. A letter asking for prayer was also sent to the 3,000 churches that belong to the International Full Gospel Fellowship.

The team members gathered together on a regular basis to discuss practical issues, share their dreams, pray, and have fellowship together. It was wonderful to see God building the team He would use to achieve His purposes. Nervousness—over visa applications and over visiting a country about which so little is known—soon disappeared. That being said, an outburst of violence following elections held in Myanmar a week before our visit did give some relatives and friends sleepless nights!

There was also a matter of raising thousands of dollars to cover the costs of the trip. As team members sent out newsletters, sold things they no longer needed, talked to church groups, and got themselves second jobs in order to make money, God came through in a big way. Three weeks before their departure, they had accumulated only half the amount needed; but by the time they returned from Myanmar, the full amount had been raised.

The process of applying for and being granted visas looked to be another difficult hurdle. Yet, true to His faithfulness (and despite the fact that some visas took longer to come through than others), God supplied every visa we requested.

Three days prior to the team's departure, Wytze flew to Yangon where he held a two-day meeting with pastors and other spiritual leaders. Wytze provided teaching about prayer and intercession and interceded with the group to ask God to pour out His Spirit during the Gospel Music Festival.

On a cold and rainy Saturday morning, the rest of our team departed for Myanmar from Schiphol Airport in the Netherlands. The excitement was tangible; the time of intense preparation was over and the time for our journey to the "special" place God had ordained was upon us. Our baggage carried not only our personal effects, but also many carefully chosen toys, pencils, stickers, and even non-prescription medications that had been requested by several children's homes in Yangon.

Accompanying us was Professor Willem Ouweneel, a Dutch professor of theology, who would join me to preach and teach at both the Gospel Music Festival and the pastors' training conference.

Our two-hour stopover in Singapore gave us a chance to gather together over coffee. The level of excitement among the team members continued to be truly awesome. We knew we were on our way to one of the greatest adventures of our lifetimes as we simply obeyed God's command to go into the world and preach the Gospel!

We arrived in Yangon, Myanmar, to be greeted by Wytze and a temperature that soared into the mid-30sC. How different it was from the near-zero temperatures we'd left behind in the Netherlands. Pastor Philip and his team also came to meet us, and what a grand reunion it was! They had so much to tell us that we all took turns to listen and talk. The expectation of what God was about to do among the people of Yangon in the next few days was *exciting!*

Almost 150 pastors attended the training sessions that were given by Professor Ouweneel and me. Many of the pastors had not met each other before; the conference was an ideal opportunity to make friends, pray with other leaders, and learn about the work and power of the Holy Spirit. Many were strengthened and encouraged; their expectations of the mighty work God would perform in their country increased daily.

When the day of the long-awaited Gospel Music Festival arrived, we were all nervous, but excited. After breakfast, we made our way to the Myanmar Conference Centre. The empty hall seemed massive, but the rehearsing choir and dancers filled the place with color, sound, and movement.

At 9 A.M., people began arriving. By the time the first session started an hour later, there were more than 3,000 people seated and eagerly waiting to hear what the Lord would say to them.

Between 3,500 and 4,000 people attended the meetings every day. As the presence of God became more and more obvious to them, they shed their inhibitions and started shouting and clapping and dancing to the music. Several bursts of laughter filled the air. I will never forget this joyful sound of people freely praising and worshiping our God.

We preached about several topics: whether a nation could be saved in a day, the cloud of Elijah, healing, repentance, and becoming a follower of Jesus. Deeply moved, people streamed to the front of the hall for prayer. The unexpectedly large number of young people and children among those seeking prayer was encouraging to us. The weeping among those being prayed for was intense and prolonged. Many danced for joy as they told us they felt they had been set free. Others testified, saying that the burden of fear they had lived with for so long was now lifted. Others tearfully interceded, asking God to touch and heal their nation.

We had a special area near the side of the stage where people could receive prayer for healing, which many did. Afterward, they filled out forms describing what had initially been wrong with them and explaining how they believed they had been healed. There was great rejoicing among us as we witnessed the Lord's faithfulness and goodness. His Word is the same yesterday, today, and tomorrow; and from what we saw, He proved that He is still the God who heals us, even today!

On the last day of the festival, we held an extended time of prayer during which many people were touched by God. They held hands and formed circles and laughed and sang joyfully to the Lord. No one wanted the festival to end. Strengthened and encouraged, having their numbers increased, and having made many new friends, people left promising to come back for the next year's Gospel Music Festival.

Our team was constantly overcome with awe as we watched God sovereignly move among His people. All we had to do was identify the dream He had put in our hearts; then, without doubting (and like the donkey that carried Jesus into Jerusalem), all we had to do was to be willing. As a result, He allowed us to carry His glory into places we never dreamed possible.

The "last word" in this chapter has to be from Pastor Philip Thang as he was the one God used to help me realize my dream to travel to Myanmar and "reach out to both the saved and unsaved there, to do what I could to help strengthen the church and see the Spirit of God bring the people a fresh wind of hope and healing."

Here are Pastor Philip Thang's own words:

> During the four-day Festival, many accepted Jesus as their Savior. Many more were healed and many

reported feeling that they had been set free from the things that were holding them back from becoming all that God wants them to be. The praise and worship, times of prayer, times of meeting and fellowship with people from various denominations was all so special and something we will all remember for a very long time.

The Gospel Music Festival has been the most wonderful and historical Christian event to be held in Myanmar for generations, and despite being constantly reminded by others that holding a meeting like this was not possible, the results, in the end, proved the truth of Mark 9:23: *"Everything is possible for one who believes."*

People are still asking for decision cards on which they state they have accepted Jesus as their Savior, and we expect the harvest of souls from the festival to continue growing for a long time. Churches are reporting a growing number of people attending their services and an increase in testimonies about what God, in His grace and mercy, is doing in various people's lives. The intimacy and joy experienced during the times of praise and worship at the festival have also encouraged traditional churches to consider using more contemporary forms of worship music.

Many people feel the Holy Spirit working [and] bringing revival and transformation. They feel more love for each other, enjoy praising the Lord with people from other denominations, and feel a greater, more urgent call to obey the Great Commission and gather in the souls waiting to be harvested.

I am seeing that what Brother Mattheus says is right. When I started to see the impossible happening in my country, God made it possible.

We have booked a stadium which can hold 10,000 people for the next Gospel Music Festival we will be holding with Mattheus and TRIN in 2011.

CHAPTER 12

DEPRESSION AND BURNOUT

It is important for me to address this subject because I suffered from depression and burnout, which greatly affected my ability to achieve God's will for my life. These common complaints can and do have a major influence on those trying to achieve their God-given dreams.

According to statistics from the World Health Organization, more than 340 million people around the world suffer from depression, and the number of new cases being diagnosed is increasing daily. Approximately 16 percent of people in Europe and 22 percent in the United States suffer from some form of depression and according to figures I have accessed on official Websites, about one in four people will suffer from depression at some time in their lives.[1] To me this means that suffering from depression is not unusual.

Depression is described as an illness which affects a person's thinking, energy, feelings, and behavior. Burnout is described as a state of emotional, mental, and physical exhaustion caused by excessive and prolonged stress. The symptoms include feelings of being overwhelmed and unable to cope with demands in the course of daily living. As the stress continues, so the motivation to start or complete tasks that need to be done diminishes, which can also hinder spiritual growth.

Perhaps lately you have been feeling somber or sad and have little interest in anything that is going on around you. Maybe it's because you have recently had something unhappy or traumatic happen to you, so it's quite understandable that you are feeling depressed. It can also be that there is no clear reason for the change in the way you feel, but your unexplained tiredness, restlessness, and somber outlook can indicate the onset of depression.

In many Christian churches, particularly the more Charismatic ones, depression and burnout are seldom spoken about because the emphasis is on the gifts of the Holy Spirit, which include the spirit of joy. As joy is the complete opposite of depression, it is often difficult for Christians to admit they have a problem with it. If they do, they are often accused of a lack of faith or told that perhaps that they are not where they should be in their relationship with God.

I cannot give you a professional explanation about these illnesses, but I hope to help you by telling you about my own personal experience and what I learned from it.

YOU ARE NOT CRAZY!

My symptoms of depression and burnout started in December 2001 and lasted for two years. In the beginning, I did not understand what was happening to me and neither did anyone else among my family and friends. As the symptoms of this illness started affecting every area of my life, I thought I was going insane and would have to be admitted to a mental institution for care.

I was in a very lonely place, and I often told those around me that I would rather have a broken leg because it would be easier to diagnose and within six weeks I would be healed. With my unexplained illness, not only did I not know what was wrong, but I also did not know how long it would take to heal.

As I tried to get a grip on my situation so I could understand it better, a chance meeting with a pastoral assistant provided the answer I had been looking for. She listened to what I had to say, and recognizing the symptoms, was able to sensitively explain that I appeared to be suffering from depression and burnout. As she described the symptoms, it became clear to me that this was what I was suffering from. Once I had a name to attach to the problem, I was immediately able to set about working toward being healed.

During my healing process I came across many other Christians suffering from burnout and depression, but they were too frightened to admit it in case others reacted negatively or did not understand. Often the advice they received from those they did dare to tell was very unhelpful. Some were told to pull themselves together and get on with their lives, others were told they needed deliverance from the demons in them that were causing the problem, and yet others were told they needed to fast and pray more often. The effect of these sometimes Scripture based but mostly pious suggestions was often very detrimental to the person suffering from the illness, as they became increasingly guilt-ridden and their feelings of isolation increased.

Depression and burnout do not come from God but are rather a sure sign that the devil is busy working in your life. John 10:10 says that Jesus came to give us life, and life in abundance, while satan came to rob, kill, and destroy all that God has given us. When we are depressed we are often robbed of the ability to hear God's voice or feel His joy.

Once satan has opened the door and gained access to your mind, a seemingly never-ending stream of negative thoughts and feelings enters your mind. If this situation continues for long enough, the resulting feelings of hopelessness and despair can start affecting your physical *and* mental health. The balance of chemicals produced by your brain to keep your feelings and emotions in check is often negatively affected, which makes the situation worse. With all the condemnation coming from both within, as well as outside of you, it feels as if you will never emerge from this seemingly never-ending situation.

If satan is then allowed to rampage unchecked through your mind, the resulting hopelessness and despair could lead to thoughts of suicide, with tragic consequences. A person committing suicide leaves their extended family and friends with wounds and scars that can last for the rest of their lives.

If you recognize these symptoms either in yourself or someone close to you, then writing this chapter will have been worthwhile. Even if you don't know anyone with these symptoms, but would like to know more about it, know that depression is a sickness; and while sufferers may at times feel they are going mad, most people recover. I was surprised to find out that many pastors, leaders, and even worship leaders experienced periods of depression and burnout. It feels like no matter what one does in the lonely wilderness called depression, there is no escape and no one can help you. Nevertheless, it *is* a place from which you can, if you have the right attitude, escape. Not only escape, but emerge much stronger and live to be a real overcomer!

DEPRESSION IN THE BIBLE

In the Bible, there are examples of people suffering from depression. King David went through periods in which he felt depressed and hopeless. In Psalm 69:2-3 he writes:

> *I sink in the miry depths, where there is no foothold. I*
> *have come into the deep waters; the floods engulf me. I*

am worn out calling for help; my throat is parched. My eyes fail, looking for my God.

Another example is in First Kings chapters 18 and 19 in which Elijah has a major victory over the Baal priests. As he prayed, fire fell from Heaven and brought revival into the camp—all Baal statues and false prophets were destroyed. This was an extraordinary happening in which the power of God was clearly demonstrated, yet within 24 hours, Elijah was sitting under a bush in the wilderness feeling so depressed that he contemplated suicide!

God tells us in the Bible that He works all things together for our good; and while depression is not a sign of weakness, but a symptom of an illness, it can be healed. We can learn not only to discern the symptoms as they appear, but also how to fight against them. We can also learn how to avoid getting the illness in the first place.

Each case of depression is different, so the way each person's depression is treated is different. I personally was healed through a mixture of pastoral care, talking to a Christian psychologist, prayers for deliverance, as well as taking medicine. As I went through the healing process, I learned more and more about myself, which I consider to be a good thing. Everyone should make time to get to know themselves better!

My period of depression was a springboard toward bigger dreams and mighty breakthroughs. As I healed, so the opportunities for me to achieve my dreams increased, and I was eventually able to devote myself completely to achieving God's goals for my life.

God's presence stayed with me as I went through the process of dying to myself and my own desires, a period of being pruned and having all things removed from me that were not from God. At last I rediscovered my soul and who I really was. The depression, which so often felt like a curse, eventually lifted, and I became abundantly blessed. If you are going through depression, know that God is for you and is busy working all things together for your good. You can expect to be victorious!

WHAT IS DEPRESSION?

Many people suffer from depression without actually knowing they have it. If a persistent mood of dejection is not obvious, then unexplained sleep problems, reduced appetite, listlessness, and forgetfulness will appear as the first physical symptoms that something is wrong. Feelings of prolonged and deep unhappiness, hopelessness, being short-tempered, and not being able to enjoy normal, everyday life often go unrecognized as symptoms of depression.

There is obviously a difference between a full-blown case of depression and going through a phase of mourning the loss of a loved one, being deeply unhappy about something, or feeling less motivated. Normally, we understand why these feelings are occurring, and know that, in time, we will get over them.

Depression, on the other hand, starts for no obvious reason and can last for weeks, months, or even years. Deeply-felt unhappiness that is not the result of depression can sometimes be put aside in order to do something that is fun or exciting, but with depression this is not possible.

When people are depressed, it seems to be impossible to enjoy doing anything and they feel as if they are different from the happy, healthy people around them. They feel quite dead inside, and each person experiences different levels and different types of feelings during their depression. It can also happen at any age and can vary from a light attack, which is soon dealt with, to an attack that is so heavy it can debilitate a person for a prolonged period of time.

In children and young people, depression can often manifest as behavioral problems or learning disabilities. In older people, it can manifest itself as forgetfulness and can often, mistakenly, be diagnosed as dementia.

Based on my own experience, I have found that genuine depression is a sickness with two predominant symptoms:

- A somber, sad, depressed attitude and a feeling of emptiness

- A loss of interest and pleasure in taking part in activities one previously found pleasant to do, the inability to feel happy, and not being able to enjoy doing anything

To be able to speak of a genuine depression, one or more of the following complaints or symptoms are present over an extended period:

- A feeling of worthlessness and guilt

- Difficulty sleeping

- A greater or lesser desire to eat with accompanying weight gain or loss

- Tiredness and too little energy

- Problems concentrating and an inability to make decisions

- Inertia or ongoing physical unrest

- Repeated thoughts of death or suicide

If you think you have the two main symptoms and one or more of the other symptoms, it is possible that you are suffering from depression. I would advise you to see your doctor, pastor, a spiritual father or mother or, at the very least, someone who is mature enough to know what to do and how to advise you.

Sometimes depression is also accompanied by feelings of panic, anxiety, being constantly tearful or unable to cry at all, feelings of hopelessness and lacking power over one's own life, physical problems that don't have a cause, the feeling that life is meaningless, or neglecting one's home or social contacts.

CAUSES OF DEPRESSION

Depression can have many causes; often it is not possible to pinpoint the exact cause. For most sufferers, it's a combination of character traits and events in life that leads to depression. The following is information I have gathered since 2002. They come from various sources such as talking to psychiatrists, reading credible Websites, and various other forms of documentation about these illnesses, and, of course, from my own personal experience. Keep in mind that every individual is unique, so this information may or may not address your particular situation. Consulting a medical or mental health professional and your spiritual adviser is strongly recommended if you have any questions about this subject.

Character traits and circumstances that can cause depression:

- *Heredity.* Research shows that some families are more prone to depression than others. Some people have, because of inherited traits, a greater chance of suffering from depression than others, but this does not mean that people from families with a history of depression will automatically suffer from it.

- *Illness.* A chronic or sudden illness can cause the onset of depression. There are also physical illnesses that can bring on depression. These include brain hemorrhages, diabetes, Parkinson's Disease, various types of cancer, and a malfunctioning thyroid gland. Illnesses such as mononucleosis and influenza can also cause depression.

- *Medicine.* The side effects of various medicines can also bring on symptoms of depression, especially those used for the treatment of high blood pressure and sleeping difficulties. Side effects resulting from combining different medications, suddenly stopping medication, using certain medications for a long time, and even the combination of medicines taken by someone who drinks alcohol can cause depression.

- *Character and personality.* People who perceive themselves as having little personal worth, who are naturally pessimistic, or are overly dependent on others, have a greater chance of developing depression than someone who is naturally self-confident and optimistic.

- *Childhood experiences.* Experiences such as abuse or neglect can affect children so badly that they can suffer from depression when they are adults.

- *Loss.* Here one thinks of the death of a loved one, but it can also apply to divorce, becoming unemployed, or a deterioration in health, retirement, or changing physical environments. It is normal to feel dejected, depressed, and sorrowful at these times, but if the emotional feeling of loss does not lessen over a period of time, it may well be that the person has become depressed.

- *Stress.* Problems at work, conflicts within a marriage, being a long-term caregiver to someone who is sick, or the birth of a child and the resulting hormonal changes, can all lead to stress resulting in depression.

Sometimes depression is the result of a person's physical environment. To help overcome depression caused by this, I have devoted a few pages to knowing what Jesus said about illness. This enables us to start feeling faith-filled and hopeful, and then help us turn our environments into positive places to be.

We need to have our thoughts renewed by replacing negative thinking with the thoughts and words of Jesus. No matter what the cause of the depression, Jesus can and will set you free from it and heal you. He wants to rescue you from the dark cell you live in; and for every sufferer, He has a different way out. Jesus once applied mud to a blind person's eyes, and after He did so, they could see. Another blind person was healed just by Jesus laying His hands on him; and on yet another occasion, someone was healed just by Jesus speaking a few words to him.

Whatever method He decides to use to heal you, know there is hope; know that He wants you out of what seems to be a bottomless, dark pit—and know that Jesus has already paid the price to set you free. Just believe, speak His Word over your situation, leave your negative thought patterns and environment, and choose positive ones instead. Talk to people you can trust and who are prepared to help you overcome this illness.

HOW DEPRESSION INFLUENCES CHRISTIANS

Depression affects all our relationships, including our relationship with God. It will make Christians feel as if all the joy they felt when they became born again has vanished and they no longer feel God's presence. To depression sufferers, God feels far away and unreachable. To take part in praise and worship services or other joyful Christian activities is almost impossible as those suffering from depression are often unable to feel anything emotionally.

It is at this stage that those suffering from depression start feeling that God has abandoned them because they have done something wrong or committed an unforgivable sin. As their guilt mounts, they start feeling that God, their only hope in their time of trouble, has turned His back on them and they can no longer reach Him.

Most suggestions by concerned friends on how the sufferer should deal with their depression involve spending more time in prayer or Bible study, which often is not possible because of the person's inability to concentrate. Pastors sometimes tell members of their congregations that they have depression because of something they have personally done, or not done; this sort of accusation is normally counterproductive and only increases the sufferer's inability to cope.

Self-help books, DVDs, and CDs, are sometimes used, occasionally with pastoral help, to try and lift a depression. These methods can work provided depressed people are able to take control of their thought patterns. However, if they cannot control their thought patterns, using these methods may well lead Christian sufferers to feel that there is no hope and that they will never be healed. Depression can be especially painful for Christians as the illness is often misunderstood. But there is hope! I am living proof of that!

TREATMENT OF DEPRESSION

After recognizing that something more than a mild depression is taking place, it's important to get professional help as soon as possible.

In most countries, the first professional person to talk to would be a family doctor who will want to know what symptoms are being experienced, and then decide the best way to help the patient. This will often be a combination of psychological help as well as prescribed medication. For Christians, speaking to a pastor as well as receiving dedicated prayer is a helpful addition to this treatment.

In the past few years I, as well as my wife and best friend Rebekah, have seen countless numbers of people healed and set free from depression. The people who were depressive and did not know Jesus and then accepted Him as their Savior, were, in every instance, completely healed and set free.

People who suffered from depression and did know Jesus as their Savior often had to go through a process of restoration before they were healed. Try and find out what the root of your depression is and then talk to a trained counselor who understands the way you feel. If necessary, ask for prayer for inner healing and deliverance.

Here are a few different types of help that are available to those suffering from depression.

TALKING

Finding someone who will listen to your problems can have a positive effect on your situation. Talking to a Christian counselor can help relieve the problem, although a more systematic approach to the problem involving talking to a mental health professional on a regular basis may be necessary.

The ideal situation would be to actually seek the help of a Holy Spirit-filled Christian psychologist or psychiatrist. Research done before you start treatment will tell you whether the recommended person is trustworthy and able to do deliverance when necessary, and if they are able to pray effectively for your healing.

PRAYING AND PROCLAIMING

People suffering from depression should find a small group of Christians they can meet with regularly to discuss their progress and to bring to the Lord in prayer any issues that are proving difficult for them to handle.

In the Bible it often tells us to proclaim the Word of the Lord. When someone has depression, as with any other problem, it is wise to search the Bible looking for God's Word on the subject, as well as His promises of help, and then proclaim them over the problem boldly. In Romans 10 it tells us that we can build up our faith by hearing the Word of God; and so as we proclaim it, we begin to believe it. Eventually, the negative thoughts about our situations are replaced with godly, positive thoughts, and we will begin to heal.

MEDICATION AND SPORT

People suffering from depression often have to take a course of prescribed medication. This is normal, and I had to take antidepressants for a time. Unfortunately, it takes between two and four weeks before their positive effects are noticed, and the side effects vary in intensity between one type of antidepressant and another.

At first I thought having to take medication was a sign of weakness. It was only when I went to a church in Canada and the worship leader told us he battled with a similar problem, that I realized that I did not need to feel ashamed or embarrassed. The illness I had was a normal illness and many people suffer from it at some time in their lives.

Serotonin is a substance manufactured in the brain which keeps us in a "happy" frame of mind. When people are depressed, they often need to take antidepressant drugs that contain ingredients that either supplement the brain's supply of serotonin or help the brain to make better use of the serotonin it does produce.

There are many ways to *naturally* increase the brain's production of serotonin. Physical exercise is one of them. People suffering from depression should consider some form of exercise for 30 minutes a day, five days a week.

SELF-HELP

A person suffering from depression has done nothing to cause this unpleasant illness to take hold of them and has no need to feel ashamed or embarrassed. I intend living a healthy life for 120 years and claim and proclaim it. However, in reality this is hardly likely to happen! We need to view our physical situations soberly and realize we live in a sinful world and are liable to suffer from illnesses, including depression, from time to time; therefore, we must do what we can to guard against them.

A few general tips we can use to help ourselves when we suffer from depression:

- Try and find out if your depression is the result of a specific event in your life or if it has its roots in an underlying problem.

- Talk to someone with whom you can discuss the feelings that are troubling you, and formulate a plan with them about how and when to seek professional help.

- Go to bed at a set time and get up at a set time.

- Find healthy outlets for your physical tension and mental stress. Run, walk, cycle, or join a gym.

- Stay socially active and do not neglect your friends.

- Do not go on vacation if you know you are not going to enjoy yourself.

- Do not make decisions that have far-reaching consequences or that you may regret making later on.

- Don't look for something destructive to distract you like pornography, alcohol, or illegal drugs.

- Listen to worship music regularly and spend time meditating on the Word.

- Play what is now referred to as soaking music during which you clear your mind and focus on God, or join a group that focuses on soaking and where you will receive prayer from others.

- Find Christian friends with whom you can do enjoyable things and who are prepared to fast and pray for you.

WHAT FAMILY AND FRIENDS NEED TO KNOW

When people in your direct surroundings suffer from depression, it is not always easy to get along with them. Living with and caring for them is often a less-than-pleasant task. It's easy to become irritated and despondent about someone who does nothing but complain, doesn't want to do anything, and is interested in nothing. You may even feel guilty because you feel so good while the depressed person feels so bad or may even feel that perhaps something you have done or didn't do has led to his or her suffering.

I have listed the following tips on how to get along with someone suffering from depression and I trust they will be helpful:

- Do not allow the person suffering from depression to be overwhelmed with the well-meant, but misguided, advice of others. Such advice often has the opposite effect, causing the situation of the sufferer to go from bad to worse.

- If possible, get together a group of friends to fast and pray with you for the sufferer and regularly proclaim God's promises over the person for whom you are praying.

- Don't be critical and don't become overly involved.

- Make sure that you do not get overtaxed by having to deal alone with the person. Call on others to help you cope and make sure you get enough rest.

- Make definite plans about what needs to be done regarding getting help for the person suffering from depression, and set a time frame in which you are going to do it.

- Be alert for signs that the person is considering suicide. Get outside help when necessary, and don't forget that God is with you in the situation. Make sure you call on Him for help, too.

- Pray that the person suffering from depression will soon get a breakthrough and healing.

MY PERSONAL STORY

During 2000, I started working in Kosovo to help those widowed and orphaned by the war there to rebuild their lives. I became increasingly tired and couldn't sleep, but continued working between 70 and 90 hours a week to alleviate the suffering of those I had come to help. Eventually, I realized that all the joy I had experienced in what I was doing had gradually disappeared.

It was during this time that I had not only the stress of coping with my increasing tiredness and lack of sleep, but had to try and adjust to working in a traumatic environment so alien to my own. To add to my difficulties, a crisis arose within the organization I was working for, which I found very hard to deal with.

A Funeral

Just before Christmas that year, a five-year-old boy named Besart was playing in the remains of his burnt-out home. He was kicking a football against what remained of the ceiling and as he did so, the wires holding it up slipped and the ceiling fell on him. Besart was badly injured and died soon afterward. As there were few vehicles available in the area, we offered, along with our Albanese team, to use our car to take his body to his parents' home.

His parents were strict Muslims whom we knew personally as they fetched bread from our bakery every day. They were victims of the war and had lost their home, and many members of their family had been killed. They were now trying to pick up the pieces and rebuild their lives.

The morning after the accident, Besart was laid out on a wooden plank in his family's front garden so people could come and say their final farewell to him. The women and men streamed out of the nearby village of Gjakova and stood near him, with the men separated from the women according to Muslim tradition. The grief and sense of loss was immense, and I was deeply moved.

As our team stood around him, I felt I had to lay hands upon him and call him back to life in Jesus' name, but as I placed my hands on him I was so overcome with grief I could not speak. I was overwhelmed with anxiety, fearing that if I prayed, he would not come back to life. After the funeral I started to feel incredibly guilty at what I saw as my failure to do what God expected me to do. I started to sink mentally into a very deep, dark hole. That was the drop that made my bucket, which had been so filled with grief, horror, and shock since I came to Kosovo, overflow into what was to become a deep depression.

Yes, my time in Kosovo had been successful from the point of view that I and my team had been able to help many widows and orphans restructure their lives after the tragic war, and I am happy that I was able to do so. On the other hand, the horrors and helplessness I had witnessed and the constant pressure I put on myself to work all hours of the day and night to do what needed to be done, had all been too much for me. I needed a break to clear my head and get a grip on my life.

A Black Hole

I flew back to the Netherlands just before Christmas; and when I saw my parents, I collapsed. I felt as if I had fallen into a large, black hole that I would never be able to get out of.

When we got home, I went to my bedroom and stayed there, feeling as if I never wanted to leave it again. I cried a lot and just wanted to crawl under my duvet and hide from the world. I even began to doubt that God existed. I was unable to read either a book or the Bible and, having lost my close connection to God, started to feel an overwhelming sense of loneliness. The emotional pain I felt seemed to come from deep within my heart. I was overwhelmed by what seemed to be the never-ending stream of negative thoughts going through my head. I started wondering how I was going to free myself from the dark hole into which I had mentally fallen.

Even though I was 25 years old at the time, I started feeling that I wanted to stay very close to my parents. I needed their attention and for them to confirm who and what I was. It was during this time that I started examining my overwhelming need to prove myself and receive the approval of my parents and the people around me. If I did not receive the approval and confirmation I needed from them, I felt lonely and insecure. Then I would double my efforts to gain their approval. I also realized that I had a bad self-image and had no idea what I wanted to do with my life.

As these problems engulfed me, I spent hours laying on the couch like a small child while my parents held me, talked to me, and comforted me. Miraculously, I felt as they held me and talked to me, that they were bringing healing to a part of me that had been deeply wounded in the past. I began to feel that God loved me unconditionally, and that I had no need to prove myself to anyone. Gradually my self-image began to improve as I saw myself from God's point of view instead of my own. I started accepting and loving myself and slowly I started climbing out of the black hole I had been living in; I started to see a clear, blue sky above me.

In retrospect, I wish I had spent more time listening to God telling me, "My son, I love you and am so proud of you." If I had believed those words of approval from my heavenly Father instead of searching for approval from my parents and others around me, I could have prevented much of the pain and abandonment I felt during those dreadful, dark days.

Your Father Loves You

One day, an older couple invited me to accompany them on vacation to Italy to take part in winter sports. I was immediately anxious as I did not think I would enjoy doing anything away from my parents and my safe environment at home. It took a lot of persuasion from my parents and friends before I agreed to go. As we left the Netherlands on our way to Italy by car, the people with me enjoyed the passing winter scenery, while I got more and more depressed, and eventually I could hardly speak. All I wanted to do was go home.

On the first day in Italy we went to the top of a high mountain so that I could learn how to ski. I found this horrifying and, at one stage, broke free from the person holding me and slid out of control, and at an ever-increasing speed, down the side of the mountain, and landed on the hard, compacted snow. My nose was bleeding and I had wrenched my knee. As I lay there, so filled with pain and anxiety, and so far from home, all of a sudden I imagined how silly I must look lying there, and I began to laugh. While I was lying there laughing, I had an enormous sense of how much God loved me.

That evening, sitting in front of a crackling log fire, I picked up a pen and paper. God told me to draw a heart representing His heart for me, and then to look up every verse in the Bible that expressed His love for His children. I went to the family I was on vacation with and together we looked up every verse we could find about the Father Heart of God. It was a beautiful night and, for the first time in a very long time, I noticed how clear the sky was. I was delighted when I saw the stars twinkling overhead.

The family I was with showed me an article in a magazine about the revival happening in a church in Toronto, Canada. On the cover were the words "The Father Loves You," and inside was information about a conference starting in Toronto a week after we were due to return home from Italy. I had a very strong feeling that I needed to be there. When I returned home, I booked a ticket to fly to Canada and attend the conference.

It was a wonderful week during which what happened to me, and what I felt, confirmed the overwhelming, unconditional love that God first revealed to me while I was lying in the snow. Luke 15:11-32, the story of the lost son who returned to his father, spoke to my heart; and I saw myself in the older son and in the lost son. God convicted me of the wrong image I had of Him and about the negative image I had of myself. He also spoke about my desire to please others, and seek other's approval, rather than looking to Him.

This wonderful revelation of God's Father Heart for me laid an important foundation for what has happened in my life since I returned home from that truly blessed week in Toronto.

OUR FIGHT IS NOT AGAINST FLESH AND BLOOD

The larger your vision or dream is, the more you will experience opposition because the devil is terrified that the children of God are going to fulfill their destinies, change the world, and that His Kingdom will come more rapidly. Christians fulfilling their destinies will trigger the return of the Lord Jesus and this means a definitive end to satan and his accomplices. Satan will do everything in his power to have you believe his lies. He will try and put you in situations where you have too much responsibility to cope with, or into other situations that will effectively silence you.

A perceived lack of time as well as lies are means that satan uses in trying to eliminate people. We live in a time that is so rushed and stressed that we can hardly keep track of ourselves. There seems to be a lack of real friendships, and instead so much coldness. We barely know our neighbors; families are split by work, adultery, or lies. I know children and teenagers who go to bed at night feeling alone and whose families haven't eaten a meal together or shared their day with each other for a long time. They have no real idea what their parents do and have no intimate relationship with them. We need to set priorities and spend time with our children and families again.

Similarly, the time we spend with our heavenly Father is so short, or so busy, that He has no chance to speak to us or to share His heart with us, His children. Make an appointment every day in your schedule by setting time aside as "Time With God." It will prove to be life-changing!

There is a difference between dejection and depression. When you are dejected, you can still experience joy. There are moments you enjoy during the day, and you can put your feelings into words. If you are depressed, you can't do this. Life becomes like a black hole that you cannot escape from.

Often, visionaries, leaders, and pioneers are affected by depression and burnout. If I look back at what happened to me, I can only thank God that there were people to help me through the dark times. These were periods during which my character was formed, my faith was tested, and everything that was not pure and not in line with the Word of God in my life was exposed and removed. My foundation had to be rebuilt. I am not saying that it was God's desire that I should be depressed or unable to function normally, but I do know that in all things the Lord works for the good of those who love Him (see Rom. 8:28). While healing my depression, God dealt with what was inside me that was not from Him. Despite my flesh and evil forces trying to undermine me, those things did not succeed because God is so much bigger and more powerful than they are.

In everyone's life there is a certain emptiness, a vacuum that can only be filled by God. Many of us try to fill this vacuum with all kinds of addictions, gossip, talking and thinking negatively, watching too much television or spending too much time on our computers; but time will show that only God can fill this vacuum, this emptiness. We know, from experience, that when we finally find time to be with the

Lord, we wonder why we don't make time to be in His presence more often. When that vacuum is filled with His presence, we experience His peace and love. Make a promise to God to do this every day.

However, because we are dealing with two powers—the power of God and the power of the world (and many of us have not yet learned to discern between the two)—every day we are subjected to these two forces: the Spirit of God and the spirit of this world. Our body, our "flesh," is very attracted to the spirit of the world (satan's power). For most men it is easier to sit late at night behind their computers or in front of the television rather than sitting in a quiet place in the house to be alone with God, listening to worship music, reading His Word, or praying with their wives. We must realize that we are subject to these two forces, but that the Spirit of God is much stronger. Many of us have filled the emptiness in our lives with lies, boredom, impurity, and with attitudes of unforgiveness, guilt, shame, and rejection.

The Spirit of God is living in every Christian and is trying to convince us of our sins and uncleanness, but many of us do not dare to enter the light. That is why there is a constant battle in our thinking and understanding. I certainly believe in spiritual warfare and intercession, but I think the biggest spiritual struggle takes place in our own thinking. Hence, the apostle Paul encourages us to be transformed by the renewing of our minds (see Rom. 12:1-2).

Some of us are so polluted by the spirit of this world, that we have become blind to it. A veil has come over our minds and lives, and we have accepted that we will live a mediocre life. We go to church, take part in religious activities, work for our employers, pay our taxes, and go on vacation periodically. The Bible calls this an abnormal life; and I agree.

The normal life that God wants us to live is the place where the heavenly gates are open and we have His Kingdom in us. The Lord wants to bless us abundantly so that we lead lives of miracles and signs of His presence; live as Jesus' hands and feet on Earth;

and cause our surroundings to change from glory to glory. Many Christians live without real hope and keep standing in front of the barrier that *was* between us and God, but do not see that the barrier *has been removed.*

What does all this have to do with depression? Everything! Until we fill up the vacuum in our lives with the Spirit of God, our spirit will be oppressed. We are created to live abundantly! The spirit of the world wants to destroy us. Just read John 10:10:

> *The thief comes only to steal and kill and destroy; I [Jesus] have come that they may have life, and have it to the full.*

God wants us to come to life. We come to life if we know who we are in God, when we finally start loving ourselves as we are and not as the world says or thinks we should be. We come to life when the seed, the DNA, the potential that God has placed in us, is released.

We come to life as we walk with God as Adam and Eve did before the Fall, hand in hand with the Father in His glory. We have heard so much about the Fall and the sinners that we are convinced that we will always live in sin and lead difficult lives. However, Jesus died on the cross on Calvary so that the glory that existed before the Fall would be restored, and we can walk again with God in purity and innocence.

Do you believe it? Do you believe that you really have access to the Father right now, access to His glory and to all heavenly treasures? It really is possible, because through the blood of Jesus, the curtain that formed the barrier between us and God has been removed and we are free to enter the throne room of God.

If we want to see the things of God, we should spend time in His presence. That is one of the keys—that we are not always striving, but that we relax in His peace and glory. Spending time with the Father is vitally important at this time, a time in which few people even know what real friendship is. God wants us to be with Him so we can see that there really is an open door in the heavens. We now have access to this door. Come and let us enter the heavenly realm together through the open door and see what's happening on the other side.

After the resurrection of the Lord Jesus, John received a revelation from the Lord. We read in Revelation 4:1-11:

> *After this I looked, and there before me was a door standing open in heaven. And the voice I had first heard speaking to me like a trumpet said, "Come up here, and I will show you what must take place after this." At once I was in the Spirit, and there before me was a throne in heaven with someone sitting on it. And the one who sat there had the appearance of jasper and ruby. A rainbow that shone like an emerald encircled the throne. Surrounding the throne were twenty-four other thrones, and seated on them were twenty-four elders. They were dressed in white and had crowns of gold on their heads. From the throne came flashes of lightning, rumblings and peals of thunder. In front of the throne, seven lamps were blazing. These are the seven spirits of God. Also in front of the throne there was what looked like a sea of glass, clear as crystal.*
>
> *In the center, around the throne, were four living creatures, and they were covered with eyes, in front and in back. The first living creature was like a lion, the second was like an ox, the third had a face like a man, the fourth was like a flying eagle. Each of the four living creatures had six wings and was covered with eyes all around, even under its wings. Day and night they never stop saying:*

"Holy, holy, holy is the Lord God Almighty, who was, and is, and is to come."

Whenever the living creatures give glory, honor and thanks to Him who sits on the throne and who lives for ever and ever, the twenty-four elders fall down before Him who sits on the throne, and worship Him who lives for ever and ever. They lay their crowns before the throne and say: "You are worthy, our Lord and God, to receive glory and honor and power, for You created all things, and by Your will they were created and have their being."

The place being written about here is our final destination! We will be close to the throne of God! We will be with Him forever! I read this Scripture in the Bible regularly because this is my final destination, the glory of God in Heaven. This is also your final destination, but right now we are still on Earth and subject to the two powers of this world. In the meantime we can prepare ourselves for the second coming of Jesus; He will be back soon, much sooner than we perhaps think. Now we must live under an open Heaven: the door is open, and the only thing we have to do is to enter in. The throne room is at our disposal to manifest His Kingdom on Earth more and more.

ENDNOTE

1. "Statistics on Mental Health," *Mental Health Foundation*, http://www.mentalhealth.org.uk /information/mental-health-overview/statistics/; (accessed January 10, 2011), and "Depression: Facts and Statistics," *Satellite Corporation*, http:// www.depressionperception.com/depression /depression_facts_and_statistics.asp.

CHAPTER 13

THE FATHER HEART OF GOD

The story of the lost son in chapter 15 of the Book of Luke in the Bible is a well-known story about a father who has two sons. This is a parable that applies to every one of us. The young son is self-centered, and after taking his inheritance from his father, moves to a distant land. After he has spent all his money, he returns to his father's house. Instead of being turned away in disgrace, he is welcomed back with deep, unconditional love by his father.

When I was skiing in Italy and fell in the snow, I realized I had a lot of the younger, lost son's characteristics. Prior to the revelation I had of the Father Heart of God and His unconditional love for me, I was selfish and mostly interested in what God could do for me. My attitude was "Give me! Give me!" instead of "Change me! Change me!" In other words, "Give me Your strength and gifts, but I'll do things my way. Not Your will, but my will be done."

After the revelation of God's overwhelming love for me and how He felt about me as His child, my attitude changed to one where I could say, "Your will not mine." The emptiness in my heart was filled with God's love, and I was no longer interested in building my own kingdom, but longed to build His Kingdom.

GOD LOVES US!

Many Christians have the wrong idea about how God feels about us as His children. They cannot relate to His immense, unconditional love as it is written about in the Bible:

> *For God so loved the world that He gave His one and only Son, that whoever believes in Him shall not perish but have eternal life* (John 3:16).

In Romans 8:14-17 it says:

> *For those who are led by the Spirit of God are children of God. The Spirit you received does not make you slaves, so that you live in fear again; rather, the Spirit you received brought about your adoption to sonship. And by Him we cry, "Abba, Father." The Spirit Himself testifies with our spirit that we are God's children. Now if we are children, then we are heirs—heirs of God and co-heirs with Christ, if indeed we share in His sufferings in order that we may also share in His glory.*

This verse is meant to remind us (or perhaps tell us for the first time) of God's unconditional love for us. The word *Abba* written in this verse means Daddy or Papa and refers to the intimate relationship that exists between a father and his child. This is the sort of relationship God wants to have with each of us. If we do not have a revelation of the truth of this statement, we will probably end up in a place of aggressive striving, religious activities, or perhaps we will fall back into sinful ways.

It is unfortunately not possible to cover all the important things necessary to understand God's Father or Mother Heart for us in this one chapter, and I would like to encourage you to search out and read one of the many excellent books written on this subject in order to acquire this life-changing revelation for yourself.

EARTHLY FATHER RELATIONSHIPS

Many of us have the wrong idea of God's Father Heart for us. It is well-known that the relationships we have (or had) with our earthly fathers greatly affect the relationship we have with our heavenly Father. During interviews while evangelizing on the streets, we found that the people who had bad relationships with their earthly fathers often had the wrong image of God as a father figure. What happens in the natural world often affects our spiritual world.

Our earthly fathers, because of their own limitations, do not always set good examples of what a father is or what he is supposed to do. Often, because of the hurt they carry with them from their own pasts, they have faulty images of fatherhood that they pass on to their own children. This, in turn, adversely affects the view that these children have of God as a father.

Often Christians have this view of God: if they sin or fail, God will be extremely angry, and so they run away from Him to avoid His anger. They also believe that Jesus came to stand between us and our angry God in order to protect us. They hide for a while thinking He wants nothing more to do with them and that only after doing a lot of good things can they win back God's love and acceptance. Often they are very afraid of God, but this is the wrong fear to have because God says in the Bible that His perfect love drives out fear. It is important to respect God, but that is very different from being afraid of God.

It is so important that we each receive a personal revelation of God's unconditional love. *Unconditional* means we don't have to do anything in order to be loved by God. A baby who is conceived and born in love receives, from the moment the baby is born, abundant, seemingly endless love from the parents, family, and friends. This despite the fact that all the baby is capable of doing is crying, sleeping, drinking, and often keeping his or her parents awake at night!

I speak from experience because, when our beautiful son Zephaniah was born, all we as his parents could do was cry as we felt the Father Heart of God for both us and our new son. Zephaniah was born at home with a midwife and nursing sister present to help with the birth. We had soaking music in the background and as he was born we started to cry. At this very important time of our lives, both my parents as well as my sister, Viviane, were present.

Rebekah, who had a very unpleasant past, had not spoken to her father, who lived in the United States, for seven years. This fact nagged at her, but due to the things that had happened between them, she chose to have no contact with either him or her step-mother. This situation had an enormously negative impact on her as well as her relationship with her heavenly Father. As her husband, I had tried a few times to persuade her that it was important to forgive her father and to restore contact with him. She had already forgiven him, but was trying hard to forget him, and certainly never wanted to see him again.

That is, until Zephaniah was born! A minute after he entered this world, Rebekah was crying from both joy and sorrow at the same time because she now wanted to speak to her father again. By super-natural means, she knew her father's telephone number, and before Zephaniah's umbilical cord was even cut, she phoned him to tell him she had just given birth to his first grandson. It was a highly emotional and blessed time.

Three months later we flew to America to meet her father, stepmother, and sister. It was a very special time when forgiveness was spoken out for all past hurts and misunderstandings. On Zephaniah's first birthday, Rebekah's father and stepmother flew to the Netherlands to attend his birthday party.

The relationship between father and daughter was completely restored, and Rebekah was then able to receive the Father Heart of God and His unconditional love for her. This brought both healing and reconciliation into her life and in her relationship with others.

THE FATHER WANTS TO BLESS YOU

God's love for us is unconditional; it is not based on anything we do. If you think of God as your heavenly Father, does that make you happy? What sort of thoughts do you have when this is mentioned? The way you answer this question will tell you a lot about what sort of relationship you have with God. If you don't feel at ease in God's presence, you will not feel at ease with yourself or others, either.

God is a father who wants to hug you and forgive you; and instead of running away from Him when we sin, we need to learn to run *to* Him. To be in a loving relationship with Him is one of the greatest blessings we will experience in our lives. First John 4:16 says:

> *And so we know and rely on the love God has for us. God is love. Whoever lives in love lives in God, and God in them.*

God the Father is not a boring father. He delights in being involved in His children's lives, even their parties! He let His Son Jesus do His first miracle on Earth at a party. He was at a wedding feast when He turned water into wine. We know that Jesus did nothing He had not seen His Father do. He changed water into wine, not into grape juice as some Christians say, and it was the best wine served that night.

God is the best winemaker, and He enjoys celebrations! God wants to bless you and He wants to bless the sinners, the righteous, the unrighteous, the murderers, the liars, the good, and the bad people. It is in God's character to bless you. God, as a Father, has no negative thoughts about you or dark plans for your future. Even if you live in deep sin, through His great mercy, He still wants to live in love and intimacy with you. You are His child, and He wants to free you, heal you, and be reconciled to you. In Jeremiah 29:11, He says:

> *"For I know the plans I have for you"* declares the Lord,
> *"plans to prosper you and not to harm you, plans to give*
> *you hope and a future."*

Satan, on the other hand, only wants to judge you and make you feel guilty. God, through the Holy Spirit and His Word, wants to convict you of sin, and that is completely different. Forgiveness and salvation are available to everyone, even right now.

Put this book down for a minute and concentrate on God, seeing Him as your Father. Let Him draw you to Himself and His love and hold you in His arms. Ask for forgiveness for your sins and receive healing, deliverance, and forgiveness from Him. Do you know that every time God thinks of you there is a broad grin on His face? God is always happy to see you, because you are the crown of His creation. God is always humble and filled with compassion.

In John 5:19 we read that Jesus only did what He saw the Father do. Jesus washed the disciples' feet (see John 13:5). This was a service that was normally done by a servant before guests entered a house. They did this because at the time, the streets were full of dust, animal droppings, and mud. It was normal to wear simple, open sandals in those days so foot washing was done for practical reasons, namely to keep the home clean and hygienic. Jesus washing the feet of His disciples was not done for any religious reason, but only to clean them. By His acting as a servant, we see in Jesus the servant heart of God the Father as He expresses His overwhelming love for us.

THE WAY TO THE FATHER

In John 14:6 Jesus says, *"I am the way, the truth and the life. No one comes to the Father except through Me."*

A road always goes somewhere and so has a reason for its existence. Jesus is the road or way to the Father; and therefore, the Father is the purpose for Jesus to exist. Jesus came to reveal the way to the Father. In John 14:7, He says, *"If you really know Me, you will know My Father as well..."*; and in verse 9 He says, *"Anyone who has seen Me has seen the Father...."*

In John 14:23, Jesus says, *"Anyone who loves Me will obey My teaching. My Father will love them, and we will come to them and make our home with them."* This means that God is looking for a place to live, and that place is in your heart. This does not mean just a short visit or a brief period of refreshing. He wants to come and live in your heart, as your Father, forever!

Jesus says in John 8:14, *"...I know where I came from and where I am going...."* My question is, "Where did Jesus come from and where was He going?" He is in the most intimate place in the universe. Look what is written in John 1:18, *"No one has ever seen God, but the one and only Son, who is Himself God and is in closest relationship with the Father, has made Him known."*

Jesus, the only Son of God the Father, rests on His Father's heart. We can also go to this most holy and intimate place to be with the Father. The barrier that separated us from God was completely removed through the blood of Jesus, His death, and resurrection.

Let us all go to this very special place! It will change our lives!

THE LOST FATHER

Let us once again look at the wonderful example we read about in Luke 15 about the lost son, or, as a speaker at the Vineyard Church in Toronto called him, "The lost father." If we make the decision not to be the son or daughter of our heavenly Father, He will still always love us and call us back to Him.

Religion tells us this unusual story is about the faults and sins of the lost son because religion always focuses on the sins committed by a person rather than what God has done to reconcile us to Him. This parable tells us not only about the rebellious son, but about the love of a father who longs for an intimate relationship with his child.

This parable is popular in church services and Sunday schools. I have heard the story several times and am always fascinated by it. In Russia, in the well-known Hermitage museum in Saint Petersburg, there is a painting depicting the lost son painted by the well-known Dutch artist, Rembrandt van Rijn. It shows the father welcoming home the lost son. The father's one hand is painted as a father's hand and the other as a mother's hand. In the background, it shows the oldest son, jealous and angry and not wanting to take part in the feast to welcome his brother home.

I stood studying this painting in the museum for a long time, and when I returned home I read the book written by Henri Nouwen and titled *The Return of the Prodigal Son: A Story of Homecoming.* In it, the author describes the painting beautifully. I strongly recommend that you read it.

Often the parable of the lost son is used to explain how much God loves us and His plan for our salvation. However, when Jesus starts to tell the story it becomes immediately obvious that this is not the story about how to become a reborn Christian. The two sons, the younger and the older, were both members of their father's household. They had a relationship with him and often spent time with him.

This parable does not tell us how to start a new relationship with God but rather how to repair the relationship we once had with Him. It is about coming home to the love of the Father after we have broken or damaged the intimate relationship we had with Him.

The younger son did not value the relationship he had with his father. He was selfish and valued his father only for the material wealth he could give him rather than for the love he received from him. Eventually he turned his back on his relationship with his father after taking as much material wealth from him as he could. Immature people mostly think only of their own interests and not the desires of others. They focus on the gifts God gives rather than on the Giver of the gifts.

In this parable, we read that at a certain moment in time the son made the decision to leave his father's house and take control of his own life. At that point the father was no longer able to extend to him the advantages of being his son. He remained his father's son but was no longer under the protection of his father. If we behave the same way toward God by taking whatever He can give us but not wanting a relationship with Him, it will also lead us into a wilderness, a dry and barren place.

We should monitor our behavior to make sure there does not come a time when we also want to do everything ourselves by taking control of our lives away from the Father. Let us not say to the Father, "Give me my inheritance and let me go and do things my own way," otherwise we, too, will leave the protection we have in the Father's arms.

Whenever our attitude to God is, "Give me, give me, give me," we have already left the intimacy of the Father's protection and entered into a place of being competitive, divisive, full of striving, lust, and other bad behavior that leads only to heartache.

EMPTINESS IN OUR HEARTS

In 2007 as a result of several research projects done among Christians, it was estimated that a surprisingly large percentage of Christian men wrestle with thoughts of pornography, adultery, and even homosexuality.[1] It is thought that after prayer meetings, home cell meetings, or other Christian activities, many men wait until their wives have gone to bed, or are busy doing something else, and then go on the Internet to satisfy their lust for pornography.

It only takes a few seconds before they log on, access a site, and then start feeling ashamed of what they are doing and lose their close relationship with God. They have opened the door to satan, and his lies have found a way to enter into their lives. They find themselves in a lonely, vulgar mental pigsty, and awake the next morning feeling guilty and disappointed in themselves.

How can Christians who are filled with the Holy Spirit and who want to follow Jesus become addicted to the filth of this world by looking at pornography on the Internet, in magazines, and on television? I think this happens when Christians start valuing the Father for what He can do for them rather than what He can be in their lives through His love and intimacy. This leads to people seeing the fulfillment of their own selfish desires as being more important than the joy they experience when they are in relationship with God, their heavenly Father.

Where I live in the Netherlands, we are known around the world for our pornography, sex shops, bad language, suggestive photos, and the prostitutes who sit behind the windows of the buildings in the Red Light District selling their services. There are even "Open Days" where anyone, including families, can visit these brothels and sex shops to find out what they are about. The annual Gay Parade, which is held on boats on the canals traversing Amsterdam, was visited by half a million people in 2007. Even the mayor was involved in the parade and was very angry with those who did not agree with the parade being held.

Our whole culture, like many others worldwide, is sliding into the gutter, and one day we will regret allowing this to happen.

The emptiness someone feels inside is meant to be a place we allow God to fill, not our own selfish desires. If we live according to what the flesh wants, we will start moving in a downward spiral until we realize that what we have been chasing after to satisfy our lusts is only temporary and does not make us happy.

Only then will people realize that they have a deep desire for love and intimacy—a deep human need only God can fill. This is why it's important for us, as Christians who know the presence of God and what it is like to be loved and cared for by a loving Father, to reach out to the lost. We need to show them how to reach out to God for themselves and build a relationship with Him that will ultimately give them what they are looking for: peace and the sense of belonging and being loved.

A HOLY LIFE

I think we should be more aware of the relationship between living holy lives and our longing to see revival in both our own lives and in our nations. Seeing God's glory and, as a result, real transformation, can only happen if we lead holy lives.

This is something we see, for example, in the lives of Ananias and Sapphira in Acts 5. There was a revival taking place in their land and there was a healthy fear of God, His holiness, and His glory among the people. The presence of God was so strong that people were selling their homes and fields and laying the money they received for them at the feet of the disciples so they in turn could help other Christians.

This is also what Ananias and Sapphira did, but they tried to deceive God. They told Peter that the money they were giving him was the entire amount they had received from the sale, but they had held part of the money back for themselves. Had they told the truth, there would have been no problem; but the fact that they lied in the powerful presence of God caused them both to fall down dead.

Ananias and Sapphira, after they had been born again, were knowingly living in sin during a time of revival. In Hebrews 10:26 it tells us, *"If we deliberately keep on sinning after we have received the knowledge of the truth, no sacrifice for sins is left."* I find this a powerful statement from God's Word, but I think it brings a healthy balance between mercy and the holiness of God. We must repent, and yes, God is forgiving, but there are also boundaries to His forgiveness if we keep on sinning and show no sorrow for the sins we have committed.

If we have left the house of our heavenly Father and forsaken our intimate relationship with Him, we must listen to that still, small voice within us saying, "Beware! You are about to fall into a trap! You are about to hurt those nearest to you!" If we ignore this warning, we will not only lose our intimate relationship with God, but we will start trying to replace it with what I can only call the false intimacy one finds in this world. It can start with one thought, but can lead to our doing things and becoming addicted to things that cause us to live, as the lost son did, in mental pigpens where we feel dirty, lonely, and ashamed.

How can it happen that well-intentioned children of God can find themselves in situations similar to a pigpen? I think that through discouragement and false expectations, jealousy and lies, even the most committed Christians, the mighty men and women of God, can lose their intimate relationship with Him. They find themselves in a place of deep sin and feel that they cannot repair the damage they have done.

The mental pigsty, the place of shame and self-condemnation, becomes their new spiritual home. It will remain so until they realize that the place where they belong, where their emptiness, shortcomings, and needs will be met, is in God's love. The way back is the way of repentance and returning to the Father and to let Him embrace them. He is still watching for their return. He longs to say to each one of them, "Welcome, My son, My daughter, at last you are home."

It was at his deepest point of sorrow that the lost son realized that he had made mistakes and that he needed to change. In place of, "Give me. Give me!" he changed his request to, "Change me. Change me!" If we read further in the Book of Luke, chapter 15, then again we will be surprised at the patience and love of the returning son's father. What love this father had for his son! Before he had even left him and his home to go into the world, the father had already forgiven him. His love for his son was not based on his behavior.

Even when we are unfaithful to God, our heavenly Father, He remains faithful to us and will always love us. We read in Second Timothy 2:13, *"if we are faithless, He remains faithful, for He cannot disown Himself."* And in Jeremiah 31:3 it says, *"I have loved you with an everlasting love; I have drawn you with unfailing kindness."*

When we fail, the Father comes to us with outstretched arms. If we show remorse and repent, He is ready to welcome us back into His embrace with love and forgiveness. Through our pride and reticent behavior, we can stop this from happening and the guilt for the wrong things we have done follows us. The lost son said, "I am no longer worthy to be your son." The son said this, not the father. Nevertheless, the father welcomed the son and accepted him back into his household, treating him like royalty. He gave him the best clothing, a golden ring as his inheritance, and had the fattened calf slaughtered in order to hold a feast to celebrate his lost son's return.

SHAME AND GUILT

Then the man and his wife heard the sound of the Lord God as He was walking in the garden in the cool of the day, and they hid from the Lord God among the trees of the garden (Genesis 3:8).

Many children of God are living under the yoke of judgment and shame because of the sins they have committed in the past. They are embarrassed before God and hide from Him, something that began in the Garden of Eden.

When Christians fall into sin they immediately feel as if they have failed. This failure often leads to feelings of shame and guilt because they have fallen short of God's expectations of them. These feelings lead to anxiety: anxiety that they won't be accepted, anxiety that they will be rejected, anxiety that the sin will be revealed to others, and anxiety about God's judgment. The natural reaction to this anxiety is to hide, and that often leads to isolation and loneliness.

When Adam and Eve sinned in the Garden of Eden, they became imprisoned in this cycle and tried to hide themselves from God. God the Father visited them in the cool of the evening to spend time talking, laughing, and just being with them. Man was the crown on God's creation.

It must have been a dark day for God when He entered the Garden one evening and realized something was wrong. Adam and Eve did not come forward to meet Him as they usually did. He called out to them, but they had hidden themselves from Him, overcome with embarrassment and remorse. An unfamiliar, strained, and unwelcoming atmosphere filled the place. They had eaten fruit from the Tree of the Knowledge of Good and Evil, the only tree God had told them not to eat from and, overcome with guilt and shame, they had lost their innocence.

The devil had deceived them and led them into sin. Their shame led them to pick fig leaves to cover their nakedness. The spiritual manifests in the natural; today Christians don't use real fig leaves to cover their sins, but rather spiritual fig leaves such as hyper-religious activities, to try and hide their real selves.

Right now God wants to change our fig leaves and shame for robes of righteousness. He wants to place His ring on our finger and return us to our rightful place as His sons and daughters in His family, complete and restored.

Hear God's words as He calls out to you, "My child, I love you. Return to Me and everything will be all right. Don't give up; I will always be with you."

PRAY THIS PRAYER

Please pray this prayer:

"Dear heavenly Father. Thank You for Your love that passes all understanding. I long to return to Your house. I confess my sins. Please forgive me for placing more value on what You can do for me than on having an intimate relationship with You. I have been focused more on what is in Your hand than what is in Your heart. I have taken from You and given in to my lusts and desires. I have left Your house to follow after my own desires and interests, and have sinned. I now long to return to You. Today I make the decision to leave the pigsty of sin and shame. Please let me feel Your compassion. Run to me, welcome

me back as Your child with love and outstretched arms.
Restore me to Your love, Father, in Jesus' name. Amen."

The good news is that we can once more walk with God and communicate with Him the way Adam and Eve did every evening. We so often hear about their fall from God's grace, and the dreadful consequences of their disobedience; but Jesus, the Son of God, died to pay the price for our sins so we may be reconciled to God our Father. Jesus is the way to the Father, and all barriers between us and Him have been destroyed.

Once again, in our newly restored innocence, we can walk with God. What wonderful news! The glory has been restored! Let us come out from behind the trees and bushes where we have been hiding from Him; let us be ourselves and once more walk with our God. God is currently giving many dreams, prophecies, and visions to His children. He wants to remove any spiritual fig leaves and other stumbling blocks from our lives. Can you dare to dream God's dreams for your life and then go and achieve them?

I heard this story recently about someone's aunt who is a potter. He was visiting her, and she had made him a lovely pot. He placed the pot carefully in his bag saying he would put it on his windowsill as soon as he got home. His aunt was a little upset. She told him it was a pot made to contain honey, and when he got home he should place honey in the pot because that was its purpose and the reason she had made it.

The pot was made by its creator to fulfill a specific purpose—just as God made each of us to fulfill a specific purpose. If you follow Him, He will show you exactly what this purpose is.

ENDNOTE

1. Dr. Archibald D. Hart, *The Sexual Man: Masculinity Without Guilt* (Nashville: Thomas Nelson, 1995).

CHAPTER 14

PREGNANT WITH DREAMS AND VISIONS

God can make you spiritually pregnant with a dream or vision. To get pregnant in the natural, there needs to be an ovum and a spermatozoa, otherwise impregnation is not possible. Mary was impregnated with a seed from God that was planted in her by the Holy Spirit. A heavenly conception took place and Jesus, the Son of God, was born.

You have in you a spiritual egg waiting to be fertilized by God. Once the impregnation has happened in your spirit, you will be pregnant with a vision or dream to achieve whatever God has planted in your spirit. You cannot forget it because it has become part of you. As in a normal pregnancy when the fruit takes time to grow, so it is in the spiritual when the dream or vision you have conceived will also take time to grow and develop. When the time to deliver the dream or vision arrives, you will need people around you to act as midwives, both men and women, to help you give birth to your dream.

It sounds silly, but I am regularly pregnant with a dream or vision. Eventually people around me begin to recognize I have a new dream or vision just as people know a woman is pregnant when her waistline starts to expand. I have spiritual mothers and fathers around me to help me give birth to my dreams and visions and turn them into reality. After the vision or dream becomes a reality, it needs to be protected from outside influences. Also, you have to make sure no one picks up your newborn dream or vision and runs away with it. This child has been entrusted to you!

At a young age, children sometimes experience dreadful, traumatizing things like violence or abuse. Loving parents will do everything they can to stop this from happening. Unfortunately, there are parents who abuse their own children, with dreadful consequences. This can also be seen in the spiritual realm—spiritual mothers and fathers should not abuse their spiritual children for their own gain, but rather shield them from outside influences, which can be harmful.

VULTURES

Wherever God is working and things are happening, there is fruit. Fruit often attracts the attention of outsiders and the media. Sometimes people come and try to steal the anointing for their own glory. To me they are like vultures that come to steal and destroy. These are imitation Christians who come to a place where the anointing of God is strong and they try and get involved, sometimes with hostility, in the anointing or the movement.

They appear to be very pleasant at first, but soon disappear when things get too hot for them or they have damaged something. They then move on to the next scene, and their pictures are often seen in their newsletters making it look as if they personally were responsible for making the dream become a reality. They even try and raise money or get attention by pretending the vision was theirs and that the anointing to achieve it rests on them.

This type of activity is detestable as the growth process of the project or dream can stagnate and the movement of God can become dirtied. Therefore, be careful who you trust and confide in. Unfortunately, people are not always as honest or well-meaning as they first seem to be.

TOUCH NOT GOD'S ANOINTED

You will know you are on the way to spiritual maturity when you are not only walking in your destiny and achieving your own God-given dreams, but you also become a "spiritual midwife" and help someone else to birth their dreams and visions. This is part of the circle God has created; it cannot be stopped.

One thing that worries me is that I see many dreams and visions that God has given to others fail to become reality. In the last few years I have seen many projects and movements of God start off well, but come to nothing. In each such case, I have, when possible, asked all parties involved what happened, and there is a similarity among all of them.

In every case, on their way to maturity (and some were already mature), those who had given birth to the vision or the movement, those who were the pioneers or had set up a work, were pushed out by people within the movement, with devastating consequences. In every case, the people in administration had control over the important things within the organization and wanted to exercise control over the ministry. By doing this, they worked the person who was originally given the dream or vision out of the organization.

People who work in administration, including bookkeepers, managers, and administrative staff, all have a servant role to play in the organization; but too often they sabotage moves in God's Kingdom. They are often the reason that there are so many splits and so much disunity in an organization, leaving many of God's children wounded. This tactic is a powerful weapon that satan uses to destroy the things of God.

I ask you most urgently to have nothing to do with these things; make sure you do nothing to jeopardize the position of a person who has brought a dream, vision, or any other work of God, to fruition. In Psalm 105:15 God says, *"Do not touch my anointed ones...."* If you don't obey this command, you will most certainly have God's wrath upon you. You see, the person who sets up a work or ministry still has God's anointing and favor on his or her life. It is painful at first for the person who is pushed out of leadership through the betrayal of those he or she trusted; but after a while the person will begin a new work, and that too will flourish, quite often bearing more fruit than the original work.

What if a founder of a ministry sins and shows no remorse? In this situation, I would advise that if the sinner does not change after several warnings and admonitions, that you remove yourself from the situation. God Himself will judge the situation; don't devise any plots to remove the person from the position yourself. This is my suggestion after seeing many disastrous results from this sort of intervention. Rather, keep yourself busy with whatever God has given you to do and mind your own business.

YOU CANNOT ACHIEVE YOUR DREAM ALONE

No one can achieve their dreams by themselves. God always wants other people involved.

At our TRIN head office, we have many full-time staff, but whenever we have a new applicant for a job, the first thing we ask is what we can do to help them achieve their dreams. If we feel that their dream fits in with ours, we always work together to help them achieve it.

For example, some people who came to work at TRIN had the same idea about setting up a partnership system like those we read about in the Bible. That sounded like an enormous task, but within five months TRIN had 600 new partners.

Someone else dreamed of setting up a better bookkeeping system and another dreamed of having teams prophesying over people in the streets. Someone else wanted to build orphanages, and yet others wanted to start prayer evenings. As we helped each other achieve our various dreams, it was a mutually beneficial situation.

This is how we help each other build God's Kingdom. Giving others the room they need to bring their dreams to fruition often leads to them reaching their goals. All I do is see the potential every person has, then acknowledge it and encourage them. I then give them the room to develop their potential and achieve their goals.

Sometimes I see TRIN as a large car God has given to me and my wife. Others can ride in the car and even learn how to drive the car so that they can eventually drive their own cars and start their own ministries. This is the way we work, and it works well because when people are given the chance to achieve their dreams, they come to life!

I have seen people come into the offices feeling totally hopeless. They had many problems, and some even considered committing suicide or were battling with depression. After a few discussions with them during which we tried to identify what the person wanted to do, we then gave them positive input, so they could, within the boundaries of TRIN, have the opportunity to develop, make mistakes, and learn to take responsibility.

Within three months they become completely different people, full of hope with new friends, a new vision, and shiny eyes! This new outlook led to doors opening both within and outside of TRIN. I have sometimes worked with people who stayed only a short time but left completely refreshed and wanting to start a new ministry by themselves. When this happens, there is only happiness in my heart, not jealousy or a feeling of competition.

I always laugh and cry when the time comes for people to leave TRIN and strike out on their own. I laugh because I am proud of them and cry because I will miss them. This is God's heart; He wants each of us to come alive. What a glorious change would happen within a congregation if the leadership team had face-to-face meetings with every church member to find out what their dreams and visions are, and then asked how they and the congregation could help them achieve their dreams.

This is a Kingdom attitude, and it breaks the hold of religious, controlling, or passive spirits. It sets people free and allows them to become all that God intends them to be without leaving their churches in search of other churches that would be willing to help them achieve their God-given goals.

People know they are in the right place when they feel they have come to life and found their purpose. This is something we cannot do for them, but we can provide opportunities for them.

PREPARATION TIME

It is possible that we have personally not yet reached the right time to birth the dream or vision God has given us. This is healthy and normal, or as it says in Ecclesiastes 3:1, *"There is a time for everything."*

There are also seasons during which we must learn and develop. If this is where you are, search for others who have similar dreams to yours, then dedicate and invest yourself in helping these people bring their dreams to fruition. This is an important key to seeing your own dreams become a reality.

Before I could live out my dream, or achieve my God-given purpose, I served many other people who had dreams and ministries. These were very good learning experiences for me. During this time I worked for: Youth With a Mission, Mercy Ships on the MV *Anastasis,* Derek Prince Ministries, and De Brug. I was the ambassador for Brazilsending (Brazil Mission); I led a team during the Soul Survivor outreach, and many more.

I encourage you to join a team or organization and be faithful to them. Let your yes be yes and your no be no. Strive for a spirit of excellence in everything you do, and be faithful in the small things. God Himself will open new doors for you to achieve bigger things. Not everyone is called to start their own ministry, so if God hasn't called you to do so, remain in the organization where you feel you have been called to serve.

It takes many people, and a lot of hard work, to bring a dream to fruition. There are people at TRIN whose dream and purpose is to work for TRIN, and they plan to work for the organization for the rest of their lives. They have adopted the vision I have for TRIN and do not find it necessary to go elsewhere to achieve a different vision. For me, having these people in my life is wonderful and very, very necessary. By working together, we can go a lot further than if we work alone. Without my faithful TRIN team, I could not achieve my dreams.

Make sure that, whether you are living out your own dream or you have made someone else's dream your own, your attitude to what you are doing remains real and honest. Keep your eyes on Jesus, and make sure you never talk negatively or disparagingly about others because, as you judge, so you will be judged. Make sure you have removed the plank from your own eye before you try and remove a splinter out of someone else's eye. The favor of God will come on your life and God will open new doors for you. He will make you prosperous and successful in all your undertakings. Remember that if God closes a door, it is for your own benefit.

An old saying rings true: When God closes one door He opens many others. God really cares about you; and your future with Him will be both hopeful and happy. Do not give up, prosperous child of God! Go for it!

BETRAYAL

You will, no doubt, experience betrayal as you attempt to live out your dream, and it is one of the most frustrating things that can happen to you. It has been my experience that as you leave your comfort zone and set about doing what God has called you to do (and which gives you a sense of satisfaction), you will automatically have to deal with the jealousy of others.

Unfortunately, the jealousy will not come from those who are in the world; they will not be your neighbors, or non-believing friends, but your close circle of Christian acquaintances. When TRIN became a reality in the Netherlands, some Christian leaders in the country spoke very negatively about what I was doing. These were leaders with a lot of influence in various churches and other organizations.

One evening, I suddenly felt a tremendous pain in my back. It was so bad I had to go to a hospital to find out what was wrong. The next day a pastor from Rotterdam, the place where I was born, telephoned me to tell me that the previous day he had been to a meeting where several Christian leaders had been present. Both I and TRIN were discussed in a very ugly manner. This had a spiritual and physical affect on my body because the pain I experienced in my body happened at exactly the same time they started talking about me.

Not one of the negative-speaking people had ever attended a TRIN meeting or tried to contact me in order to start a relationship. I made the decision to forgive these leaders and, as I blessed them, the pain disappeared. Fortunately, I was later able to meet these leaders, and we were not only able to discuss our different points of views, but were also able to lay the foundations for a deep and lasting relationship with each other.

I think few Christians, including leaders, have any idea of how powerful their words are. We are called upon to bless one another; but if we talk negatively about each other, we curse each other. As a leader, I call upon leaders to stop betraying others by talking badly about them. Stop being jealous. Become a humble servant, someone who washes the feet of others.

A 2010 Update

Along with my friend and brother-in-law, Jop van der Bijl, we founded Revival Alliance Network. The focus of this fast-growing organization and its members is to bring about revival and transformation. By not giving up, always staying humble, and being respectful to other leaders, God gave us their favor and trust. So regardless of the negative things leaders or others may say about you, if you know you are walking according to God's will for your life, do not give up. Try and share your heart with the leaders who do not understand you; and, if possible, spend time with them and let God do the rest.

A JUDAS IN YOUR LIFE

Sometimes God allows things to happen in your life to teach you how to bless your enemies. This is what David did as he eluded the spear Saul threw at him twice, and in love, stayed silent.

Betrayal is always painful. It is a very traumatic experience; but with the right attitude in your heart, you will emerge from the pain a stronger person. Even Jesus was betrayed. He had built very strong relationships with His disciples, and He called them His friends. He chose them, was with them day and night for three years, and they became His best friends. He spent more time with His disciples than He did with His mother or other family members. He gave them as much training as He could so that when His Father called Him home, they could take over His ministry. He taught them many things about God's Kingdom and how they could establish it here on Earth. He taught them about anointing and character.

It was one of the darker times in Jesus' life when, as He sat eating with the disciples one evening, Judas excused himself and went off to tell the Roman soldiers where they could find Him. To tell the soldiers which man was Jesus, he would kiss Jesus on the cheek. I believe this caused Jesus deep pain even though He knew it was going to happen to Him. His friend, with whom He had spent three years and whom He had taught so much, betrayed Him in return for a small sum of money.

A few hours after Judas betrayed Jesus, he committed suicide. It was Jesus' silence, His unwillingness to defend Himself that convicted Judas about the terrible thing he had done.

When those you trust the most and whom you least expect to betray you do just that, it will cause you considerable pain. Judas held an important position among Jesus' disciples as he was the one who looked after the money matters; he was the bookkeeper for the group. Betrayal, unfortunately, often occurs through people with important servant roles in ministry. They smell power and become jealous of the one whose dream or vision they are helping to achieve, and are often people who do not love themselves.

I experienced this in an organization I worked for years ago. There were Judases who accused my employer of wrongdoing that they themselves had done. Years later, my employer found out that those accusing him were guilty of doing the same thing.

I followed my employer for years after this to see how he dealt with this betrayal and what he had learned from it. I found out that not only was he a lot stronger from having to face the crisis, but he had learned to know himself better and found out who his real friends were. His relationship with God is now a lot deeper and more intense, and he has a very successful ministry. I learned from him to never be bitter, to bless and forgive my enemies, to distance myself from the situation, to not give way to the pain, and to move closer to Jesus.

I have also experienced incredibly painful betrayal by people in ministry whom I considered to be my friends. They wrote malicious letters and made vindictive phone calls to plant doubts about my integrity. Of course God is a God of righteousness and He came and quickly put a stop to the hurtful situation.

However, the feeling of being betrayed went deep into my family and our ministry team's heart, and it took almost a year to completely forgive and release the perpetrators of this potentially destructive plot from any condemnation or judgment from our side.

Chester and Betsy Kylstra from Restoring the Foundations in Hendersonville, North Carolina, helped us through this difficult period and through them we learned several new tools to help us work with the Holy Spirit to deal with betrayal and learn to trust again. We learned to stand on the promises of God, to unmask the ungodly lies we were told, and to replace them with God's truth.

In the long run, this experience has ultimately made us much stronger in the Lord. Our ministry is growing faster and bearing a lot more fruit. Remember, you may have an encounter with a Judas, but handling it successfully can make you much stronger in the long run.

To be successful in achieving your dreams, you need to be prepared if people within your own camp try and turn others against you. My experience is that God allows these Judas-like people into our lives to strengthen us; and that through it, we actually achieve our goals a lot more quickly. Your attitude in these situations is very important and will influence how well you survive. Don't fight back unnecessarily or insult your adversary; rather bless and forgive them and keep your heart pure, because God will see the way you have chosen to conduct yourself and bless you.

If you have been used as the Judas in someone else's life, you need to ask the person you have hurt to forgive you for the pain and damage you have caused. It could be that you were spiritually blind when you harmed someone else, and by the grace of God He worked all things together for good to come out of the situation. Maybe you are jealous, angry, or even disappointed by the person concerned. Maybe you enjoy hearing that things are not going well with them, or that they are not being successful, or maybe you have said negative things about the person in order to get your own way. If this is the case, then I advise you to put this book down and ask God to forgive your arrogant and proud attitude right now.

Be careful what you say about others, because what comes out of your mouth as judgment and gossip about others will eventually return to you. You cannot sit on God's throne judging others because whatever seeds you sow will eventually bring you a harvest. Remember this: whatever you hear about others is normally only half the truth and secondhand information at best. There are always two sides to a story; but we so often stand ready to judge, just like Judas did, and then have a spirit in us which undermines others. This offends God and removes His presence from us very quickly. It is the spirit that killed Jesus, a spirit of religion, a spirit of treachery and betrayal. Unfortunately, many of us have given room to these spirits to operate in us at some time in our lives.

Repent from these things as they are blockages that stop you from achieving God's plans for your life. God wants you to think positively about people and to bless them, and to react, not according to the way the world thinks, but rather as the Kingdom of God thinks. Fortunately, even though we all make mistakes, God can change us. The Spirit of God in you will teach you to renew the way you think and speak every day.

CHAPTER 15

GO!

J esus said to them:

> ...*Go into all the world and preach the gospel to all creation. Whoever believes and is baptized will be saved, but whoever does not believe will be condemned. And these signs will accompany those who believe: In My name they will drive out demons; they will speak in new tongues; they will pick up snakes with their hands; and when they drink deadly poison, it will not hurt them at all; they will place their hands on sick people, and they will get well* (Mark 16:15-18).

These verses are called the Great Commission and while there is much to say about this, I will limit it to one word, *Go!* As I have said earlier in this book, we often wait for a voice from Heaven or run from conference to conference hoping for a prophetic word to tell us what to do; but if we are born again and filled with the Holy Spirit, God's command to make disciples is for us, and we need to start doing that right now.

If you have given your life to Jesus and are baptized in the Holy Spirit, then the Holy Spirit is able to communicate with your spirit. The Holy Spirit knows everything that is on God's heart and wants to share His secrets with you. He wants to show you the way and teach you how to live according to God's will for your life. During our services, God regularly points out someone to us and it's a joy to prophesy over them. Often it is a confirmation of what God has already placed deep in the heart of the person, and the prophetic word activates the truth of it for them.

If you wonder what to do if you don't get picked out and given a specific word during a service, do not worry. Just listen to the Holy Spirit and do what God has placed on your heart to do. Don't wait for a voice from Heaven to tell you what to do because it will probably never happen! In most instances, you need to take the first step yourself and take responsibility for your own decisions. Then you will see that, as you take a step toward realizing your dream, you will be abundantly blessed and doors will start opening for you.

You do not need a specific calling to love others, to help the widow, to visit and encourage the sick, to send a card to a friend in need of encouragement, or to pray for someone. God has given us everything! His Son, His Holy Spirit, His Word in the Bible, gifts, talents, angels, authority, and faith. What more does He need to give us to persuade us to *Go*? The world is in turmoil, most probably because Christians have not stood up and taken their rightful positions, but instead have become lukewarm toward the things of God. We have locked ourselves in our warm, cozy churches, while outside the world is in dire need and in the process of destroying itself.

BLINDERS ON YOUR EYES

I once had a vision that featured a lovely white house. It was beautifully built and freshly painted. On the roof of the house was a huge, wooden cross. It was Sunday morning and the house was filled with well-dressed people. A wonderful praise and worship band was playing and there was lots of food and drink. I saw many people talking and laughing, and then the church service began.

When the service was over, the doors were opened for people to leave. I saw demons waiting for the churchgoers and putting blinders on their eyes, much in the same way as people put blinders on horses.

From what I could see, sick people were lying on the ground outside the building. I saw worms and maggots coming out of the rotting wounds in their flesh. Children and teenagers were lying helplessly on the ground, writhing and groaning in pain, calling out for someone to help them. There were also people who looked lost and whose eyes were filled with fear and hopelessness. They were dying spiritually because there was no one who cared enough to tell them about the love that God has for them and the sacrifice Jesus made to save them.

As the doors of the house opened and the blinders were put on their eyes, the well-intentioned Christians walked out of the building. They were talking about the music that was a little too loud, the preaching that was excellent, and the way the leadership talked too long about the necessity to give money. While continuing to talk and laugh with each other, they stepped over the bodies of the sick and injured and failed to see the pain and suffering of the spiritually desolate all around them.

They then jovially bid each other good-bye and made their way back to their homes where they would stay, comfortable and going about their business, until the church service the following Sunday.

This vision shocked me deeply. It was a simple example of one of the many buildings that we, as Christians, go into to hide away. We live on our own, safe island of religion. Many of us have become similar to the Dead Sea. We drink from the River of Life, but that life does not flow out of us to give life to others. We keep all the water to ourselves until it eventually turns into a stinking pool of stagnant water.

It is time to take our blinders off and see the world as Jesus sees it. We need to be moved by the need in the world and go look after those nearest to us. There is so much to do, and so much need around us. Everyone can love someone in their own way or extend a hand to help someone in need. Start by doing the small things, and as God sees you are trustworthy, He will give you bigger things to do.

My cry is *Go!* You have received all the power and authority from Jesus that you need to *go* and make a difference in this world.

DO NOT BELIEVE LIES

Many people allow themselves to be influenced by their negative circumstances and start believing the lies and "facts" of this world. One fact I was told at 14 years of age: I could not learn because I had difficulty concentrating. Medical practitioners diagnosed me as having a form of ADHD (attention deficit hyperactivity disorder) but my motto was "Always serve God." No pills can come against that!

As I have written in Chapter 1, I was told it was impossible, because of the ADHD, for me to achieve anything higher than a lower level, technically-orientated course at school. I chose not to believe this and, through faith in God, determination, and a desire to see my dream to be a marine officer fulfilled, I completed a course I was not supposed to have been able to do—and passed. I then went to join Mercy Ships as a marine officer aboard their ship, MV *Anastasis*.

Rebekah, as you have read in her testimony, was surrounded by satanists from the time of her birth. As she went through traumatic times and witnessed despicable actions by those around her, she felt trapped. She longed to be like a butterfly and fly away, leaving behind the bondage she was in; and despite death threats and ongoing harassment, that is exactly what she has done!

Many people believe similar lies about themselves and hear from satan all the reasons why they cannot achieve their dreams. At this point many people stop dreaming and accept the idea that they will never achieve the desires of their hearts, the dreams God has given them.

In Matthew 19:26 Jesus says, *"With man this is impossible, but with God all things are possible."* It's time that we left our old ways of thinking behind and set about renewing our minds. It's time to look at ourselves positively and start believing the promises of God for our lives. Let's close our eyes and imagine not what is now impossible, but what God can make possible.

My question to you is this: How and where do you see yourself in five years' time? Write down your dream, find people who believe in you. Remember that nothing is impossible for God, and that He wants to bless you. There is not enough time to write down all the miracles God has done for us, but through them we have learned that we can trust God to achieve the impossible every day in our lives. Believe it and it will happen to you, too.

FREEDOM FIRE

An example of God doing the impossible happened to us in 2006 when the area we were using to hold our meetings became too small. One week before we were due to hold the Freedom Fire conference, we still had not found a larger facility. I went before the Lord and asked Him for advice about this problem. We had 700 people due to attend the conference including 23 overseas guests; and with our $650 budget, we couldn't even afford to rent a field let alone a hall to accommodate everyone!

Once more I closed my eyes and this time imagined the conference being held in a luxury hotel in the city of Ermelo, not far from our offices in the Netherlands. I then phoned the manager of the hotel and made an appointment to see him. An hour later, I, my leadership team, and several of the conference speakers, went to see the manager. With less than a week to go, it did not seem possible to organize a conference in the hotel's conference facility—but for God it was possible!

After discussing the conference with the manager, I signed a contract for an amount of money I did not have, but it was really unusual that such a wonderful facility was available to us at such short notice, and I felt it was the right thing to do. The conference took place with no problems, and many people were deeply touched by the Lord. During one of the sessions we felt we should take an offering to cover the cost of renting the room, and after counting it we found that it was exactly enough to pay for the conference facility.

Many of those who came to the conference knew that most of our conferences are free, so to be able to attend a conference in this wonderful, but expensive, facility at no cost was a real surprise. When they asked us how we had managed it, the only answer I could give them is that when we believe in the impossible, God will make it possible.

HEAVEN ON EARTH

Another example of God making the impossible possible happened when Rebekah and I were on the island of Hawaii to spend time with our friends, Bob and Kathy Fitts and their family. While they were showing us around the island, Bob was singing a song from a CD they had given us. The song was about all nations of the earth praising God. I quickly closed my eyes and saw a picture of people from every nation seated in a big stadium. They had come together for four days to praise and worship God together.

I shared this picture with Rebekah who had seen something similar while Bob was singing. We talked to God about this and together laid our ideas at His feet. After that we started to react to the pictures practically by writing down on paper what we had seen. Shortly after that, we were invited to Kelowna in Canada to take part in the Eyes and Wings Conference organized by Wesley and Stacey Campbell.

At one point while we were there, we were on a podium along with five other young people. We were all about 30 years old and were accompanied by our spiritual mothers and fathers. I realized that we, as young pioneers, needed to come together regularly, along with our spiritual mothers and fathers, to encourage and help each other, and to receive guidance and instructions from God regarding the parts we would play in the end-time movement. I shared this picture with Stacey and immediately we got out our diaries and decided to meet each other again straight after The Call conference, which was to be held in Nashville, Tennessee, a year later on July 7, 2007.

I then shared the pictures I had seen while Bob was singing. Everyone encouraged me to start working to achieve what I had seen in my dream by taking practical steps as soon as I returned to the Netherlands. Immediately upon my return home I set up a Website, invited other people to come and hear my vision, and eventually a work group was formed. The conference was to be called Heaven on Earth. As God opened the doors for me and I saw the impossible become possible, many international speakers wanted to come and take part in the conference.

It was almost July 7, 2007, and we went to Nashville to attend The Call Conference. It was one of the most inspiring gatherings we have ever attended. About 80,000 people of all ages had decided to come together for 12 hours to fast and pray and to ask God for forgiveness for all the wrong things that had been done in America's past. It was a very impressive time, and we know that God heard us. The prayers of a group of people who go before God wanting to live holy lives, causes the fire of the Holy Spirit to fall and remove the false gods from among them. This leaves space in their lives for God's Spirit to move and, through them, to reach out to touch others with God's fire and love.

What really moved me was how Christians took responsibility for things that had gone wrong and sins that had been committed in the land.

After this experience at The Call, we went to Kelowna to meet up with the others as planned. It was good to see 20 young pioneers from all around the world, along with their spiritual parents, attend the meeting. Lou Engle, Mike Bickle, James Goll, Dutch Sheets, and Wesley and Stacey Campbell attended the meeting, too. During the times of prayer, the Holy Spirit came in power, and history was written in the hearts of the young pioneers and their spiritual parents. I shared my vision with them of a stadium and a conference that would be attended by people from many nations. The favor of God opened the doors and everyone encouraged me to keep dreaming and to turn the dream into a reality.

A 2010 UPDATE

I did keep going, and God did turn the dream into a reality! In May 2008 at the Ahoy sports stadium in Rotterdam, we held our first giant Heaven on Earth conference with 7,500 people from many nations attending and many national and international speakers taking part. The Holy Spirit and God's presence were tangible, and many were blessed and touched during this special time.

In May 2009 we held the second Heaven on Earth conference, this time in Zwolle in the Netherlands, and thousands of people attended and again heard many national and international speakers preaching. Many were saved, healed, and set free from bondage as they accepted Jesus Christ as their Savior. Heidi Baker baptized dozens of people during one of our services and we give all the glory to God for the wonderful things He is doing through the dream he gave to both Rebekah and me.

In May 2010 we held our third Heaven on Earth Conference, this time in the city of Ede here in the Netherlands. Once again God, our faithful, merciful Father, was present and signs and wonders manifested as we went before Him in gratitude for all that He continues to do among us.

This proves that if you can see the invisible, as we did, that God can do the impossible—so why are you waiting? Start dreaming and stop thinking that your dream will never become a reality. God wants to bless everyone with the blessings of Abraham, Isaac, and Jacob—if you are a child of God, this favor and blessing are on your life. It is the favor and blessing that open the doors to bring you to a higher level. He wants to promote you and bless you with all good things.

PETER AND PAUL

Let's look at two great examples from the Bible: two normal Christians with normal daily cares, but as they went about their normal lives, God used them powerfully.

Let's first look at the life of Peter. After the outpouring of the Holy Spirit in the upper room where Jesus' disciples were gathered, Peter was empowered to preach the Gospel, and 3,000 people accepted Jesus as their Savior. After this, according to Acts 9, Peter set out to travel to various towns and villages to encourage and pray for the people.

In a town called Lydda in Israel, with only a few thousand residents, Peter heard from the new Christians that there was a man who had been lame for eight years and that he spent his days lying on a mat. His name was Aeneas. Peter immediately went to his home, probably with many of the new converts following him. When he entered the house and saw Aeneas, he took him by the hand and said, *"Jesus Christ heals you. Get up and roll up your mat"* (Acts 9:34). Immediately the power of God streamed through Aeneas' body, and he was healed. I can just imagine that Aeneas would have started to jump and dance and praise God, and the new Christians would have run out of the house to tell the whole town what had happened.

We read in the Bible that all the residents of Lydda, as well as the nearby town of Sharon, accepted Jesus as their Savior after witnessing the healing miracle God had done for Aeneas.

This would not have happened if Peter had not been prepared to leave his comfort zone and go to the towns and villages, then meet Aeneas and pray for him. Then the news of the resulting miracle persuaded thousands of people to accept Jesus as their Savior. I invite you to be like Peter; step out of your comfort zone, do what you feel God is telling you to do, and see the miracles happen. It's that simple.

RAISED FROM THE DEAD

We also read in the Bible that friends of Peter's who lived in Jaffa, a few hours walk from Lydda, on hearing he was in their neighborhood, immediately went to him. A woman in their community, who had always looked after the poor, had died. Her name was Dorcas, and she not only looked after the widows and orphans, but made clothing for them, too. She had died at a relatively young age and the entire neighborhood was deeply upset. As her body lay wrapped in burial clothing and surrounded by grieving women, Peter's friends went to fetch him.

When he arrived at the house, he sent all the grieving women out of the room.

Peter knelt before the lifeless body, looked at God instead of what so clearly lay in front of him, and took Dorcas' cold, lifeless hand in his. The power of God immediately started to stream through Dorcas and she began to breathe again. She slowly got up and sat on the edge of the bed, then walked to the kitchen to make Peter and his friends something to eat (see Acts 9:38-42).

The whole village celebrated the wonderful miracle that had happened, and many believed and accepted Jesus as their Savior. Even today God is healing people and resurrecting people from the dead, and God wants to use you to do miracles like these. There is the need to see God's hand everywhere, from the supermarket to the school playground, and even where you work. God will use you to demonstrate His power and love in places like these. All you have to do is *go!*

A WRECKED SHIP

In another example, in Acts chapters 27 and 28, we see Paul on a ship with prisoners and soldiers. He was on his way to Rome in Italy where he would ultimately die. The ship was well-built and had capable, experienced men sailing it.

The soldiers on the ship guarded the prisoners but treated them harshly. Because he had the favor of God resting upon him, Paul was treated well. On their way to Italy, a giant storm blew over the ocean and the ship tossed and rolled on the waves. Panic broke out among every one except Paul who had a dream in which an angel told him about the storm and that everyone would survive. He kept his eyes on the Lord and remembered the stories the disciples had told him. They had told him about being in a boat during an enormous storm and how panic had broken out among them, and as they cried out to Jesus to help them, the storm was stilled.

From this Paul learned that when a storm occurs, he should not panic, but rather put his trust in the Lord. The storm got worse and eventually the ship broke into pieces and all those who had been sailing in it were left clinging to wreckage that was floating in the water.

A SNAKE BITE

Due to the favor of God on Paul, everyone had survived the drama of the wrecked ship and made it safely onto dry land, the island of Malta. The people who lived on Malta quickly came to the shipwrecked people's aid and did what they could to help them. Paul and the others were soaked, so they decided to make a big fire to warm themselves.

As Paul gathered wood for the fire, a poisonous viper attached itself to his hand and bit him. Immediately the Holy Spirit reminded him of Jesus' words, now recorded in the Gospel of Mark:

> And these signs will accompany those who believe... they will pick up snakes with their hands; and when they drink deadly poison, it will not hurt them at all... (Mark 16:17-18).

The residents of Malta, the Roman soldiers, and Paul's fellow prisoners stood rooted to the ground. They were all waiting for Paul to fall down dead. This did not happen, and not even his hand or arm was swollen. The news of this miracle spread like wildfire around the island until it reached the ears of Publius, the governor of Malta.

He invited Paul and his fellow travelers to stay with him in his large, luxurious home for three days. Publius' father was terminally ill and he asked Paul if he would go and pray for him. Paul went to the ill man, laid his hands on him, and as he started to pray, the power of God flowed through the old man's sick body and he was healed. After this miracle, all the sick people on the island were brought to Paul for prayer and all of them were healed.

After that, another boat was found for Paul and his fellow passengers to continue their trip to Rome; they left Malta loaded with gifts and other riches the people had given them.

Both Peter and Paul had lived their lives as normal citizens and were not moved by negative circumstances. The environment they found themselves in did not affect them, but rather they affected their environment. They went, they kept their eyes upon Jesus, they remembered His words, and they applied His words to their situations in practical ways.

LIFEBOAT OR CRUISE SHIP?

As a maritime officer, I sailed on various ships; I know former colleagues who were fortunate enough to sail on cruise ships. The ships were luxurious and only the best food and drink was served to the passengers on board.

These ships regularly sailed past the poorest countries in the world and, while people lay dying of hunger on the beaches, the ship passed by in luxury and splendor. Just as I saw in my vision of the white house, churches have to be careful not to become cruise ships instead of lifeboats. The purpose of the Church is to rescue people from spiritual death, a hell that really exists.

Are we prepared to roll up our sleeves and get dirty rescuing people who are outside the Church and drowning spiritually, or are we going to remain inside our churches and pretend they don't exist or are not our business? One day we will face God and will have to give an account of ourselves, both what we did, and what we should have done but didn't do, while we were here on Earth. Yes, I believe in God's mercy and forgiveness, but I also believe He will judge us for neglecting to do what we should have done. Have a look at Matthew 25:31-46, and you will see what is expected of you. Then read the following:

> Then I heard the voice of the Lord saying, "Whom shall I send? And who will go for us?" And I said, "Here am I. Send me!" He said, "Go..." (Isaiah 6:8-9).

As God's eyes look for those He can send, be the one to shout out, "Yes, Lord, here I am! Send me!" and ask the Lord of the harvest how you can be useful to His Kingdom.

YOU ARE A WINNER!

Do not let your past determine your future. You cannot be an overcomer with a victim mentality. Speak words of victory instead of failure over your life. You were born a winner, born to live a truly great life, and created to succeed.

It all began at your conception when the sperm from your father raced for the egg that had been released in your mother's womb. The strongest sperm cell got there first, fertilized the egg, and you were created! You were a winner from the very beginning. Congratulations!

Since then, satan and the world have tried to destroy you by telling you various lies about yourself. However, the truth is that you are valuable, perfectly made, have a good heart, and God wants to bless you. If this is not the way you see yourself, break out of the negative, vicious cycle you are in and start seeing yourself the way God sees you.

To get over any victim mentality you may have, start being thankful for what you do have. Write a list of at least ten things you are grateful for. Things like having fresh water to drink. (Do you know that two thirds of the world does not have access to fresh drinking water and that every day 30,000 children die from the lack of clean water to drink?)

Thank God that you have a roof over your head because millions of people don't. Instead, they spend their lives homeless and begging.

Be grateful that you are healthy and that you can buy fresh bread every day. Be grateful that you perhaps have a small garden, clean clothes, a cell phone, etc.

CHRISTIAAN

One of my heroes is someone named Christiaan. From his birth he has had physical problems that have confined him to a wheelchair; at times he can hardly speak. Some people avoid him and cannot talk to him because they find his situation difficult to deal with.

Christiaan could have chosen to spend his life locked away in his room being miserable, bitter, lonely, and thinking about the things he couldn't do. He could have spent his life blaming God and others for the unfairness of his situation—but he didn't. Instead, he made the decision to ignore what he didn't have and couldn't do and to focus on what he did have and what he can do.

Several years ago he heard about the desperate need of those living in the aftermath of the war in Kosovo. He cried when he heard about the terrible things that had happened to the widows and orphans there and came, in his wheelchair, to ask me what he could do to help them.

After talking to him, he came up with the idea of raising money through a sponsored ride in his wheelchair around the town of Voorthuizen where he lived. He then went ahead and raised sponsorship funds, did the ride, and raised several hundred dollars to send to Kosovo to help the widows and orphans.

We took Christiaan to Kosovo so that he could hand over the money he had raised from the sponsored ride himself. He made his way in his wheelchair over the sandy path between bombed houses with tears in his eyes. He handed the money to the widows and remaining children and, in doing so, made a great impression on us all.

In the Netherlands, the press heard about him and wrote articles about his efforts to help the war victims in Kosovo. Now, several years later, Christiaan has grown spiritually and has become a well-known person who is often written about in newspapers or featured on radio programs.

His sponsored ride has now become an annual event and not only goes throughout the Netherlands but into Belgium as well. He has raised many thousands of dollars and helped many Kosovarans rebuild their lives.

What has been just as important as his money to those needing help in Kosovo is Christiaan's attitude. They have learned from him not to look at what they don't have or what they can't do, but rather to look at what they do have and what they can do. Through Christiaan they have learned that giving is one of the most important things anyone can do.

What can you do to help someone?

GIVE AWAY WHAT YOU DO NOT HAVE

The widows in Kosovo lost everything in the war: their husbands, their homes, and their hopes for the future. In fact, their entire future looked dark and depressing, until they realized that they could not let their pasts dictate their futures. This became obvious when they heard about the desperate plight of orphans in Uganda. When we showed them pictures of the home we were building for the founder of the children's village there, Joseph Lubega, they decided to work with other widows and their children to do something to help the children in Uganda.

Please realize that these women get less than $76 a month to live on, which is far too little to meet all their needs. They could have been miserable, unhappy, and felt hard done by; instead they decided to give away part of their income to help Ugandan orphans. When Joseph heard of their generosity, he said these wonderful, true words: "They have learned the secret of giving away what they do not have, and that gives life."

Giving of ourselves is often painful, but Christiaan and these Kosovaran widows are wonderful examples. If you meet the widows now, you will see faces that shine with the love of God and lives filled with the Holy Spirit and joy. They have chosen to exchange their negative, traumatized thoughts for God's thoughts. They have begun to think positively and are acting from this place within themselves that has changed their lives completely.

MAKE A DECISION

Make a decision today to leave behind your victim mentality and self-pity. Get up and go and help someone out of their pain or need. Go to a retirement or nursing home and hug and help an elderly person. Help a neighbor. Write a lovely card to someone who needs a word of encouragement, or sponsor a child in a third world country. React to every negative thing in an opposite, positive spirit.

If someone insults us or does something wrong to us, our first thought is to say or do something unpleasant to them in return. It would be better, however, to react in the opposite spirit by training our thoughts to do God's will and to bless them instead. Often, instead of blessing others, we gossip about them, which negatively influences our thoughts. At times, the Christian world looks like a battlefield where there is little trust and far too many people are damaged by the lack of mutual love. No wonder Paul wrote the following:

> For the entire law is fulfilled in keeping this one command: "Love your neighbor as yourself." If you bite and devour each other, watch out or you will be destroyed by each other (Galatians 5:14-15).

Make the decision today to love each other (love is a decision, not an emotion), and follow the biblical principle of forgiving each other, and bless even your worst enemy. By doing this you will change your life forever.

CHAPTER 16

YOUR CALLING, IDENTITY, AND TIME IN THE DESERT

Perhaps, after reading this book you will say, "Mattheus, I don't really have a vision or dream, or even a calling on my life—in fact, sometimes I think God doesn't even know I exist. Maybe I'm really not important to Him."

Or you may be on the point of giving up on your dream because it seems too difficult to achieve, and every time you try to progress toward achieving it, things get worse instead of better!

For these reasons I am going to use this last chapter to try and clear up any remaining confusion about your calling, destiny, and what to do when you seem to have arrived in a spiritually dry and desolate desert.

YOUR CALLING AND IDENTITY

In Genesis, we see the calling God gave to Adam and Eve:

...Be fruitful and increase in number and fill the water in the seas, and let the birds increase on the earth (Genesis 1:22).

...Be fruitful and increase in number; fill the earth and subdue it. Rule over the fish in the sea and the birds in the sky and over every living creature that moves on the ground (Genesis 1:28).

In verse 26 it is written: *"Let us make mankind in our image, in our likeness, so that they may rule...."*

As we know, Adam and Eve lost their mandate because they sinned. In Genesis 3:3 God tells Adam and Eve not to eat fruit from the Tree of the Knowledge of Good and Evil, saying, *"...you must not touch it, or you will die."* However, in Genesis 3:4 satan introduces doubt into Eve's mind by saying, *"You will **not** certainly die."* In verse 5, satan goes on to say that if they eat the fruit they "will be like God."

Unfortunately, Adam and Eve did not understand that they were created in God's image and that He had called and anointed them to rule over the earth. As a result, when satan tempted them to eat fruit from the Tree of the Knowledge of Good and Evil in order to "be like God," they sinned by eating it, fell from grace, and lost their God-given calling.

Jesus, who is often described as the second Adam, later paid the price for their and mankind's sins by dying on the cross. This means that the mandate Adam and Eve had to rule, subdue, fill the earth, rule over it, etc., has been restored; it is now our responsibility to carry it out.

If you wrestle with your identity and do not know or realize who you are in God's eyes or that you, too, are created in His image, you may also have lost your way or taken things into your own hands and it hasn't worked out. You may feel as if the darkness has overwhelmed you or that your wings have been clipped and you are unable to fly.

Maybe you even feel imprisoned and far from reaching your destiny, much as Joseph must have felt at times during his exile in Egypt.

If this is how you feel, then let me pray for you right now. "Dear Lord Jesus, in *Your* name I rebuke every lie and proclaim victory and breakthrough in every area in the life of the person reading this. Right now Holy Spirit please confirm to the reader that he or she is paid for with the blood of Jesus, made in God's image, and that he or she is created to rule on Earth as a king and priest. I also ask, Holy Spirit, that You would open up the heavens above this reader and let the words *My beloved* be heard in his or her spirit. Amen."

Please remember, that no matter where you are in your walk with God, Jesus has paid the price to redeem you from any sin you may have committed or any presumption you may have made. Repent and submit to the Holy Spirit and you will have a much clearer idea of who you are in God's eyes, what authority you have, and what your calling is.

INTO THE DESERT

What happens when you know you have a calling on your life, you know you have received the anointing from the Holy Spirit to do what you have been called to do, and you have received prophetic words to confirm it, but just the opposite seems to be happening in your life?

You get frustrated, doubt your calling and prophetic words, and after several years of walking in the desert, you are ready to abandon your dreams and go back to living a "normal" life again. Does this sound familiar?

Recently I have been sharing this scenario with the congregations I preach to in various churches; then I ask them if they ever feel like abandoning their dreams. Normally more than 75 percent of the people raise their hands; but during ministry time afterward, the Holy

Spirit moves powerfully on them, reigniting their passion to once again rise up and pursue their dreams.

Let's take a final look at the stories of some of the powerful men and women in the Bible who faced similar situations, how they reacted, and what ultimately happened to them.

David was one of these people, and we first read about him when he is a young boy. He was the youngest of eight brothers who loved the Lord passionately and worked in a field every day tending his father's sheep. One day the prophet Samuel, at God's bidding, visited David's family, released God's anointing on David's life, and then prophesied that he would become the king of Israel (see 1 Sam. 16:13).

David was excited and told his brothers he had been anointed to be the king of Israel. He received a less-than-enthusiastic response from them. (Here we see that God's favor on David's life did not automatically mean he would have favor with his brothers!)

Ten years later we see David still very far from being a king and, in fact, he was fleeing from King Saul who wanted to kill him. This was not, I am sure, where David imagined he would be when Samuel anointed him to be king of Israel.

We see in First Samuel 22 that:

> David left Gath and escaped to the cave of Adullam. When his brothers and his father's household heard about it, they went down to him there. All those who were in distress or in debt or discontented gathered around him, and he became their commander. About four hundred men were with him (1 Samuel 22:1-2).

I am sure when David was first anointed he imagined he would live in a beautiful palace fit for a king, not a cold, distant cave with his parents, brothers, and a motley collection of vagrants, misfits, and other people society had rejected. Yet despite what he was seeing in the flesh, David never gave up believing he would one day achieve his destiny; he took the anointing on his life very seriously. In fact, in almost every situation he found himself in, he behaved as if he were already a king and priest.

God used these unpleasant circumstances to train David for his future position as king. He did not complain about his situation or give up on what he knew God had in store for him. We see in the selection from First Samuel that he walked in his anointing and calling, and became the leader of 400 men. These men, who were with him in the cave and were described as "distressed, or in debt or discontented," became a triumphant army!

A quick look at the story of Joseph reveals that he had a dream that God was going to give him an important position in society and that his brothers were going to bow down to him. The next morning he told his brothers about the dream and they scoffed at him, eventually getting so jealous and angry that they sold him as a slave to passing merchants just to get rid of him (see Gen. 37).

In the story of Joseph, we see again as we saw with David, someone who was leading a good life when God called and anointed him. He was then led into his own personal desert and became a slave and then a prisoner. He was falsely accused, condemned, and abandoned. In this seemingly hopeless situation where God's plans for him seemed impossible to achieve, Joseph acted as if he was already walking in his calling. After many trials and tribulations, God gradually increased the favor on Joseph's life until he was in a position of great honor and influence and was able to do all God had called him to do. (And his brothers did, indeed, bow down before him!)

We also see this same preparation for ministry in the life of Jesus. As we read in the Gospel of Matthew:

As soon as Jesus was baptized, He went up out of the water.
At that moment heaven was opened, and He saw the Spirit
of God descending like a dove and alighting on Him. And
a voice from heaven said, "This is My Son, whom I love;
with Him I am well pleased" (Matthew 3:16-17).

In this way God affirmed Jesus as His Son, confirmed His calling, and anointed Him with the power to accomplish it. One would expect that after this Jesus would have gone to one of the larger cities and started His ministry immediately, but as we read in Luke 4:1-2:

Jesus, full of the Holy Spirit, left the Jordan and was led
by the Spirit into the wilderness, where for forty days He
was tempted by the devil. He ate nothing during those
days, and at the end of them He was hungry.

Please note that the *Holy Spirit* led Jesus into the wilderness, not satan!

I often meet Christians who have received their calling and anointing and complain that they suddenly find themselves in the wilderness or desert, and then blame their uncomfortable situation on satan. Then they launch into spiritual warfare binding satan, not realizing that they are, in fact, fighting against the Holy Spirit! He is the One who leads us into the desert to confirm our calling and to find out if we know who we are in Christ.

Jesus did not eat or drink for 40 days and when He was in a very weakened state, satan came to Him to tempt Him. Using the same potentially destabilizing tactics as he did with Eve, satan tried to introduce doubt into Jesus' mind saying, *"If you are the son of God"* (Matt. 4:3,6). However, Jesus remembered quite clearly that God had called Him "My Son" when He came up out of the waters of the Jordan River after being baptized, so He knew exactly who He was. Note that He did not argue with satan, but rebuked him for trying to tempt Him and then said, *"It is written"* (Matt. 4:4,6,10) and quoted the relevant verse from the Bible.

Satan tried three times to tempt Jesus, and when He responded in the same way every time, satan left Him alone and Jesus left the wilderness to start His ministry.

This is the most important lesson for us to learn. When tempted by satan, rebuke him in the name of Jesus, and then say, "It is written." Then quote the relevant Scripture verse.[1]

Speaking out the Word over your future is so important, and the devil hates it. Proverbs 18:21 and James 3:3-10 tell us there is life and death in our tongue, so we need to start using it to proclaim and decree God's promises for our lives. We were made to be God's priests and kings, and we need to start behaving as such. The moment we start doing so, God will activate His plans for our lives, and we will soon see the fruit.

This is the same calling God gave Adam and Eve in Genesis 1:28 and which has now been restored to us through the sacrifice of the second Adam, Jesus. So let us not waste time, but step into the calling and anointing on our lives and walk by faith and not by sight to fulfill it.

OUR DESTINY

Revelation 5:7-10 says:

> *He went and took the scroll from the right hand of Him who sat on the throne. And when he had taken it, the four living creatures and the twenty-four elders fell down before the Lamb. Each one had a harp and they were holding golden bowls full of incense, which are*

the prayers of God's people. And they sang a new song saying: "You are worthy to take the scroll and to open its seals, because You were slain, and with Your blood you purchased for God persons from every tribe and language and people and nation. You have made them to be a kingdom and priests to serve our God, and they will reign on the earth."

Here we see that each of the elders and the four living creatures has a gold bowl in their hands, a gold bowl filled with incense, which are the prayers of God's people. These are prayers not only prayed by this generation but by our ancestors in generations that are long gone. They are prayers for revival, transformation, and for God's Kingdom to come on Earth as it is in Heaven. In these endtimes, God is going to answer these prayers.

This is why we hear so much talk of revival and transformation among the nations. More and more the Gospel is spreading to hard-to-reach parts of the world through our persistence and passion for the One who sacrificed His all that we might spend eternity with God.

The dreams He has given us are to assist God in achieving His goals in this, the last days of the endtimes. The result of the prayers and fasting from past generations will be that God opens the flood gates of Heaven and equips us to work with Him to see these prayers for our families, streets, towns, and nations answered.

In Revelation 5:10 it tells us that those of us who are purchased by the blood of Jesus are *"to be a kingdom and priests to serve our God, and* [we] *will reign on the earth."*

This means we have been set apart for the Lord, and have been given the anointing and power required to be the servant kings and priests in the areas God has put us in. This includes our family, friends, work colleagues, communities, and our country. So take authority over your own life and start acting as a king and priest set apart for the Lord in your area of influence. You have a divine mandate to love, take care of, and to rule over the earth—and most of all, to see God's Kingdom come on Earth.

I want to encourage you with the following Scriptures:

> *"The Lord your God is with you, the Mighty Warrior who saves. He will take great delight in you; in His love He will no longer rebuke you, but will* **rejoice over you** *with singing. I will remove from you all who mourn over the loss of your appointed festivals, which is a burden and reproach for you. At that time I will deal with all who oppressed you. I will rescue the lame; I will gather the exiles. I will give them praise and honor in every land where they have suffered shame. At that time I will gather you; at that time I will bring you home. I will give you honor and praise among all the peoples of the earth when I restore your fortunes before your very eyes," says the Lord* (Zephaniah 3:17-20).

> *Whoever dwells in the shelter of the Most High will rest in the shadow of the Almighty. I will say of the Lord, "He is my refuge and my fortress, my God, in whom I trust."*

> *Surely* **He will save you** *from the fowler's snare and from the deadly pestilence. He will cover you with His feathers, and under His wings* **you will find refuge**; *His faithfulness will be your shield and rampart. You* **will not fear** *the terror of night, nor the arrow that flies by day, nor the pestilence that stalks in the darkness, nor the plague that destroys at midday. A thousand may fall at your side, ten thousand at your right hand, but it will*

not come near you. You will only observe with your eyes and see the punishment of the wicked.

If you say, "The Lord is my refuge," and make the Most High your dwelling, no harm will overtake you, no disaster will come near your tent. For **He will command His angels concerning you to guard you** *in all your ways; they will lift you up in their hands, so that you will not strike your foot against a stone. You will tread on the lion and the cobra; you will trample the great lion and the serpent.*

"Because he loves Me," says the Lord, "I will rescue him; I **will protect him,** *for he acknowledges My name. He will call on Me, and I will answer him;* **I will be with him** *in trouble, I will deliver him and honor him. With long life I will satisfy him and show him My salvation"* (Psalm 91).

But now, this is what the Lord says—He who created you, Jacob, He who formed you, Israel: "Do not fear, for I have redeemed you; I have summoned you by name; you are mine. When you pass through the waters, I will be with you; and when you pass through the rivers, they will not sweep over you. When you walk through the fire, you will not be burned; the flames will not set you ablaze" (Isaiah 43:1-2).

ENDNOTE

1. In Hebrews 4:12 we are told that the Word is a two-edged sword. In Ephesians 6:16-17 to use the Word as a shield of faith to protect ourselves from the *"flaming arrows of the evil one."* Write down

and try to memorize verses from the Bible that you can use as a sword and shield when praying for yourself as well as for others. I am assured by mature Christians that the more skilled you get at doing this, the less satan will bother you.

EPILOGUE

This is my prayer, my absolute passion: that you will dare to start dreaming and step out in faith. Spend time with God getting to know Him and His will for your life, then set about prayerfully achieving your God-given destiny. Have as little as possible to do with people who discourage you from being all God called you to be, people who themselves dare not to dream.

Don't give up. Be open to new ideas, concepts, and revelations from God. Decide to give everything required of you in order to achieve God's purpose for your life. Be the person God created you to be—not a copy of someone else, but an authentic individual.

Do not doubt that as much as you want to talk to God, God wants to talk to you—personally. This happens in various ways, sometimes with an audible voice or perhaps through impressing something deep into your spirit. He can also do it through a prophecy, dream or vision, and, of course, through His Word, the Bible.

Live as Jesus lived. Learn, preach, heal, bring deliverance, touch the untouched, and demonstrate the Kingdom of God through the power of the Holy Spirit. Love the Word of God. Study the Bible from the beginning to the end. Learn from what you read and apply it to your life. Practice the godly principles you learn and see God do the impossible in and through you. Don't give up, regardless of how you feel. Do not make hasty decisions without thinking about the long-term consequences. Faith will always make a way. God will always send others to help you. Do whatever God tells you to do even if it makes you unpopular with others.

The call on your life, as well as on the lives of all believers, is clearly written in the Great Commission in the Bible. In Matthew 28:18-20 Jesus says:

> All authority in heaven and on earth has been given to Me. Therefore go and make disciples of all nations, baptizing them in the name of the Father and of the Son and of the Holy Spirit, and teaching them to obey everything I have commanded you. And surely I am with you always, to the very end of the age.

In John 20:21 Jesus says, "Peace be with you! As the Father has sent Me, I am sending you."

Another version of the Great Commission is in the Book of Mark. Mark 16:15 says: "Go into all the world and preach the gospel [Good News] to all creation." Please note it does not say shut yourself up in a church and live as normal a life as possible.

Mark 16:16 says, "Whoever believes and is baptized will be saved, but whoever does not believe will be condemned." Hold spontaneous baptismal ceremonies for newly saved Christians. It is not God's will that anyone should be lost, which is why He calls those who do believe to tell those who do not know Him.

Mark 16:17-18 says:

"And these signs will accompany those who believe...." This means you!

"In My name they will drive out demons;" which means that with the authority we have in the name of Jesus, we should drive out demonic forces in people and set them free, as the disciples did in Mark 6:13.

"...They will speak in new tongues;" which is a sign that one has been baptized in the Holy Spirit and has been empowered to witness about Jesus to the ends of the earth (see Acts 1:8).

"...They will pick up snakes with their hands...." The snake is the symbol of the devil; as you resist him, he will flee from you.

"...And when they drink deadly poison, it will not hurt them at all...." Of course we do not go around physically drinking poison, but I see this verse meaning that when we are mature followers of Jesus and someone tries to give us the poison of a teaching that is not from God, the Holy Spirit will warn us that what we are hearing is a lie. Therefore, we will avoid it and all the potential harm it can do to us.

"...They will place their hands on sick people, and they will get well." Sickness is not from God. As His child, and in the name of Jesus, you are empowered to lay hands on the sick and see them healed.

Do not be fooled by people who say that these things were only done 2,000 years ago by the disciples. This is a lie from the devil to make sure you do not do the same things the earliest disciples did. It says in Mark 16:17: *"And these signs will accompany those who **believe**..."* and that includes you.

You have a choice; you can either live in faith or die in doubt. Seeing the invisible and doing the impossible has happened to me and many others who live by faith. You can do the same, and it will change your life completely. Obey God, whatever the cost. When things look dark and hopeless, Jesus will give you a revelation, a word, or bring someone across your path to help you. He will help you get through your dark period. Stay close to God; it's the safest place in the world to be. Keep proclaiming God's Word over your life, and speak out with conviction and belief about what God promises you in the Word. Let critical comments directed at you only serve to strengthen you as you obey God. Look to God, and not to people or things to provide what you need. God is Almighty; He is sovereign over Heaven and Earth and will rescue you from all your enemies.

Do you realize that you are working in conjunction with God and that He is working in conjunction with you? Give a tenth of all that you earn to the Kingdom of God because what you sow you will reap. You have to plant a seed before you can reap a harvest. With every disappointment or loss, sow a seed in hope. React as the Holy Spirit advises you to, and not in the spirit of this world. When you sow a seed expecting to receive a miracle in return, you are then in a position of hopefulness and will receive whatever it is you are hoping for.

Give your own testimony to people you meet. It is written in the Bible that through the blood of Jesus and the word of your testimony, satan will flee. Even if you are going through a difficult time, give your testimony and call upon the blood of Jesus. Expect a breakthrough and miracles in your situation and you will be amazed at what will happen. Obey God, and remain humble in your own eyes.

Ask yourself the correct questions when you experience opposition. Do not fight your enemies, but rather bless them and pray for them. Set them free by holding nothing against them. Silence does not throw oil on a fire. You will be surprised at what happens when you give God room to bring justice into unjust situations. Go with God, with your own Chief and Leader. Do not be a follower of others, but rather a follower of Jesus.

I finish my epilogue with the important call that God placed on your life: *The Spirit of the Sovereign Lord is on you, because the Lord has anointed you to preach good news to the poor. He has sent you to bind up the broken-hearted, to bring freedom to those in bondage, to comfort those who mourn,* to rebuild where there is now only devastation, to care for the widows and orphans, and bring God's Kingdom to the whole world (see Isaiah 61:1-4).

A 2010 Update

Since writing this book and publishing it in Dutch three years ago, an amazing amount of activity has happened. I have been overseas more than a hundred times, led hundreds of thousands of people to the Lord, seen astounding outpourings of God's Spirit, and witnessed many miracles, signs, and wonders—but never before have I felt the coming of the Lord to be so close, and I am not alone.

In 2009, Rebekah and I attended The Call conference in Kansas City in the United States with Lou Engle and Stacey and Wesley Campbell. Mike Bickle, the founder of IHOPU (International House of Prayer University) spoke to us, and what he said both shocked and excited us.

In the Bible it says, *"And this gospel of the kingdom will be preached in the whole world as a testimony to all nations, and then the end will come"* (Matt. 24:14). Most of us know that when "the end comes" is the time when Jesus will return to Earth to claim His Bride, those whose sins are forgiven, and who have accepted Him as their Lord and Savior.

I, like so many others, thought preaching the Gospel to every tribe and nation in the world would take many more years, but, according to Mike, at a meeting of the CEOs of the world's top missionary organizations, they estimated that 5,600 of the approximately 6,000 tribes and nations in the world had already been reached! This leaves about 400 unreached people groups and, with mission agencies concentrating their efforts on these groups for the next few years, the CEOs estimated that by 2020 every group in the world will have been reached.

That's only ten years or approximately 3,650 days from now!

First John 2:18 tells us, *"Dear children, this is the last hour."* Romans 13:11-14 tells us:

And do this, understanding the present time: The hour has already come for you to wake up from your slumber, because our salvation is nearer now than when we first believed. The night is nearly over; the day is almost here. So let us put aside the deeds of darkness and put on the armor of light. Let us behave decently, as in the daytime, not in carousing and drunkenness, not in sexual immorality and debauchery, not in dissension and jealousy. Rather, clothe yourselves with the Lord Jesus Christ, and do not think about how to gratify the desires of the flesh.

You may feel that now is the time, as a Christian, to avoid the darkness in this world by going into hiding and waiting for Jesus to come back, but you are *wrong!* Take heart; be encouraged, because it is written in Isaiah 60:1-3:

Arise, shine; for your light has come, and the glory of the Lord rises upon you. See, darkness covers the earth, and thick darkness is over the peoples, but the Lord rises upon you, and His glory appears over you. Nations will come to your light, and kings to the brightness of your dawn.

This Scripture tells us that the darker it gets in the world, the brighter we will shine with the light and glory of God upon us. Despite the earthquakes and famines that have come and mark the arrival of the last days, there is a great release of God's favor and revelation on His people right now.

I implore you to wake up, step into your destiny, bring God's Kingdom to this earth, and rule and reign like a priest and king over the area God has called you to. As you see the invisible, God will reveal the true potential He has created in you and, despite any adverse circumstances, He will give you the anointing and wisdom to do the impossible—and you *will* walk in your destiny.

MORE WORLDWIDE
READER REACTIONS

Our mutual hunger and desperation to see the power and presence of God break out in our churches, cities, and regions brought about a divine connection between Mattheus and myself from the very first time we met. God has put a powerful and fiery anointing on Mattheus, and it is a true spirit of revival. I see incredible miracles, signs, and wonders happening through him and his ministry. He has a passion to see God's people consumed with the fire and purpose of God. I pray you will be inspired to follow your own destiny after reading this book.

ABRAHAM KUCHIPUDI
Founder, CEO
Save the Unsaved Ministries, India

In the Netherlands we have posters and postcards that often feature strong, thought-provoking sayings. My favorite text translates to *It takes courage to live as one should*. I like people with courage and like to support such people. Mattheus is a person with courage. He lives his life to the full because he has dared to step out of his comfort zone and open up new paths. I hope and expect that this book will encourage many more to do the same.

THEO AERTS
Former CEO of Soul Survivor
Well-known Netherlands publisher

An inspirational and honest book. It challenges you to become active for Jesus, and that is good!

HERMAN BOON
Pastor and television personality

In a disarming but riveting way, Mattheus knows how to touch people's hearts to get them to move and influence the world with the power and values of the Kingdom of God. He is a real encourager!

GERARD DE GROOT
Pastor, teacher, author
Leadership team, Revival Alliance Network

People like Mattheus and Rebekah van der Steen show what God can do through young people who have surrendered their lives to God.

DANIEL HOOGTEIJLINGE
Missionary in Africa

For a long time I have dreamed about young men and women who dare to dream about a spiritual breakthrough in our nation, and who have the courage to stick their necks out and work toward achieving these dreams. Mattheus is exceptionally good at both dreaming and achieving what he dreams of doing. I hope that many young, as well as older people, will be inspired both by his book as well as his work.

PROFESSOR DR. WILLEM J. OUWENEEL
Mentor and spiritual father
Author of 138 books

When I was 17 years old, Jesus came into my life and from that moment my dream was to become a missionary. I have followed this dream with fire and passion, and it became a reality. Now, back in the Netherlands, I have met a young man who has been touched by Jesus and has a dream, a dream to touch the nations and influence them with the Gospel of Jesus Christ. This young man is Mattheus, and to him I say, "Mattheus, you have a dream that God gave you—go after it, and it will come true."

JAN SJOERD PASTERKAMP
Pastor and apostolic leader
Board member, Derek Prince Ministries

Believing in Jesus Christ and in the One who sent Him for our salvation is necessary for obtaining that salvation. In my experience, Mattheus and Rebekah believe this promise completely, with all the positive results that come from salvation in its full, biblically correct meaning. According to me, believing in, and being obedient to God is necessary for those wishing to become a fruit-producing instrument in the hand of our Three-in-One God for this time and in this place. Mattheus and Rebekah inspire me in this area. May they now also inspire you and bring you into a deeper understanding of God's call on your life.

FATHER MARC VAN ROSSEM
Catholic priest

I read this book in one breath. I am completely inspired by it!

PETER VLUG
Founder of Tiener Toekomst,
a well-respected youth movement

More Reader Comments

...At last! I have been waiting for a book like this for years. All the pieces of the puzzle of my life have fallen into place. I have been a Christian for 30 years and wish I had this book to read a long time ago.

…This book really sets you free to live and, together with God, to do the impossible.

…Mattheus, I just sat and cried with emotion and joy when I read your book, *Dare to Dream*. I recognized so much of what you have written about as having happened in my own life. Reading this book has set me free to dare to dream and to work toward making these dreams become realities.

ABOUT THE AUTHOR'S MINISTRY

TOUCH, REACH AND IMPACT THE NATIONS (TRIN)

Touch, Reach and Impact the Nations (TRIN) is a Christian organization that operates internationally and is called to touch the untouched, reach the unreached, encourage the discouraged, and to teach those who do not know about the Person, love, and power of Jesus Christ.

TRIN reaches out and helps orphans, widows, families in need, victims of war, refugees, missionaries, church leaders, and various groups of Christians around the world.

TRIN also has a sponsorship program called Operation Held that is currently feeding, clothing, and schooling 900 children in various third world countries. There is an ongoing program to build homes to house children who are currently homeless.

TRIN regularly holds Fire Nights and Worship Celebrations in various places in the Netherlands and hundreds of people attend every meeting. The ministry also organizes regular conferences and campaigns in both the Netherlands as well as overseas, and hundreds of thousands of people across the world have accepted Jesus as their Savior through this ministry. TRIN is also involved in raising up and training revivalists to reach the world with the

Good News of Jesus Christ. (A free online course can be found on the Revivalists Website listed below.)

TRIN believes in a united Church devoted to God, filled with followers of Jesus, and led by the Holy Spirit—a Church able to teach, lead, and equip people to achieve both their dreams and their God-given purposes.

FOR MORE INFORMATION PLEASE VISIT:

www.trin.nl

www.mattheusvandersteen.nl

www.revivalists.nl

Facebook: Mattheus van der Steen

Email: info@trin.nl

For conference bookings and to book

Mattheus as a speaker

pa@trin.nl

Phone: 0031(0) 341 42 47 85

Our physical address, should you wish to write, is cited on our Websites.

IN THE RIGHT HANDS, THIS BOOK WILL CHANGE LIVES!

Most of the people who need this message will not be looking for this book. To change their lives, you need to put a copy of this book in their hands.

> But others (seeds) fell into good ground, and brought forth fruit, some a hundred-fold, some sixty-fold, some thirty-fold (Matthew 13:8).

Our ministry is constantly seeking methods to find the good ground, the people who need this anointed message to change their lives. Will you help us reach these people?

> Remember this—a farmer who plants only a few seeds will get a small crop. But the one who plants generously will get a generous crop (2 Corinthians 9:6).

EXTEND THIS MINISTRY BY SOWING
3 BOOKS, 5 BOOKS, 10 BOOKS, OR MORE TODAY,
AND BECOME A LIFE CHANGER!

Thank you,

Don Nori Sr., Publisher
Destiny Image
Since 1982

DESTINY IMAGE PUBLISHERS, INC.

*"Speaking to the Purposes of God for This Generation
and for the Generations to Come."*

VISIT OUR NEW SITE HOME AT
WWW.DESTINYIMAGE.COM

FREE SUBSCRIPTION TO DI NEWSLETTER

Receive free unpublished articles by top DI authors, exclusive

discounts, and free downloads from our best and newest books.

Visit www.destinyimage.com to subscribe.

Write to: Destiny Image
            P.O. Box 310
            Shippensburg, PA 17257-0310

Call: 1-800-722-6774

Email: orders@destinyimage.com

For a complete list of our titles or to place an order
online, visit www.destinyimage.com.

FIND US ON FACEBOOK OR FOLLOW US ON TWITTER.

www.facebook.com/destinyimage   facebook
www.twitter.com/destinyimage   twitter